THE SEVEN SAGES OF ROME

(MIDLAND VERSION)

EARLY ENGLISH TEXT SOCIETY
No. 324
2005

Cambridge, University Library, MS Dd.1.17, f.54 r

THE SEVEN SAGES OF ROME
(MIDLAND VERSION)

EDITED FROM
CAMBRIDGE, UNIVERSITY LIBRARY, MS Dd.1.17
BY
JILL WHITELOCK

Published for
THE EARLY ENGLISH TEXT SOCIETY
by the
OXFORD UNIVERSITY PRESS
2005

OXFORD
UNIVERSITY PRESS

Great Clarendon Street, Oxford OX2 6DP

Oxford University Press is a department of the University of Oxford. It furthers the University's objective of excellence in research, scholarship, and education by publishing worldwide in

Oxford New York

Auckland Cape Town Dar es Salaam Hong Kong Karachi Kuala Lumpur Madrid Melbourne Mexico City Nairobi New Delhi Shanghai Taipei Toronto

With offices in

Argentina Austria Brazil Chile Czech Republic France Greece Guatemala Hungary Italy Japan Poland Portugal Singapore South Korea Switzerland Thailand Turkey Ukraine Vietnam

Oxford is a registered trade mark of Oxford University Press in the UK and in certain other countries

Published in the United States by Oxford University Press Inc., New York

First published 2005

British Library Cataloguing in Publication Data
Data available

Library of Congress Cataloging in Publication Data
Data applied for

ISBN 0-19-722327-3

Typeset by Anne Joshua, Oxford
Printed in Great Britain
on acid-free paper by
The Cromwell Press, Trowbridge, Wiltshire

FOR DAD
AND IN MEMORY OF MAM

PREFACE

The Middle English verse *Seven Sages* had a long textual history, undergoing many stages of copying and transmission. Its extant manuscripts span a period of two hundred years from the early fourteenth to the early sixteenth century, and this process of time and transmission has resulted in different versions of the text. The manuscripts used for the editions published by Killis Campbell (1907) and Karl Brunner (EETS, 191, 1933) all belong to the version known as the Y-group. Within the Y-group, these two editions represent two sub-groups: Campbell's text gives the Northern, and Brunner's the Southern Version of the poem. Separate from both of these is the Midland Version of the *Seven Sages* edited here. It occurs in only one known manuscript, Cambridge, University Library, MS Dd.1.17 (hereafter referred to as D).

Of the Middle English versions, the Midland Version has been the most neglected, perhaps because of the lack of a modern edition. Until now, the only edition has been that of Thomas Wright for the Percy Society in 1845; it is not widely available and contains a number of errors. Furthermore, Wright offered no critical or textual analysis of the version of the *Seven Sages* that he had chosen to edit, preferring to devote his introduction to *The Book of Sindbād*, the work from which the *Seven Sages* is ultimately derived.

This new edition comprises not only a corrected text with critical apparatus, but also the first full study of the Midland Version of the *Seven Sages*, its relationship with the other Middle English versions, and its originality. I am grateful to Cambridge University Library for permission to print the text of *The Seven Sages of Rome* from Dd.1.17, and to include a plate as the frontispiece.

The edition is a revised version of my Ph.D. thesis '*The Seven Sages of Rome* and Orientalism in Middle English Literature, with an Edition of the Poem from Cambridge, University Library, Dd.1.17' (University of Cambridge, 1998), undertaken at Darwin College, Cambridge, with British Academy funding, and I am grateful to both these institutions. I am indebted to all those people who advised me during its progress, most importantly to my supervisor Jill Mann and to my examiners Christopher Page and Rosamund Allen for their comments and suggestions. I am also grateful to Richard Beadle for invaluable help on the poem's dialect, to Jeremy Dimmick, and to James Simpson, my first teacher of medieval literature. Special thanks go to Robert Whitelock for support and advice on drafts of the thesis and the edition.

Helen L. Spencer, Editorial Secretary of the Early English Text Society, and the Society's anonymous readers made numerous invaluable suggestions for the revision of the thesis. I am also grateful to everyone at the Department of History and Philosophy of Science in Cambridge who encouraged me whilst completing these revisions. The staff of the Department of Manuscripts of Cambridge University Library deserve particular mention for repeatedly fetching the enormous, weighty manuscript that contains the text, and I am grateful to Jayne Ringrose for help with the manuscript description and for allowing me access to unpublished notes in the Department's possession.

Finally, a special thanks to my family and Rob Ralley for all their help and support.

CONTENTS

ABBREVIATIONS

Manuscript Sigla

A Edinburgh, National Library of Scotland, MS Advocates 19.2.1 (Auchinleck)
Ar London, British Library, MS Arundel 140
As Edinburgh, National Library of Scotland, MS Asloan Manuscript (the Middle Scots version)
B Oxford, Balliol College, MS 354
C London, British Library, MS Cotton Galba E.IX
D Cambridge, University Library, MS Dd.1.17
E London, British Library, MS Egerton 1995
F Cambridge, University Library, MS Ff.2.38
R Oxford, Bodleian Library, MS Rawlinson Poet. 175

Versions of 'The Seven Sages of Rome' Referred to in the Edition

Y-group the version representing all the Middle English manuscripts except for D

A* used here to represent the Old French prose *Sept Sages*, the source of the Middle English versions (and here designated A* to distinguish it from the Middle English Auchinleck text), though in fact group A* includes versions in Italian, Swedish, and Welsh, as well as French and Middle English (see Campbell, *Seven Sages*, pp. xxxii–xxxv). The Middle English Y-group and Midland Version are sub-groups of A*.

D* the Old French 'Version Dérimée' (here designated D* to distinguish it from the Middle English manuscript D; shares a common parent version with K (see Campbell, *Seven Sages*, p. xxx))

Dolopathos a different version of the story, extant in the Latin prose of Johannes de Alta Silva (late twelfth century) and the Old French verse version of Herbert (translated from the Latin towards the end of the first quarter of the thirteenth century (see Campbell, *Seven Sages*, p. xix))

H the group of manuscripts and editions of which the Latin prose *Historia Septem Sapientum* is the prototype (derived from A*, and composed *ca.* 1330, with translations into

	most European languages (see Campbell, *Seven Sages*, p. xxvii))
I	the 'Versio Italica' (Italian, and one Latin, versions derived from A*; probably not earlier than the fourteenth century (Campbell, *Seven Sages*, p. xxix))
K	the oldest extant version of the *Seven Sages*, in Old French verse, written *ca.* 1155 (see Campbell, *Seven Sages*, p. xxvii)
Midland	the Middle English version represented by D
S	the version as transmitted in the Latin prose *Scala coeli* of Jean Gobi (*fl.* 1320–50) (see Campbell, *Seven Sages*, p. xxiii)

Editions and Secondary Works

Brunner	Brunner, Karl, ed., *The Seven Sages of Rome (Southern Version)*, EETS, 191 (1933)
Campbell, *Seven Sages*	Campbell, Killis, ed., *The Seven Sages of Rome*, The Albion Series of Anglo-Saxon and Middle English Poetry (Boston, 1907)
Campbell, 'Study'	'A Study of the Romance of the *Seven Sages* with Special Reference to the Middle English Versions', *PMLA*, 14 (1899), 1–107
Chaucer	All quotations are taken from Larry D. Benson, gen. ed., *The Riverside Chaucer*, 3rd ed. (Oxford, 1988)
CRAL	Section de traitement automatique des textes d'ancien français du CRAL, Université de Nancy II, *Les Sept Sages de Rome: Roman en prose du XIIIe siècle d'après le manuscrit no 2137 de la B.N.*, Travaux du CRAL, 2 (Nancy, 1981)
Wright	Wright, Thomas, ed., *The Seven Sages, in English Verse, Edited from a Manuscript in the Public Library of the University of Cambridge*, Percy Society: Early English Poetry, Ballads, and Popular Literature of the Middle Ages. Edited from Original Manuscripts and Scarce Publications, 16 (London, 1845)

Works of Reference

Goff	Goff, F. R., *Incunabula in American Libraries: A Third Census of Fifteenth-Century Books Recorded in North American Collections* (New York, 1964)
IMEV	Brown, Carleton, and Rossell Hope Robbins, *The Index of Middle English Verse* (New York, 1943)
IPMEP	Lewis, R. E., N. F. Blake, and A. S. G. Edwards, *Index of Printed Middle English Prose*, Garland Reference Library of the Humanities, 537 (New York, 1985)
ISTC	The British Library, *The Illustrated ISTC on CD-ROM*, 2nd ed. (Reading, 1998)
LALME	McIntosh, Angus, M. L. Samuels, and Michael Benskin, *A Linguistic Atlas of Late Mediaeval English*, 4 vols. (Aberdeen, 1986)
Manual	Severs, J. Burke, and Albert E. Hartung, gen. eds., *A Manual of the Writings in Middle English, 1050–1500* (New Haven, CT, 1967-)
MED	Kurath, Hans, *et al.*, eds., *Middle English Dictionary* (Ann Arbor, 1956–2001)
OED	Simpson, J. A., and E. S. C. Weiner, prep., *Oxford English Dictionary*, 2nd ed. (Oxford, 1989)
STC	Pollard, A. W., and G. R. Redgrave, comp., *A Short-Title Catalogue of Books Printed in England, Scotland, & Ireland and of English Books Printed Abroad, 1475–1640*, 2nd ed., rev. and enl., begun by W. A. Jackson & F. S. Ferguson, completed by K. F. Pantzer (London, 1976–1991)

INTRODUCTION

1. *THE SEVEN SAGES OF ROME* IN MEDIEVAL LITERATURE

The Seven Sages of Rome was one of the most popular works of medieval literature, with versions in nearly every European language.[1] It is a framed tale collection of fifteen stories, in which the tales are told by the Empress of Rome and the Seven Sages in order, respectively, to justify and refute the charge of attempted rape brought by the Empress against her stepson the Prince.[2]

When his son is seven, Diocletian, the Emperor of Rome, decides it is time to begin the child's education. The task falls to the Seven Sages, who take the Prince outside the city to a specially built palace, whose walls are decorated with images of the seven liberal arts. The child learns quickly, but while he is away from home, his mother dies and his father is advised to remarry. The new Empress begins to plot the Prince's death, and persuades his father to send for him. Through necromancy, the Empress contrives the Prince's death should he speak in the next seven days; however, before leaving for Rome, the Sages consult the stars and discover the Empress's plan. The Prince determines to keep silent, and asks each of the Sages to save his life for one of the seven days.

At Rome, the Prince's silence angers his father, and the Empress requests a private hearing with her stepson, promising to make him speak. When they are alone, the Empress attempts to seduce the Prince; rebuffed, she tears her clothes and her face and accuses him

[1] Campbell, *Seven Sages*, p. xxi. For bibliographical information on the *Seven Sages* and *The Book of Sindbād*, see Hans R. Runte, J. Keith Wikeley, and Anthony J. Farrell, *The Seven Sages of Rome and The Book of Sindbad: An Analytical Bibliography*, Garland Reference Library of the Humanities, 387 (New York, 1984), and Hans R. Runte, Ralf-Henning Steinmetz, and other members of the Society of the Seven Sages, 'Supplement to *The Seven Sages of Rome and The Book of Sindbad: An Analytical Bibliography*', Society of the Seven Sages, http://myweb.dal.ca/hrunte/ABSupp.html#UP (accessed 12 June 2005). For a summary of the different versions of the *Seven Sages*, see Campbell, *Seven Sages*, pp. xvii–xxxv.

[2] The following summary is based on the version of the *Seven Sages* in Cambridge, University Library, MS Dd.1.17 edited here. See below, 'The Relationship of D with the Other Manuscripts' and the 'Textual and Explanatory Notes' for details of how the Midland Version of D differs from the other Middle English versions and their Old French source.

of attempted rape. The Emperor instantly condemns his son to death, but the execution is stayed until the morning at the request of the earls and barons. So begins the tale-telling, with the Empress each night persuading her husband to kill his son, only to be thwarted by the intervention of one of the Seven Sages the next day, saving the Prince's life with a countering tale. Generally, the Empress tells stories about usurping sons or calculating counsellors, whilst the Sages employ tales of wicked women. At the end of the seventh day, after fourteen stories, the Prince finally speaks, declaring his innocence and illustrating it with a tale of his own telling. The Empress confesses her guilt and is executed, and the Emperor never remarries, leading a chaste and virtuous life until his death.

The history of this popular work spans centuries from the first surviving version written in France around the middle of the twelfth century, into the era of printing and beyond.[3] In fact, it dates even further back than this, for the *Seven Sages* was adapted from *The Book of Sindbād*, a work of perhaps the fifth century B.C.,[4] and most likely to be Persian, Hebrew, or Indian in origin.[5] In Britain, as well as the Middle English verse versions there are versions of the *Seven Sages* in Welsh and Middle Scots;[6] there is also a Middle English prose *Seven Sages.*[7] None of these is directly connected to the Middle English verse versions.[7] Eight manuscripts of the Middle

[3] In addition to the *Seven Sages*, there is an adaptation of the work known as the *Dolopathos*, written in Latin by Johannes de Alta Silva in the late twelfth century, and translated into Old French verse towards the end of the first quarter of the thirteenth century.

[4] Campbell, *Seven Sages*, p. xi.

[5] For recent discussions, see Stephen Belcher, 'The Diffusion of the *Book of Sindbād*', *Fabula*, 28 (1987), 34–58, and Jill Whitelock, 'Transmitting Tales: Myths of Origin and the Atavistic Text', ch. 2 of '*The Seven Sages of Rome* and Orientalism in Middle English Literature, With an Edition of the Poem from Cambridge, University Library, Dd.1.17', unpubl. Ph.D. thesis (University of Cambridge, 1998). There are extant versions in Syriac, Greek, Hebrew, Old Spanish, Persian (three versions), and Arabic. *The Book of Sindbād* has the frame-story and usually four tales in common with *The Seven Sages of Rome* (*Canis*, *Aper*, *Senescalcus*, and *Avis*).

[6] On the Welsh version, see Campbell, *Seven Sages*, p. xxxiii. The work is edited by Robert Williams, '*Seith Doethion Ruvein*', Selections from the Hengwrt MSS. Preserved in the Peniarth Library, vol. II (London, 1892), 301–24. Vol. II also contains an English translation by G. Hartwell Jones, '*The Seven Wise Masters of Rome*', pp. 647–62. For the Middle Scots version, see the edition by Catherine van Buuren, *The Buke of the Sevyne Sagis: A Middle Scots Version of The Seven Sages of Rome Edited from the Asloan Manuscript (NLS Acc. 4233), c. 1515*, Germanic and Anglistic Studies of the University of Leiden, 20 (Leiden, 1982).

[7] *IPMEP*, no. 613, printed three times between the late fifteenth and mid sixteenth centuries and a translation of Version H of the *Seven Sages*, most likely from an early printed edition of the Latin *Historia Septem Sapientum* (see Campbell, *Seven Sages*, pp. lx–lxi). The three editions were printed by Richard Pynson (1493, *STC* (2nd ed.), no. 21297),

English *Seven Sages* survive—a significant number—and examination of their textual affiliations suggests many more must have been lost, again attesting to the work's popularity. The earliest extant manuscript of the Middle English *Seven Sages* is the famous Auchinleck manuscript, dated to *ca.* 1331–40,[8] and the work itself must have entered Middle English literature a little earlier than this: Killis Campbell suggested a date of around 1275.[9]

The work was clearly read and drawn upon by contemporary writers of tale collections such as Chaucer and Gower;[10] yet, particularly when compared with *The Canterbury Tales* or Gower's *Confessio Amantis,* the *Seven Sages* is less well known today. One problem has been the difficulty critics have had in classifying the work by genre. In terms of structure, its definition as a tale collection is clearly the most satisfactory.[11] In terms of content, it is also like other tale collections in its inclusion of a diverse selection of stories, ranging from the very brief and simple first tale *Arbor* ('The Tree'), to the last, much longer story *Vaticinium* ('The Prophecy'), which draws from the tradition of medieval romance. However, the *Seven Sages*'s affiliations with romance go much deeper than the occasional romance-like story, setting it apart from other tale collections.[12] The

Wynkyn de Worde (1506?, *STC* (2nd ed.), no. 21298), and William Copland (*ca.* 1555, *STC* (2nd ed.), no. 21299). For the Wynkyn de Worde edition, see *The History of The Seven Wise Masters of Rome: Printed from the Edition of Wynkyn de Worde, 1520*, ed. George Laurence Gomme, Chap-Books and Folk-Lore Tracts, 1st ser., 2 (London, 1885). The Wynkyn de Worde version was translated into Scottish verse by John Rolland of Dalkeith in 1560 (Campbell, *Seven Sages*, p. lxii). The English prose *Seven Sages*, variously adapted, continued to be printed into the early part of the nineteenth century.

[8] Alison Wiggins, 'Physical make-up', in *The Auchinleck Manuscript*, ed. David Burnley and Alison Wiggins, National Library of Scotland, 5 July 2003, Version 1.1, http://www.nls.uk/auchinleck/editorial/physical.html (accessed 12 June 2005).

[9] Campbell, 'Study', p. 85, *Seven Sages*, p. lix.

[10] See pts. 1 and 2 of my M.Phil. dissertation, Jill Denham, '*The Seven Sages of Rome*: a source for Gower's *Confessio Amantis*; *The Seven Sages of Rome*: a source for Chaucer's *The Manciple's Tale*' (University of Cambridge, 1993).

[11] It is entered as a tale collection in vol. 9 of *A Manual of the Writings in Middle English 1050–1500*, gen ed. Albert E. Hartung (New Haven, CT, 1993), 3272–3, 3561–3.

[12] The *Manual*'s definition acknowledges this: 'a collection of tales within a tale; it is sometimes classified as a romance' (p. 3272). Extracts from the *Seven Sages* have been included in romance anthologies such as those edited by George Ellis, *Specimens of Early English Metrical Romances, Chiefly Written during the Early Part of the Fourteenth Century*, 2nd ed., vol. 3 (London, 1811), 23–101, or Walter Hoyt French and Charles Brockway Hale, *Middle English Metrical Romances* (New York, 1930 repr. 1964), pp. 759–85, with Henry Weber including all of the poem from the Auchinleck manuscript in his collection *Metrical Romances of the Thirteenth, Fourteenth, and Fifteenth Centuries: Published from Ancient Manuscripts*, vol. 3 (Edinburgh and London, 1810), 3–153.

story of the frame-tale itself, with the Empress's threats to familial and political stability, to the processes of lineage and succession, connects the *Seven Sages* to the broad motif of 'the deprived boy winning back his heritage',[13] common to so many romances such as *Floris and Blanchfleur, Bevis of Hampton, King Horn, Havelok*, or the Reinbrun section of *Guy of Warwick*. Moreover, the *Seven Sages* keeps company with romances in several manuscripts, reinforcing the association. Most notably, it occurs in the romance sections of both the Auchinleck manuscript and Cambridge, University Library, MS Ff.2.38, between *Sir Degare* and *Floris and Blanchfleur* in the former, and *Bevis of Hampton* and *Guy of Warwick* in the latter.[14] In its verse form, too—the octosyllabic couplets popular to romance—and its language of common phrases and rhyme tags, the *Seven Sages* betrays many of the features endemic in the formulaic romance-style.[15]

Its genre has made the *Seven Sages* problematic for critics—is it a tale collection, is it a romance, or can it be both?[16]—but this is also

[13] W. R. J. Barron, *English Medieval Romance*, Longman Literature in English Series (London, 1987), p. 69. See also Helen Cooper's observation that the *Seven Sages* has 'a powerful frame story that could exist in its own right as a romance even without the inset tales', *The Structure of The Canterbury Tales* (London, 1983), p. 24. On the other hand, Dieter Mehl regarded *Inclusa* and *Vaticinium* as the only stories that 'could at all be described as romances', *The Middle English Romances of the Thirteenth and Fourteenth Centuries* (London, 1968), p. 285. The poem was indexed in Gerald Bordman's *Motif-Index of the English Metrical Romances*, FF Communications, 190 (Helsinki, 1963).

[14] However, the *Seven Sages* was not included in Gisela Guddat-Figge's *Catalogue of Manuscripts Containing Middle English Romances*, Münchener Universitäts-Schriften, Philosophische Fakultät: Texte und Untersuchungen zur Englischen Philologie, 4 (Munich, 1976), in spite of its presence in manuscripts such as Ff.2.38. Consequently, Guddat-Figge has to describe the final section of this manuscript as 'an almost unbroken sequence of romances' (p. 97), obviously regarding the *Seven Sages* as the weak link in the chain rather than viewing its context as evidence for a medieval appreciation of the work as a romance. There is also a tradition of the *Seven Sages* accompanying overtly didactic works in manuscripts (it occurs twice with *The Prick of Conscience*, for example: see the 'Summary Description of the Y-Group Manuscripts' below), but the romance connection is a strong one, and prompted Geraldine Barnes to include the *Seven Sages* in her *Counsel and Strategy in Middle English Romance*: 'Not all scholars consider *The Seven Sages* to be a romance, and some classify it as purely didactic narrative, but its *modus operandi* of counsel and strategy gives it a place amongst the romances in this study' (Cambridge, 1993), p. 117.

[15] Carl Schmirgel cites the *Seven Sages* as one of several texts for comparison in 'Typical Expressions and Repetitions in *Sir Beues of Hamtoun*' in *The Romance of Sir Beues of Hamtoun*, ed. Eugen Kölbing, EETS, ES 46, 48, 65 (1885, 1886, 1894), pp. xlv–lxvi.

[16] Even when the *Seven Sages* is included in secondary works on romance, it is often with reservations. Laura A. Hibbard refers to the work as 'a collection of tales rather than a romance', *Mediaeval Romance in England: A Study of the Sources and Analogues of the Non-Cyclic Metrical Romances*, new ed., Burt Franklin Bibliographical and Reference Series, 17

what makes it highly interesting to the reader. In itself the text brings together many of the different genres, many of the different modes of story-telling of its time. In addition, with its several characters and multiple narrators it plays with different perspectives on the events of the frame-tale, generating multiple points of view. On the one hand, for example, the stories of the Seven Sages draw broadly from the tradition of antifeminst *exempla*—humorous warnings of women's wiles that move in and out of numerous collections throughout the Middle Ages— and it is easy to see why some critics have preferred to focus on this, rather than on the work's connections with romance.[17] The Seven Sages as characters clearly view the frame-tale in the light of this genre, rather than that of romance, for who is the Emperor but the foolish husband of stories such as *Puteus* or *Avis*, the *senex amans* of countless comic tales, making a second marriage in his old age to a younger woman—always a bad move in this context? On the other hand, the frame-tale also reads like a romance, and the Prince himself interprets it this way, choosing to tell the romance *Vaticinium* when he recovers his speech, equating himself with the son in the story, whose father tries to kill him to avert the prophecy that his child will one day become greater than himself. As the last tale in the collection, the story the Prince chooses

(New York, 1963), 174. In contrast, French critics seem happier classifying the work as a romance: for example, Yasmina Foehr-Janssens, *Les temps des fables: Le roman des Sept Sages, ou l'autre voie du roman*, Nouvelle bibliothèque du Moyen Âge, 27 (Paris, 1994) discusses the work as a *roman de clergie*. In the French tradition, the several romance continuations to the *Sept Sages*, most of which dispense with the device of intercalated tales altogether, may have encouraged this definition. A useful description of these romances can be found in Henri Niedzielski, 'La formation d'un cycle littéraire au Moyen Âge: Exemple des *Sept Sages de Rome*', *Studies on The Seven Sages of Rome and Other Essays in Medieval Literature Dedicated to the Memory of Jean Misrahi*, ed. H. Niedzielski, H. R. Runte, and W. L. Hendrickson (Honolulu, 1978), pp. 119–32.

[17] For example, George Kane, although discussing the poem in a chapter on 'Middle English Metrical Romances', connects it with *exempla* or *fabliaux* rather than romance, *Middle English Literature: A Critical Study of the Romances, the Religious Lyrics, Piers Plowman*, Methuen's Old English Library (London, 1951), pp. 60–1. Similarly, Piero Boitani, whilst acknowledging that the work has been classified as a metrical romance, regards the tales of the *Seven Sages* as more important than the frame, and views the poem in its entirety as 'closer to the comic mode', *English Medieval Narrative in the Thirteenth and Fourteenth Centuries*, trans. Joan Krakover Hall (Cambridge, 1982), p. 116. See also John Jaunzems, 'Structure and Meaning in the *Seven Sages of Rome*', in Niedzielski, Runte, and Hendrickson, *Studies*, pp. 43–62, for a discussion of how the *Seven Sages*, as a tale collection, differs from the genre of romance. Jaunzems is right to say that classifying the work as a romance 'invites the reader to approach it with the wrong set of expectations' (p. 46); however, as I suggest below, romance, as one of several genres at play in the *Seven Sages*, is still given special prominence.

to illustrate his innocence, *Vaticinium* gives the romance genre a special prominence in the *Seven Sages*.

However, this interplay of perspectives and of genres is more than a device for maintaining the reader's interest throughout a collection of stories—it is at the heart of the plot itself. The dilemma of the *Seven Sages* centres around the problems of reading signs: its plot hinges on the Empress's contrivance of the appearance of attempted rape (she tears her clothes and scratches her face), and the Emperor has to read these visual signs, just as he will have to listen to the tales of his wife and the Seven Sages. With both, he must determine the correct interpretation. Has the Empress been assaulted by his son, or, as we know to be true, is she lying? The poem explores the difficulty of transmitting the truth in a world in which women are arch-manipulators of how things seem.

In this context, the special prominence *Vaticinium* gives to romance is derived not only from its position as the final tale in the collection—it is also drawn from the status of the Prince as its teller. We know from the account of his education at the beginning of the work that he is especially wise, and his wisdom takes the form of the skilful reading of signs.[18] This interpretative wisdom is reflected in the sort of story the Prince chooses to tell. Until this point, the Seven Sages have defended the Prince by telling stories of women's deception in order to discredit his stepmother's testimony. *Vaticinium*, however, moves the narrative strategy to a different level by offering an interpretative reading of the frame-tale scenario.[19] The stepmother's accusation of rape and subsequent stories, told to persuade the Emperor that the Sages and Prince wish to overthrow his rule, occasioned all the old Emperor's fears about being supplanted by his young son. *Vaticinium* is the Prince's way of acknowledging these fears whilst making it clear that the child in his story (and so he himself) is not to blame, since the young are

[18] The Sages test the Prince's learning, raising the height of his bed by hiding ivy leaves under the bedposts in order to see if he will deduce what has happened. The Prince correctly interprets the evidence. More importantly, the Prince can read the stars more skilfully than his masters. One of the Sages, Caton, sees that his pupil will die if he speaks on his return to court, but it is the Prince who realizes that he can save himself by keeping silent for seven days.

[19] *Vaticinium* is not in *The Book of Sindbād*, but was chosen by the redactor of the *Seven Sages* to end the work. Therefore the Prince's interpretative reading of the frame-tale scenario in *Vaticinium* parallels the redactor's own reading of his source: he saw how the *Sindbād* was thematically connected with the matter of medieval romance and wove this into his transformed text.

destined to take the place of their parents. He uses the genre of romance for this purpose.

Yet as a tale collection, it is the tensions in competing points of view that generate energy in the *Seven Sages*, however resolved. Against the dilemma of the central father–son relationship, the antifeminist perspective of the Sages themselves is inevitably a limited one, but nevertheless the work as a whole became known by their names as either *The Book of Sindbād* or *The Seven Sages of Rome*.[20] Moreover, the woman's perspective—not just in the character of the Empress, but in the women of the stories as well—makes claims on our attention as the frame sometimes struggles to contain its stories in a clear moral context. These differing perspectives were an area for possible elaboration by later redactors, and this is something in which the author of the Midland Version was particularly interested, making it the most original of the Middle English versions in terms of narrative strategy.[21]

In recent years, editors of Middle English texts, particularly romances, have begun to appreciate the value of different versions of the same poem instead of the obsessive quest to recover the lost 'authorial original' through the application of recensionist editing. As Jennifer Fellows observes:

> when it comes to popular literature such as romances . . . scribes are not *trying* to transmit accurate reproductions of an archetype—their alterations are deliberate and constructive; they are not only verbal, but often extend to transpositions, reworkings, introductions, omissions of entire episodes. Scribal activity can no longer be separated from authorial intention, because the scribes themselves have authorial status.[22]

Of course, as Fellows herself acknowledges, not all scribal activity was so constructive. For example, in the version of the *Seven Sages* in Dd.1.17, the scribe has only partially 'translated' the poem in his exemplar into his own dialect, resulting in a text that abounds with

[20] In *The Book of Sindbād*, Sindbād is the Prince's only tutor; the Sages appear later as the King's counsellors, and it is they who save the Prince from execution, not Sindbād.

[21] This is discussed further in the section on 'The Midland Version' in the 'Introduction'.

[22] Jennifer Fellows, 'Editing Middle English Romances', *Romance in Medieval England*, ed. Maldwyn Mills, Jennifer Fellows, and Carol M. Meale (Cambridge, 1991), pp. 5–16 (p. 7); see also Rosamund Allen, 'Some Sceptical Observations on the Editing of *The Awntyrs off Arthure*', *Manuscripts and Texts: Editorial Problems in Later Middle English Literature: Essays from the 1985 Conference at the University of York*, ed. Derek Pearsall (Cambridge, 1987), pp. 5–25.

variant spellings and corrupted rhymes. Nevertheless this text, when compared with the other extant manuscripts of the Middle English *Seven Sages*, constitutes a highly original, different version of the poem: at some stage in its textual history it has undergone exactly the sort of positive scribal reworking that Fellows describes. More than any of the other extant texts, this version of the poem consistently diverges from the common Old French original, bearing witness to a scribal redactor who was both reader and author, responding to his story with a keen intelligence for narrative manipulation.[23]

2. DESCRIPTION OF THE MANUSCRIPT[24]

Contents

Vol. 1[25]

1. ff. 2ra–97vb Ranulf Higden, *Polychronicon* (imperfect).[26]
2. ff. 111ra–121ra Geoffrey of Monmouth, *Historia regum Britannie* (imperfect).[27]

[23] However, D also often best preserves the French in minor details, see below, 'The Interrelationship of the Manuscripts', and the 'Textual and Explanatory Notes'.

[24] The manuscript has been described in the following works: *A Catalogue of the Manuscripts Preserved in the Library of the University of Cambridge*, vol. 2 (Cambridge, 1857 repr. München, Hildesheim, and New York, 1980), 15–26; C. David Benson and Lynne S. Blanchfield, *The Manuscripts of Piers Plowman: The B-Version* (Cambridge, 1997), pp. 32–38; Julia C. Crick, *The Historia regum Britannie of Geoffrey of Monmouth*, vol. 3, *A Summary Catalogue of the Manuscripts* (Cambridge, 1989), 67–71; M. R. James, unpublished notes on Dd.1.17, *ca.* 1930, Dept. of Manuscripts, University Library, Cambridge; George Kane and E. Talbot Donaldson, eds., *Piers Plowman: The B Version. Will's Visions of Piers Plowman, Do-Well, Do-Better and Do-Best: An Edition in the Form of Trinity College Cambridge MS B.15.17, Corrected and Restored from the Known Evidence, with Variant Readings*, rev. ed., Piers Plowman: The Three Versions (London, 1988), pp. 2–3; M. C. Seymour, 'The English Manuscripts of *Mandeville's Travels*', *Edinburgh Bibliographical Society Transactions*, 4.5 (1965–6), 167–210 (pp. 179–80).

[25] The manuscript (one volume) was rebound in 1862, and foliated as if composed of three volumes, hence the references to vols. 1–3 in the following description. The decision to foliate the manuscript in this way is discussed below.

[26] Churchill Babington and Joseph Rawson Lumby, eds., *Polychronicon Ranulphi Higden monachi Cestrensis; Together with the English Translations of John Trevisa and of an Unknown Writer of the Fifteenth Century*, Rerum Britannicarum Medii Aevi scriptores, or Chronicles and Memorials of Great Britain and Ireland during the Middle Ages, Rolls Ser., 41, 9 vols. (London, 1865–86). This copy begins abruptly in ch. 4 of Book I; ch. 33 is missing from Book V; and it ends in ch. 2 of Book VIII. These omissions are due to lost leaves. It should be noted that the Cambridge University Library manuscripts catalogue was written before Dd.1.17 was rebound, and lists the *Polychronicon* as item 23. See further below.

[27] Most recently edited by Neil Wright, *The Historia regum Brittanie of Geoffrey of Monmouth*, vol. 1, *Bern, Burgerbibliothek, MS. 568* (Cambridge, 1985). D begins in c. 117 of this edition (p. 84), due to missing leaves.

3. ff. 121ra–122vb Unidentified.[28]
4. ff. 122vb–129ra Jean Turpin, *De vita Caroli Magni* (the Pseudo-Turpin),[29] with the four appendices *De miraculis beati Iacobi*, *Qualiter Iacobus translatus est in Galiciam*, *De sollempnitate beati Iacobi*, and *De statura Karoli* (the same text as found in London, British Library, MS Royal 13.D.I).[30]
5. ff. 129ra–159ra Martinus Polonus, *Chronicon pontificum et imperatorum*, with continuation.[31]
6. ff. 159rb–160va A short chronicle of the kings of England.[32]
7. ff. 160va–203va Guido delle Colonne, *Historia Troiana*.[33]
8. ff. 203vb–204rb Attrib. John of Legnano, *Propheciae*.[34]
9. ff. 204rb–230vb Jacques de Vitri, *Historia Hierosolimitana*.[35]

[28] Heading: 'H. minister seruor*um* dei .H. illustri regi anglor*um* salutes *et* or*ati*ones'; begins: 'Cum mecum p*ropter* ea q*ue* responsione tua accepi tractarem'; ends: 'de tua generacione siue p*ro*genie sanctissima. Valete.' As Diana Greenway states, this is an unidentified text and not Henry's letter to Henry I, as was previously thought. See her edition of Henry, Archdeacon of Huntingdon, *Historia Anglorum: The History of the English People*, Oxford Medieval Texts (Oxford, 1996), p. cxxvii, n. 4.

[29] H. M. Smyser, ed., *The Pseudo-Turpin: Edited from Bibliothèque Nationale, Fonds Latin, MS. 17656 with an Annotated Synopsis*, Mediaeval Academy of America Publication, 30 (Cambridge, MA, 1937).

[30] André de Mandach, *Naissance et développement de la chanson de geste en Europe*, vol. 1, *La geste de Charlemagne et de Roland*, Publications romanes et françaises, 69 (Genève and Paris, 1961), 368.

[31] L. Weiland, ed., *Martini Oppaviensis Chronicon pontificum et imperatorum*, Monumenta Germaniae historica: Scriptores, 22 (Hanover, 1872), 377–475. The continuation is edited by O. Holder-Egger, *Continuatio pontificum Anglica fratrum minorum brevis*, Monumenta Germaniae historica: Scriptores, 30.1 (Hannover, 1896), 713–14. The text in Dd.1.17 has been designated as belonging to class IIIb by Anna-Dorothee v. den Brincken, 'Studien zur Überlieferung der Chronik des Martin von Troppau (Erfahrungen mit einem massenhaft überlieferten historischen Text)', *Deutsches Archiv für Erforschung des Mittelalters*, 41 (1985), 460–531 (p. 528).

[32] Unedited. Begins: 'Primis [*sic*] habuit kanciam; Alius westsexe; Tercius merceneriche'; ends: 'cum rege francie contra rege*m* anglie tanq*ua*m stipendiarius regis francie'. The sequence of kings runs from Bricbrigh, king of the West Saxons, to a notice of Richard II, ending with his marriage to Anne of Bohemia in 1381. However, the chronicle reads as if Richard is already dead: for example 'Iste Ricardus fuit filius edwardi . . .' (f. 160rb, ll. 58–59), 'temp*or*e istius ricardi . . .' (f. 160rb, l. 60). This would date the manuscript to 1400 at the earliest, or soon after.

[33] Nathaniel Edward Griffin, ed., *Historia destructionis Troiae*, Mediaeval Academy of America Publication, 26 (Cambridge, MA, 1936 repr. New York, 1970).

[34] Unedited. On the dubious ascription of this work to John of Legnano, see John P. McCall, 'The Writings of John of Legnano with a List of Manuscripts', *Traditio*, 23 (1967), 415–37 (p. 431).

[35] [J. Bongars, ed.], *Iacobi de Vitriaco Acconensis episcopi Historia Hierosolimitana, Gesta Dei per Francos, siue orientalium expeditionum, et regni Francorum Hierosolimitani historia a variis, sed illius aevi scriptoribus, litteris commendata*, Orientalis historiae, 1 (Hanover, 1611), 1047–1124. This copy wants the Prologue.

10. ff. 231ra–261vb Jacobus Theramicus, *Consolatio peccatorum* (imperfect), headed, in a sixteenth-century hand, 'lib*er* vocat*ur* beliall *et* viz p*ro* praxe jur*is*'.[36]

Vol. 2

11. ff. 1ra–6ra *Testamenta XII patriarcharum*, Latin translation of Robert Grosseteste.[37]
12. f. 6ra A Latin prayer.[38]
13. ff. 6ra–38va Henry of Huntingdon, *Historia Anglorum*.[39]
14. ff. 38va–56rb Marco Polo, *De statu et consuetudinibus orientalium regionum*, Latin version of Pipino.[40]
15. ff. 56rb–71ra Friar Hayton, *Flos ystoriarum terrae orientis*, Latin translation of Nicolas Falcon.[41]
16. ff. 71ra–71rb *Fides Saracenorum*.[42]

[36] Bloomfield, no. 3997. Printed by Johann Schüssler at Augsburg in 1472 (*ISTC*, no. ij00064000; Goff, J64), and several other early editions. No modern editions.

[37] *Testamenta duodecim Patriarcharum filiorum Jacob ad filias suos interprete Roberto Lincolniensis episcopa*, Patrologiae cursus completus: Series Graeca, 2, ed. J.-P. Migne (Paris, 1857), 1037–1150.

[38] Unedited. Begins: 'Audi p*ate*r om*n*ipot*ens* audi mis*erum*'; ends abruptly: 'tibi pia plorans co*m*patit*ur* vi*r*go maria *et* ⟨.⟩'. The text breaks off abruptly, being overwritten by the following item.

[39] Most recently edited and translated by Greenway, *Historia Anglorum. This is 'the abbreviated version of the text found in the HPB* [*Historia post obitum Bede*], running to 1148, continued from the "Marianist text" down to 1154': Diana Greenway, 'Henry of Huntingdon and the Manuscripts of his *Historia Anglorum*', *Anglo-Norman Studies IX: Proceedings of the Battle Conference 1986*, ed. R. Allen Brown (Woodbridge, 1987), p. 120. See also Greenway, *Historia Anglorum*, pp. cxxvii, clviii, where this version is designated Version 6, Redaction B. Dd.1.17 is one of four known manuscripts that preserve this version. The ascription in the colophon of the Dd.1.17 to Marianus Scotus ('Explicit cronica marciani [*sic*] scoti de gestis regni anglor*um* . . .') derives from the *Historia Anglorum* having been used in one manuscript as a continuation for John of Worcester's chronicle, itself a continuation of that of Marianus Scotus (see Greenway, *Historia Anglorum*, pp. clvii–clviii). The text is, however, correctly identified in the running title.

[40] No modern editions, but see the facsimile of the edition printed by Gerard Leeu, produced by the National Diet Library (*Itinerarium, Antverpiae, 1485* (Tokyo, 1949)). The title is from the colophon of the reprint: the original edition has now been assigned to the printer Gerard Leeu at Gouda, between 1483 and 11 June 1484 (*ISTC*, no. ip00902000).

[41] Edited in *Documents latins et français relatifs à l'Arménie*, Recueil des historiens des croisades: Documents arméniens, 2 (Paris, 1906 repr. Farnborough, 1967), 255–363.

[42] Unedited, title from final rubric. Begins: 'Credunt Saraceni vnu*m* deum creatorem *esse* om*nium*'; ends: 'p*er* angl*um* vltimo de p*a*radiso *et* inferno. Explicit ffides saracenorum'. Julia C. Crick erroneously claims that the same item is contained in Cambridge, St John's College, MS G.16 (184) (*Historia regum Britannie*, III.53). In fact, the item in the St John's College manuscript is part of the *Vita Mahumeti* section of Godfrey of Viterbo's *Pantheon*, and differs entirely from the item in Dd.1.17, in spite of having a similar incipit ('Credunt igitur Sarraceni unum esse Deum').

17. ff. 71rb–74vb Attrib. Ramón Martí, *De origine et progressu et fine Machometi et quadruplici reprobatione eius*.[43]
18. ff. 74vb–79rb William of Tripoli, *De statu Saracenorum*.[44]
19. ff. 79rb–79vb A life of Muhammad (imperfect).[45]

[43] Attributed to John of Wales in two manuscripts, and printed under his name by Georgius Fabricius, ed., *De Saracenis et Turcis chronicon Volfgangi Drechsleri. Item, De origine et progressu et fine Machometi, & quadruplici reprobatione prophetiae eius Ioannis Galensis Angli, liber* (Strasbourg, 1550). Attributed to Ricoldus de Monte Crucis in another manuscript. However, modern scholarship tends to favour Ramón Martí as the author: see Norman Daniel, *Islam and the West: The Making of an Image*, rev. ed. (Oxford, 1993) pp. 31, 416 (under *Reprobatio: quadruplex reprobatio*). There is a modern edition by Josep Hernando, '*De seta Machometi o De origine, progressu et fine Machometi et quadruplici reprobatione prophetiae eius*', *Acta historica et archaeologica mediaevalia*, 4 (1983), 9–63. The edited text is shorter than that of Dd.1.17 and the 1550 edition, however, but the version in Dd.1.17 is closer to the text of Hernando than that of Fabricius. This item and the following two are placed under the same running title, 'Gesta Machometi'. It is also in Cambridge, Gonville and Caius College, MS 162 (83), ff. 1^r–11^v, where it is also followed by William of Tripoli, ff. 12^r–25^v. On the lower margin of f. 71^r of Dd.1.17 are two lines determining the longitude and latitude of the Holy Sepulchre: 'hec linea qui*n*decies ducta longitudinem monstrat sepulcri d*omi*ni', 'hec nouies ducta latitudinem monstrat eiusdem sepulcri'. These lines are also in the Caius manuscript, f. 140^r.

[44] Edited with a German translation by Peter Engels, *Notitia de Machometo: De statu Sarracenorum*, Corpus Islamo-Christianum, Series Latina, 4 (Würzburg and Altenberge, 1992); H. Prutz, ed., *Guilelmi Tripolitani ordinis praedicatorum Tractatus de statu Saracenorum et de Mahomete pseudopropheta et eorum lege et fide incipit*, Kulturgeschichte der Kreuzzüge (Berlin, 1883), pp. 573–98. According to Engels, the text in Dd.1.17 is very closely connected to that in Caius, MS 162 (83), ff. 12^r–25^v, and the two are derived from the same original, seemingly no longer extant (unpublished notes on Dd.1.17, 1988, Dept. of Manuscripts, University Library, Cambridge).

[45] Unedited. Begins: 'Tempore Bonifacie p*a*pe iiij Ro*ma*ni pontifici*s*'; ends abruptly: 'Cibus cibor*um* vestentur ge*ner*ibus'. Also contained in London, British Library, MS Royal 13.E.IX, ff. 93^r–94^r, and London, British Library, MS Sloane 289, ff. 92^v–95^v (Engels, unpublished notes). According to Norman Daniel, this 'composite account of Islam' partly derives from Dialogus V of Petrus Alphonsi's *Dialogi in quibus impiae Judaeorum confutantur*, and partly represents a version of the 'Corozan' text (the popular legend of Muhammad's marriage to a lady from a province called Corozan) and perhaps the *Libellus in partibus transmarinis de Machometi fallaciis* from Vincent of Beauvais's *Speculum historiale* (Daniel, *Islam and the West*, pp. 258, 30–31; the full reference for the Petrus Alphonsi text is given on p. 422). The end of this copy is wanting due to missing leaves. According to the table of contents inside the cover of Dd.1.17, some other items were contained in these missing leaves: *Somnium beati Thome martiris post decessum ab Anglia*, *Processus fratris Nicholai Wysebeche de unxione regis Anglie etc*. A later hand has added the gloss, 'ista d*e*fi*ciu*nt'. The first of these is perhaps Thomas Becket's *Narratio de ampulla olei sancti quo reges Angliae ungi debent in coronation sibi diuinitus ostensa*. Certainly, the incipit of this work, 'Quando ego Thomas Cantuariensis archiepiscopus exsul ab Anglia fugiebam ad Franciam', is reminiscent of the title given on the table of contents for the item once in Dd.1.17. This work is short enough to have been contained in the three leaves missing from the end of vol. 2, and to have left enough space to be have been preceded by the end of item 19, and followed by the similarly themed *Processus fratris Nicholai Wysebeche de unxione regis Anglie etc*.

20. ff. 83ra–93va Gildas, *De excidio Britanniae* (imperfect).[46]

Vol. 3

21. ff. 1ra–31ra William Langland, *Piers Plowman* (B-Text).[47]
22. ff. 31rb–32rb *How Men þat Been in Heele Schulde Visite Seeke Folke*.[48]
23. ff. 32va–53vb *Mandeville's Travels* (Defective Version).[49]
24. ff. 54ra–63rb *The Seven Sages of Rome*.[50]
25. ff. 63va–87vb Clement of Llanthony, *Concordia Evangelistarum*.[51]

[46] Edited from this, and another manuscript, by [J. Josceline], *Gildae, cui cognomentum est sapientes, De excidio & conquestu Britanniae, ac flebili castigatione in reges, principes, & sacerdotes epistola* (London, 1568). Also edited by Theodor Mommsen, *Chronica minora saec. IV. V. VI. VII*, vol. 3, *Gildae Sapientes De excidio et conquestu Britanniae ac flebili castigatione in reges principes et sacerdotes*, Monumenta Germaniae historica: Auctorum antiquissimorum, 13 (Berlin, 1888), 1–85, with variant readings from this manuscript, denoted as D; and by Henry Petrie and Thomas Duffus Hardy, *Monumenta historica Britannica, or Materials for the History of Britain, from the Earliest Period to the End of the Reign of King Henry VII*, vol. 1, *Gildae Sapientes De excidio Brittaniae liber querulus* (N.p., 1848), 1–46, with variant readings from this manuscript, denoted as B. Most recently edited and translated, using Mommsen's text, by Michael Winterbottom, *The Ruin of Britain and Other Works*, History from the Sources (London, 1978).This copy wants most of the first chapter, due to missing leaves. The text has been marked up for printing: see John Bromwich, 'The First Book Printed in Anglo-Saxon Types', *Transactions of the Cambridge Bibliographical Society*, 3 (1959–63), 265–91 (pp. 273–4, and plate III, facing p. 274).

[47] *IMEV*, no. 1459, *Manual*, VII.2211–34; 2419–48. Edited by Walter W. Skeat, *The Vision of William Concerning Piers the Plowman*, together with *Vita de Dowel, Dobet, et Dobest, Secundum Wit et Resoun*, pt. 2, *The "Crowley" Text; or Text B*, EETS, 38 (1869), with variant readings from this manuscript, denoted as C. Also edited by Kane and Donaldson, *Piers Plowman: The B Version*, with variant readings from this manuscript, denoted C. On the hand used for *Piers Plowman* in the manuscript, see John H. Fisher, '*Piers Plowman* and the Chancery Tradition', *Medieval English Studies Presented to George Kane*, ed. Edward Donald Kennedy, Ronald Waldron, and Joseph S. Wittig (Wolfeboro, NH, 1988), pp. 267–78.

[48] *IPMEP*, no. 460 (Version B). Edited from this manuscript by Jeanne Krochalis and Edward Peters, *The World of Piers Plowman*, The Middle Ages (Pennsylvania, 1975), pp. 194–202.

[49] This manuscript has been designated as belonging to sub-group I of the Defective Version in the recent edition by M. C. Seymour, *The Defective Version of Mandeville's Travels*, EETS, 319 (2002), p. xvii. The edition includes variant readings from D.

[50] *IMEV*, no. 3187 (B-Text), *Manual*, IX.3272–3, 3561–3.

[51] Unedited. See Michael Lapidge and Richard Sharpe, *A Bibliography of Celtic-Latin Literature 400–1200*, Royal Irish Academy Dictionary of Medieval Latin from Celtic Sources: Ancillary Publications, 1 (Dublin, 1985), 21.

Composition of the Manuscript

Membrane. Vol. 1: 440 × 305 mm. (330 × 95 mm.), ff. 261; vol. 2: 440 × 305 mm. (330 × 95 mm.), ff. 93; vol. 3: 440 × 305 mm. (330 × 115 mm., items 21, 22; 330 × 90 mm., items 23, 25; 330 × 65 mm., item 24), ff. 87.

ff. i + 261 + 93 + 87 + i.

Vol. 1, ff. 114, 115 have been mutilated; only small upper portion remains.

Modern, accurate foliation (arabic numerals) has been added in pencil in the top right corner of each recto by Henry Bradshaw, dating from the rebinding of the volume in 1862; a '+' in pencil regularly marks the recto of the second leaf of the innermost bifolium of each quire throughout the volume. Therefore this supersedes the old foliations in ink (arabic numerals), and later in pencil, which, as a result of rebinding, are now out of sequence. The modern pencil foliation is the one followed in this description.

Ruled in crayon (except for vol. 2, ff. 1^r–71^r, ruled in brown ink), with single vertical and horizontal bounding lines, and a frame of double lines ruled in the margin (except for items 21 and 22, when there are no double vertical lines, perhaps because of the greater width of the columns of text). Pricking visible at outer edges only. Writing on lines.

Vols. 1 and 2: two columns to the page, each of 72 lines; vol. 3, items 21–23: two columns to the page, each of 61 lines; item 24: three columns to the page, each of 60–61 lines; item 25: two columns to the page, each of 71–73 lines.

Collation

Vol. I: i + 1^{12} (wants 1), 2–5^{12}, 6^{12} (wants 7), 7–8^{12}, 9^{12} (wants 2–12), 10^{12} (wants 1, 2; 6, 7 fragments), 11^{12}, 12^{12} (wants 6, 7), 13–21^{12}, 22^{10} (wants 10), 23 (wanting: see note following item 10 above).

Vol. 2: 24^{12}, 25^{12} + one (inserted after 2), 26–29^{12}, 30^{12} (wants 8–10), 31^{12} (wants 10–12).

Vol. 3: 32–34^{12}, 35^{12} (wants 1), 36–38^{12}, 39^{8} (wants 4–8) + i.

Catchwords (Hands I and III: scribal hand, boxed in, with pen flourishes; Hand II: scribal hand, boxed in, usually in red) visible in the usual place at the end of each gathering.

Various medieval quire and leaf signatures are sometimes visible. As the volume has a history of rebinding, it may be of interest to give a full account of these signatures.[52]

Vol. 1: crayon sequence sometimes visible in 1 (ii–v, struck through), 2 (i–vj), 13 (a mark resembling an open-topped *p*, followed by j–vj), 17 (bj–bvj), 18 (cj–cvj), 19 (dj–diiij, dvj),[53] 20 (ej–evj), 21 (fj–fvj), 22 (gj–gvj, with gvj crossed through, this quire being of ten, not twelve, leaves).

Brown ink sequence sometimes visible in 4 (dj–diiiiij), 7 (giiij), 8 (hiij, hiiiiij), 10 (jiiij), 11 (lj–l[iij], in red ink), 12 (m[iij]), 13 (j, in red ink), 15 (pj–piij, pv), 16 (qiij iij).

Vol. 2: crayon sequence sometimes visible in 24 (ij, ivj),[54] 25 (kj–kvj), 26 (lj–liiij, liiiiii),[55] 27 (mj–miiij, mvj),[56] 30 (nj–nij, niiij–nvj),[57] 31 (oj–ovj).

Brown ink sequence sometimes visible in 24 (6), 25 (5, 6), 26 (3), 27 (1–3, 6), 28 (3, 5).

Vol. 3: crayon sequence sometimes visible in 32–34 (varying number of horizontal lines: – for 1, = for 2, etc.; on leaf 1 of quire 33 the horizontal line is placed over a single vertical line), 36 (j, iij, iiij, struck through), 37 (iii, v, vi), 39 (i–iii, struck through).

Ink sequence visible in 33 (iiij, in brown), 38 (j–vj, in dark green or blue).

Secundo folio

q*ue* vulgares cronice

Handwriting

Hand I (vol. 1, vol. 2, ff. 71ra–93va, vol. 3, f. 63va–87vb): formal Gothic text-hand, double compartment *a*, sometimes straight-sided

[52] See also Benson and Blanchfield, *Manuscripts of Piers Plowman*, pp. 35–36, for a useful table documenting the details of the quires. Many of the signatures are now very worn, which may account for the few occasions where I have noticed a signature not in Benson and Blanchfield, and vice versa.

[53] The lower part of leaf 5 has been lost.

[54] The lower part of leaves 2–5 has been lost. Quires 28 and 29 have no signatures: 27 is signed *m* and 30 is signed *n*, though the contents run in sequence through all four quires.

[55] Benson and Blanchfield, *Manuscripts of Piers Plowman*, p. 36, transcribe this signature as *p* rather than *l*, which follows on from the previous *k* (the letter has a looped ascender, hence the confusion). Leaf 4 has been signed liij by mistake.

[56] The lower part of leaf 5 has been lost.

[57] The lower part of leaf 3 has been lost.

(more frequently at beginning of manuscript); double compartment *g*; ascenders of *b*, *h*, and *l* usually slightly hooked to the left, occasionally with a horizontal stroke to the left; ascender of *d* oblique; long *s* and capital form of short *s*; lobe of *p* usually not joined to shaft at top; 2-shaped *r* used after *o*, *b*, *p*; shaft of *t* protrudes above the headstroke; some biting between *d* and *e*, *d* and *o*. Textura, of twice the height, frequently employed for chapter headings, incipits, and explicits.

Hand II (vol. 2, f. 1ra–71ra): very similar to Hand I, but with the following differences: oblique splinters on ascenders of *b*, *h*, and *l*; ascender of *d* usually slightly curved; 2-shaped *r* used more frequently; single compartment *g*; lobe of *p* joined to shaft.[58]

Hand III (vol. 3, ff. 1ra–63^{rc}): same scribe as Hand I, writing *Anglicana formata* for the Middle English items (when switching to Latin for item 25, the scribe inadvertently uses a long, Anglicana *r* on f. 63va, l. 32, in the word *Tercius*). Ascenders of *b*, *l*, and *h* looped, sometimes hooked; ascender of *d* usually oblique, but looped form occasionally found; short *s* used at beginning of words, long *s* used at beginning and middle, and occasionally at end, and capital form of short *s* used at end of words; long *r*, with 2-shaped *r* used after *o*; shaft of *t* protrudes above headstroke; long *i* used for personal pronoun and at beginning of words, short *i* used elsewhere, and occasionally at beginning of words; *y* usually has long, hooked descender, curving to right, and is frequently surmounted by a dot. Thorn used only occasionally, yogh frequently. Occasional biting between *d* and *e*. Bastard Anglicana, of twice the height, used for headings, but with looped ascenders.

Punctuation[59]

Very rare. Some at the beginning of the text: *punctus*, above the line, at, for example, f. 54ra, ll. 23–25; mark resembling the upper stroke of a *punctus elevatus* used at the end of the line at, for example, f. 54ra, ll. 9, 12, 27, 28. Both marks indicate a medial pause but are used only

[58] None of the previous descriptions of the manuscript identifies a second hand for the Latin texts; however, the style of catchwords varies from that of Hand I (see above), and the manuscript is ruled in brown ink rather than crayon for this section, both also implying a second hand, most likely a second scribe.

[59] The following descriptions are confined to the text of *The Seven Sages of Rome* only. See the description in Benson and Blanchfield, *Manuscripts of Piers Plowman*, for the rest of the manuscript.

sporadically, not systematically, and are increasingly rare throughout the text. A *punctus elevatus* is used at f. 56^{rc}, l. 34, perhaps to mark the end of the line, as the scribe has written some of the following line on this one, and has had to cancel these words. Red or blue paraph marks are employed throughout. At the beginning, a paraph marks the introduction of each of the Seven Sages, and they are used throughout to indicate the beginning of a tale, but within the tales or the links between them there seems to be no coherent system for their use. An exception is that, of the 119 paraphs used in total (one of which, at l. 2995, is unexecuted), 36, nearly a third, mark a line beginning with the word *Quod*, and so function as speech marks of sorts.[60] Only 16 lines that begin with *Quod* are not marked with a paraph.

Abbreviations

Standard, but infrequent (except for the word *Emperour*, which is regularly abbreviated, e.g. f. 54ra, l. 1, where both the *er* and the *ur* are represented by the standard brevigraphs, and f. 56^{vc}, l. 6, where the scribe employs his frequent abbreviation *E*, which he also sometimes uses for *Emperes(se)*). Other abbreviations: *þ*^{t}, *w*^{t}, crossed *z* for 'and' (e.g. f. 54ra, l. 32); brevigraphs used, for example, for the omission of *n* (e.g. f. 54rb, l. 24), *er* (e.g. f. 54ra, ll. 1, 59), *ur* (e.g. f. 54ra, l. 1); final *e* sometimes shown by a flourish (e.g. f. 54ra, l. 32).

Corrections

The scribe was clearly very careless, making many errors. His favoured methods of correction were superimposition and expunction.

superimpositions: e.g. f. 54ra, l. 27, *oor*: *r* written over *ȝ*; f. 54rb, l. 23, *berd*: *d* written over another letter; f. 54^{rc}, l. 5, *dyuise*: *y* written over two minims.

expunction: e.g. f. 54vb, l. 1; f. 54^{vc}, l. 53; f. 55^{rc}, l. 3.

[60] Paraphs occur at the following lines: 25, 37, 49, 59, 71, 83, 91, 117, 165, 209, 261, 305, 337, 350, 404, 408, 416, 420, 448, 472, 624, 702, 712, 726, 802, 816, 844, 904, 922, 928, 990, 1007, 1030, 1046, 1154, 1164, 1173, 1188, 1280, 1299, 1312, 1319, 1333, 1446, 1474, 1514, 1648, 1662, 1674, 1709, 1728, 1786, 1836, 1862, 1872, 1876, 1917, 1936, 1948, 2004, 2072, 2080, 2095, 2123, 2127, 2141, 2187, 2203, 2229, 2261, 2269, 2283, 2289, 2389, 2393, 2399, 2407, 2431, 2443, 2457, 2467, 2581, 2609, 2617, 2643, 2645, 2740, 2750, 2754, 2766, 2768, 2772, 2778, 2784, 2786, 2796, 2798, 2843, 2847, 2861, 2871, 2899, 2981, 2985, 2995 (unexecuted), 3082, 3114, 3118, 3128, 3134, 3155, 3235, 3245, 3371, 3375, 3393, 3434, 3444, 3454.

cancellation: f. 56^{rc}, l. 34.

cancellation and expunction: f. 56va, l. 26.

interlineation with/without caret mark: e.g. f. 55ra, l. 22; f. 55va, l. 55; f. 57vb, l. 36.

erasure and rewriting: e.g. f. 55^{rc}, l. 28, *do deth*; f. 58vb, l. 3, *hed*: *h* written over another letter, over eras.; f. 59^{rc}, l. 21, *the*.

relineation: f. 55^{vc}, ll. 31–32; f. 60rb, ll. 31–32.

line(s) omitted either before or after, e.g., f. 54^{vc}, l. 33; f. 57va, l. 32; f. 57^{vc}, l. 15.

non-scribal corrections or additions: f. 57vb, l. 43; f. 58^{vc}, l. 46; f. 60^{vc}, l. 1.

There are also many uncorrected errors, such as words written twice (e.g. f. 54^{vc}, ll. 47, 53; f. 57^{rc}, l. 21), misdivision (f. 55vb, l. 2; f. 61^{rc}, l. 25), transposed letters (f. 58vb, l. 3) and so on. Full details of such errors are given in the apparatus to the edition.

Marginalia

In *The Seven Sages of Rome* a later hand (perhaps sixteenth-century) has glossed the rubrics at the beginning of each tale (starting with the second story, f. 55^{vc}) indicating the number of the tale and its teller (the Sage's name is given, or *nouerca* to indicate the stepmother). Tale 15, however (the Prince's), is not glossed. F. 56^{v}: something inked in lower margin, now faded and illegible; f. 59^{r}: various pen trials in upper margin; f. 63^{r}: various pen trials and the name *Robert M* inked in lower margin.

Elsewhere, most notably, vol. 1, f. 96^{v}: *Jane Stafford* or *Staford* pencilled in left margin three times; vol. 3, f. 34^{r}: *This is Robert morrys boke* inked in right margin;[61] vol. 3, f. 44^{v}: *Roberte* inked in left margin. Jane Stafford could be the Northamptonshire lady of that name who died in 1551.[62] Item 20, the Gildas, has been marked up for printing, as mentioned above.

[61] 'Robert morrys' is written as 'Robert bertmorrys': Crick transcribes 'Hertmory[e]' (*Historia regum Britannie*, III.70), but it is likely that 'hert' is just 'bert' from the end of 'Robert', written again (see Benson and Blanchfield, *Manuscripts of Piers Plowman*, p. 38, n. 45). As mentioned above, 'Robert M' is written on f. 63^{r}.

[62] Lady Jane Stafford, née Spencer of Althrop, Northants, widow of Sir Richard Knightley of Fawsley, Northants (Benson and Blanchfield, *Manuscripts of Piers Plowman*, p. 38, n. 44; A. I. Doyle, letter to Prof. Carley, 12 August 1986, Dept. of Manuscripts, University Library, Cambridge (copy)).

Decoration

Blue initial of three lines with red pen flourishing at the start of the *Seven Sages*, also occurring on f. 55^{vc}, the beginning of the first tale. Red and blue paraphs throughout (see above, 'Punctuation'). The entrances of the third and fourth Sages are marked by the marginal glosses *Thyrde* and *Fyde*, boxed in red; the beginning of each tale is similarly glossed, for example *Fyrst Talle*, *A Tale of þe Mayster*, *A Tale*. *N*ota *b*en*e* in the left margin boxed in red next to f. 58va, l. 19: *Old man chasty ʒong wyf*. The running title *seuene sagees* (with variant spellings) is written in the upper margin, boxed in red, with both words on each folio up to f. 55^{v}, then the first on the versos and the second on the rectos only for the rest of the text. Scribal indication of paraphs and initials to be decorated still visible.

Binding

Modern binding, dating from July 1969, by Douglas Cockerell & Son, Grantchester. 'Liber Glastoniensis' in gold letters on spine. Fragments of former binding (1862) inside front cover: brown leather, including title in gold letters, 'Liber Glastoniensis'.

From 1862, the manuscript has been foliated as if composed of three volumes but, as Kane and Donaldson remarked, 'we can find no grounds for doing so; the indications of layout, handwriting, ornament and content are that it was meant to be a single great book, differentiated only in handwriting according to whether the local text was in Latin or English'.[63] Although the manuscript may well have been written in stages as three separate volumes (vols. 2 and 3 do begin new quires), the old crayon quire signatures link the present vols. 1 and 2, further suggesting that they were never regarded as separate volumes.[64]

Also in 1862, Higden's *Polychronicon* was moved from its position after Clement of Llanthony at the end of the manuscript (where it was located from at least as early as the sixteenth century, as witnessed by the table of contents) to the beginning. This falls in line with its placement in manuscripts with similar contents, such as London, British Library, MS Royal 13.D.I, in which the Higden precedes the Geoffrey of Monmouth. The alphabetical sequence of

[63] Kane and Donaldson, *Piers Plowman: The B Version*, p. 3, n. 22.

[64] The old ink signatures, however, are different in each of the 'volumes', as outlined above, so this could be evidence that the manuscript was regarded as three separate volumes at some point in its history.

the old ink quire signatures in Dd.1.17 links these same two items here. Only one leaf is missing from the beginning of the Higden, which may have been enough to contain the start of the text, so it could well have begun the whole volume. However, the first quire of the Higden is signed on ff. 2–5 with roman numerals ii–v, struck through, and the only other quire in the manuscript in which such a signature is now visible is the final quire of the Clement of Llanthony, the last item: ff. 1–3 are signed using the same system of roman numerals, struck through.

There is no evidence from quire signatures to prove that volume 3 was intended to be bound after volume 2: the sixteenth-century contents list alone testifies to this.[65] One possibility is that volume 3, beginning with *Piers Plowman*, was originally placed at the beginning of the manuscript, followed by volume 1 starting with the Higden, and volume 2. This would mean that the Higden originally followed the Clement of Llanthony and preceded the Geoffrey of Monmouth. At some stage four leaves were lost from the end of the Clement of Llanthony, and the section containing *Piers* to Clement of Llanthony became detached, eventually being placed at the end of the manuscript. At that point, the order of quires would have been the same as today, with the Higden at the start of the manuscript. This could account for the old ink signatures, which indicate an initial position for the Higden.[66] At a later stage, but before the compilation of the contents list in the sixteenth century, some leaves were lost from the end of the *Polychronicon* and the beginning of the Geoffrey of Monmouth, and the *Polychronicon* found its way to the end of the manuscript where it remained until the manuscript was rebound in 1862. This theory makes better sense of all the old crayon quire and leaf signatures which, as seen above, could be said to link the Clement of Llanthony with the Higden. The modern sequence of volumes does not account for the possible link between the Clement of Llanthony and the Higden, unless we assume that the similarity between those quire signatures is of no importance.

[65] The alphabetical sequence of the old crayon quire signatures finishes at the end of vol. 2 with *o*, having commenced with *a* midway through Guido delle Colonne in vol. 1. Had vol. 3 followed on from vol. 2, one might have expected the first quire to be signed *p*.

[66] The signatures are first visible in quire 4, signed *d*.

Provenance

In his edition of Gildas (1568), which is partly based on the text in this manuscript, John Josceline said that the volume he had in hand (not necessarily the whole of the present manuscript) once belonged to Glastonbury Abbey, and was now the property of a lawyer from Kent.[67] This association is now usually discredited: Kane and Donaldson and A. I. Doyle are sceptical on the grounds of Middle English dialect,[68] and in N. R. Ker's *Medieval Libraries of Great Britain: A List of Surviving Books*, the connection is rejected.[69] Elsewhere, Doyle comments that 'some features of the spelling and annotation may support a northern provenance or destination, rather than the older guess of Glastonbury',[70] although the manuscript may have been moved to Glastonbury during the fifteenth century.[71] The manuscript's contents are similar to those known to have been in volumes of the Austin Friars' library at York, and Ralph Hanna remarks that 'the historical texts of the manuscript suggest origin among regular clergy'.[72]

Julia Crick suggests a close association between Dd.1.17 and London, British Library, MS Royal 13.D.I, both written around the same time, and having many items in common.[73] Royal 13.D.I is

[67] *Gildae, cui cognomentum est sapientis*, p. Aij.

[68] Kane and Donaldson, *Piers Plowman: The B Version*, p. 3, n. 25; Doyle, letter.

[69] N. R. Ker, ed., *Medieval Libraries of Great Britain: A List of Surviving Books*, 2nd ed., Royal Historical Society Guides and Handbooks, 3 (London, 1964), 91. However, in the *Supplement to the Second Edition* of Ker's work, 'Cambridge, U.L., DD.1.17. H. Huntendonensis. s.xiv/xv.¹?' is included as a questionable entry: Andrew G. Watson, ed., *Medieval Libraries of Great Britain: A List of Surviving Books: Supplement to the Second Edition*, Royal Historical Society Guides and Handbooks, 15 (London, 1987), 38.

[70] 'Remarks on Surviving Manuscripts of *Piers Plowman*', *Medieval English Religious and Ethical Literature: Essays in Honour of G. H. Russell*, ed. Gregory Kratzmann and James Simpson (Cambridge, 1986), pp. 35–48 (p. 42).

[71] Doyle, informal notes, referred to in Benson and Blanchfield, *Manuscripts of Piers Plowman*, p. 33.

[72] Ralph Hanna III, *William Langland*, English Writers of the Late Middle Ages, Authors of the Middle Ages, 3 (Aldershot, 1993), 35; Doyle, letter; Doyle, 'Remarks on Surviving Manuscripts of *Piers Plowman*', pp. 35–48 (p. 42 and n. 22).

[73] See Julia C. Crick, *Historia regum Britannie*, vol. 4, *Dissemination and Reception in the Later Middle Ages* (Cambridge, 1991), 74, 106, 135, 143, 150, n. 65, 169, 185, 205 (Dd.1.17 is referred to by the number 40, and Royal 13.D.I by 111 in Crick's work). According to Peter Engels, unpublished notes, the two manuscripts share the same scribe and initial shaper, but this claim has been rejected by A. I. Doyle (quoted in Benson and Blanchfield, *Manuscripts of Piers Plowman*, p. 37, n. 42). A plate of Royal 13.D.I is included in S. Harrison Thomson, *Latin Bookhands of the Later Middle Ages 1100–1500* (Cambridge, 1969), p. 102. On the date of the manuscript, Harrison notes an entry in one of the items 'concerning Richard II and his expedition into Scotland in 1385'. This may be compared with item 6 in Dd.1.17, which ends in 1381 with Richard's marriage to Anne of Bohemia.

known to have belonged to St Peter's, Cornhill, in London.[74] Cambridge, Gonville and Caius College, MS 162 (83) contains items 17 and 18 (*De origine et progressu et fine Machometi et quadruplici reprobatione eius* and William of Tripoli's *De statu Saracenorum*) of Dd.1.17, and also the two lines on volume 2, f. 71^{r}, which indicate the dimensions of the Holy Sepulchre. According to Peter Engels, these two manuscript texts of William of Tripoli were derived from the same original, which seems no longer to be extant.

As mentioned above, the Jane Stafford of volume 1, f. 96^{v} was perhaps the Northamptonshire lady who died in 1551, and we do know that the whole of the present volume was acquired by Bishop John Moore of Ely sometime before 1697: it is listed as being in his library in Bernard's *Catalogi* (1697).[75] Bishop Moore died in 1714, and George I bought his library and donated it to the University in 1715.

3. THE Y-GROUP MANUSCRIPTS

In addition to Dd.1.17, there are seven known manuscripts that contain the Middle English verse *Seven Sages of Rome*, but in the version known as the Y-group.[76] Descriptions of these manuscripts can be found in the editions of Brunner and Campbell, and in Campbell's dissertation.[77] Further descriptions are indicated in the

Engels also suggests that London, British Library, MS Royal 13.E.IX, which has the anonymous item 19 in common with Dd.1.17, was also probably written in the same scriptorium.

[74] Thomson, *Latin Bookhands*, p. 102; Engels, unpublished notes; Crick, *Historia regum Britannie*, III.180–3. Thomson dates this ownership to *ca.* 1450 on the basis of two *ex libris* inscriptions.

[75] [E. Bernard], 'Librorum manuscriptorum admodum reverendi in Christo patris D.D. Joannis Mori episcopi Norvicensis catalogus', *Catalogi librorum manuscriptorum Angliae et Hiberniae in unum collecti, cum indice alphabetico*, vol. 2 (Oxford, 1697), 361–84 (p. 369).

[76] The Middle Scots *Seven Sages* is not directly related to the Middle English versions, and so need not form part of this discussion. A description of the manuscript, and information on this text, can be found in the recent edition by Catherine van Buuren. Similarly, the Middle English prose *Seven Sages* is independent of the Middle English verse versions, being a translation from Version H of the *Seven Sages*, most likely from an early printed edition of the Latin *Historia Septem Sapientum*: see Campbell, *Seven Sages*, pp. lx–lxi.

[77] Brunner, pp. ix–xiii, Campbell, *Seven Sages*, pp. xxxvi–xxxix, Campbell, 'Study', pp. 37–42.

notes. The manuscripts, in approximate chronological order, are as follows.

1. A—Edinburgh, National Library of Scotland, MS Advocates' 19.2.1, 'Auchinleck'

Membrane. *ca.* 1331–40. Dialect: London.[78] The poem, item 18, occupies ff. 85ra–99vb, and is fragmentary: between ff. 84–85 one leaf has been removed, and so the end of *Sir Degare* and the beginning of the *Seven Sages* (about 120 lines) are now wanting. The end of the *Seven Sages* (*ca.* 1050 lines) is also wanting, due to the removal of gathering 15; the missing leaves also contained the beginning of *Floris and Blanchfleur*.[79] The disposition of the text may be seen in the facsimile of the Auchinleck manuscript published in 1977 or in the National Library of Scotland's digital version.[80] Kölbing's conjecture that this version of the *Seven Sages* shared a common authorship with the Kentish versions of *Arthour and Merlin*, *Alisaunder*, and *Richard Coeur de Lion* was challenged by Campbell.[81] An abstract of A, with extracts, was included in Ellis's *Specimens of Early English Metrical Romances*.[82] This text of the *Seven Sages* was first edited in 1810 by Henry Weber, for the third volume of his *Metrical Romances*.[83] Weber used C (see below) to supply the missing lines in the Auchinleck text. The text of A formed the base for Karl Brunner's 1933 edition for the Early English Text Society.

[78] *LALME*, I.88. See also Linguistic Profile (hereafter LP) 6500, III.301.

[79] Brunner, p. ix. Derek Pearsall and I. C. Cunningham, introduction, *The Auchinleck Manuscript: National Library of Scotland Advocates' MS. 19.2.1* (London, 1977), p. xxi. The extant 2646 lines correspond to ll. 120–2770 in Brunner's edition.

[80] Pearsall and Cunningham, *Auchinleck Manuscript*; Burnley and Wiggins, *Auchinleck Manuscript*.

[81] Campbell, 'Study', pp. 85–87. In support of Kölbing's theory, see G. V. Smithers, ed., *Kyng Alisaunder*, vol. 2, EETS, 237 (1957), p. 41. Pearsall and Cunningham refer to Smithers as confirming the theory of a common authorship for *Arthour and Merlin*, *Alisaunder*, and *Richard*, and 'perhaps' the *Seven Sages* (*Auchinleck Manuscript*, p. xi).

[82] Ellis, *Specimens*, pp. 23–101. Ellis used C (see below) for the end of the poem, where A is wanting. He gives an introduction to the poem in vol. 3, 3–22.

[83] Weber, *Metrical Romances*, III.1–153. An introduction to the poem is given in I.lv–lviii, and explanatory notes in III.367–74.

2. *R—Oxford, Bodleian Library, MS Rawlinson Poet. 175 (Summary Catalogue 14667)*[84]

Membrane. s. xiv $^{med.}$ Dialect: Yorkshire, North Riding.[85] The *Seven Sages* occupies ff. 109ra–131va. The text is fragmentary: after f. 125, two folios are wanting (some earlier leaves having been misbound in their place), resulting in a loss of about 350 lines from l. 3673 in Campbell's edition.[86] The manuscript also contains *The Prick of Conscience*, and a variety of other religious items. The presence of the *Seven Sages* in R was announced by Arthur S. Napier in 1899, who gave ll. 1–128 as an example of the text.[87] Variant readings from R are given in Campbell's edition.

3. *C—London, British Library, MS Cotton Galba E.IX*[88]

Membrane. s. xv $^{in.}$ Dialect: northern.[89] The *Seven Sages*, the second item, occupies ff. 25rb–48rb. It is entitled *þe Proces of þe Seuyn Sages*. The manuscript also includes *Ywain and Gawain*, some moral verses, the *Prophecies of Merlin*, *Sir Penay*, two poems on the Rood, various ballads, the *Gospel of Nicodemus*, a manual of the Seven Deadly Sins, and *The Prick of Conscience*. Weber and Ellis used this text of the *Seven Sages* to replace the missing lines of A for their edition and summary respectively. Petras printed *Avis* from this manuscript.[90] Campbell edited C for his edition of 1907.

4. *Ar—London, British Library, MS Arundel 140*[91]

Paper. s. xv^{I}. Dialect: South Lincolnshire, but mixed with various dialectal components.[92] The *Seven Sages* is the fifth item, occupying

[84] Falconer Madan, *A Summary Catalogue of Western Manuscripts in the Bodleian Library at Oxford*, vol. 3 (Oxford, 1895 repr. München, 1980), 321–2. A brief description is included in Robert E. Lewis and Angus McIntosh, *A Descriptive Guide to the Manuscripts of the Prick of Conscience*, Medium Ævum Monographs, ns 12 (Oxford, 1982), 116.

[85] Campbell, *Seven Sages*, pp. lxxiii–lxxvi.

[86] Campbell, *Seven Sages*, pp. xxxvii.

[87] Arthur S. Napier, 'A Hitherto Unnoticed Middle English Manuscript of the *Seven Sages*', *PMLA*, 14 (1899), 459–64.

[88] Also described by H. L. D. Ward, *Catalogue of Romances in the Department of Manuscripts in the British Museum*, vol. 2 (London, 1893 repr. 1962), 213–18; Albert B. Friedman and Norman T. Harrington, eds., *Ywain and Gawain*, EETS, 254 (1964), pp. ix–xii; Guddat-Figge, *Catalogue of Manuscripts*, pp. 173–6; Lewis and McIntosh, *Descriptive Guide*, pp. 58–59.

[89] *LALME*, I.106.

[90] Paul Petras, *Über die mittelenglischen Fassungen der Sage von der Sieben Weisen Meistern* (Breslau, 1885), p. 56.

[91] Also described by Ward, *Catalogue of Romances*, pp. 224–7; Lewis and McIntosh, *Descriptive Guide*, pp. 57–58; John M. Manly and Edith Rickert, *The Text of The Canterbury Tales: Studied on the Basis of All Known Manuscripts*, vol. 1, *Descriptions of the Manuscripts* (Chicago, 1940 repr. 1967), 52–54.

[92] *LALME*, I.105.

ff. 152^{r}–165^{v}, and is fragmentary (only 2467 lines remain). It begins with the preamble to the fourth tale, *Medicus*, and ends shortly after the beginning of the last story, *Vaticinium*.[93] The other items in the volume are *Ypotis*, *Mandeville's Travels*, *The Prick of Conscience*, a fragment of a religious poem upon 'Gy of Werwyke' and 'Alquyn the Deken', and Chaucer's *The Tale of Melibee*. According to M. C. Seymour, this last item was originally contained in a separate manuscript, and belongs to the second half of the fifteenth century.[94] Campbell printed ll. 1–228 of the *Seven Sages* in this manuscript (*Medicus*).[95] Variant readings from Ar are given in Brunner's edition.

5. *F—Cambridge, University Library, MS Ff.2.38*[96]

Paper. s. xv $^{ex.}$/s. xvi $^{in.}$ Dialect: Leicestershire.[97] The *Seven Sages* follows *Bevis of Hampton*, and occupies ff. 134ra–156vb. The text is fragmentary: it wants ll. 143–51, 166–84, 206–16, and 243–9 of the printed edition (f. 135 is torn), 880–1010 (f. 141 is missing), and 1257–1389 (f. 144 is missing), and the ends of several lines have been lost as a result of cropping.[98] The first part of this large manuscript is made up of various religious pieces, but the *Seven Sages* finds its place towards the end of the volume, in the middle of a sequence of romances: *The Erle of Toulous*, *Sir Eglamour of Artois*, *Sir Tryamour*, *Octavian*, *Sir Bevis of Hampton*, *The Seven Sages of Rome*, *Guy of Warwick*, *Le Bone Florence of Rome*, *Robert of Sicily*, and *Sir Degare*. A facsimile of the manuscript was published in 1979.[99] Extracts from this text of the *Seven Sages* were printed in Halliwell's *The Thornton Romances*, and in Wright's edition of the *Seven Sages*.[100] Petras

[93] Brunner, p. xi.

[94] Seymour, 'English Manuscripts', p. 184.

[95] Campbell, 'Study', pp. 94–100.

[96] Frances McSparran and P. R. Robinson, introduction, *Cambridge University Library MS Ff.2.38*, (London, 1979), p. xii. Also described in *Catalogue of the Manuscripts Preserved in the Library of the University of Cambridge*, II.404–8; Guddat-Figge, *Catalogue of Manuscripts*, pp. 94–99.

[97] *LALME*, I.67; LP 531, III.244–5.

[98] McSparran and Robinson, *Cambridge University Library MS Ff.2.38*, p. xxv; Brunner, pp. 194–5, 202, 204.

[99] McSparran and Robinson, *Cambridge University Library MS Ff.2.38*.

[100] James Orchard Halliwell, ed., *The Thornton Romances. The Early English Metrical Romances of Perceval, Isumbras, Eglamour and Degrevant. Selected from Manuscripts at Lincoln and Cambridge*, Camden Society, 30 (London, 1844), pp. xlii–xliv; Wright, pp. lxx–lxxii. Halliwell gives only a brief summary of the poem, with a few short quotations, in the context of a description of Ff.2.38 (pp. xxxvi–xlv), one of the manuscripts he was using for his edition.

printed the tale *Avis* from this manuscript in his dissertation on the manuscripts of the Middle English *Seven Sages*. Brunner prints the full text in his edition.[101]

6. *E—London, British Library, MS Egerton 1995*[102]

Paper. From the dates contained in one of the items, a chronicle of the mayors of London, we know that the manuscript was completed after 1469, but probably begun some years earlier. Dialect: Surrey.[103] The *Seven Sages*, a complete text, is the first item, and occupies ff. 3^{r}–54^{v}. The other items include medical recipes, the moral lines 'Earth upon Earth', various extracts from courtesy books, 'There was a man that hadde nought' (*IMEV*, no. 3546), Latin prognostications of the weather, names of the bishoprics in England, a piece on 'The termys of venery and the crafte . . .' and 'the namys of hawkys', a version of the 'Gouernayl of helthe', Lydgate's 'Sapiencia phisicorum', directions in verse for blood-letting, 'The assyse of brede and of alle', supposedly a statute of Henry III for 1266–7, a list of churches, monasteries, and hospitals of the city of London, *The Siege of Rouen*, verses by Lydgate on the kings of England from the Conquest to Henry VI, and Gregory Skinner's *Chronicle of the Mayors of London*. An extract from this version of the *Seven Sages* was printed by Petras in the appendix to his dissertation.[104] Variant readings from E are given in Brunner's edition.

7. *B—Oxford, Balliol College, MS 354*[105]

Richard Hill's Commonplace Book. Paper. s. xvi^{1}: the latest date given in the volume is 1536, and the earliest is 1508. Dialect: southern.[106] The *Seven Sages*, a complete text, occupies ff. 18ra–54rb. The first rubric gives the title of the work as follows: *Here begynneth þe prologes of the vij sages or vij wise masters which were*

[101] Brunner, pp. 193–210, 129–92.

[102] Also described by Ward, *Catalogue of Romances*, pp. 218–24; James Gairdner, ed., *The Historical Collections of a Citizen of London in the Fifteenth Century*, Camden Society, ns 17 (1876), pp. i–x; David R. Parker, *The Commonplace Book in Tudor London: An Examination of BL MSS Egerton 1995, Harley 2252, Lansdowne 762, and Oxford Balliol College MS 354* (Lanham, 1988), pp. 17–36.

[103] *LALME*, I.109; LP 5630, III.493.

[104] Petras, *Über die mittelenglischen Fassungen.*

[105] Also described in R. A. B. Mynors, *Catalogue of the Manuscripts of Balliol College Oxford* (Oxford, 1963), pp. 352–4; Parker, *Commonplace Book*, pp. 37–88. A digital version of the manuscript is available at http://image.ox.ac.uk/show?collection=balliol&manuscript=ms354 (accessed 12 June 2005).

[106] Campbell, *Seven Sages*, pp. xxxviii. Not analysed in *LALME*.

named as here after ffolowith.[107] The colophon reads as follows: *Thus endith of the vij sages of Rome which was drawen owt of crownycles* and *owt of wrytyng of old men* and *many a notable tale is therin, as ye beffore sayde. Quod Richard Hill.*[108] According to f. 176r, Richard Hill was *seruant to M. Wynger, alderman of London.*[109] The manuscript catalogue for Balliol College informs us that Hill was a grocer, and was born shortly before 1490.[110] Its principal contents include 'Godfrydus of Rome' (a tale from the *Gesta Romanorum*), prose treatises on the management of horses and grafting, family memoranda, *The Siege of Rouen*, *Trentale sancti Gregorii pape* (*IMEV*, no. 1653), some extracts from Gower's *Confessio Amantis*, two poems by Lydgate ('On the Virtues of the Mass', 'The Churl and the Bird'), an Anglo-French vocabulary with a bilingual text of the *Boke of Curtasie*, London annals for the years 1414–1536, and several other verses, songs, carols, and miscellaneous pieces of information. The existence of the *Seven Sages* was first noted in this manuscript by H. Varnhagen.[111] Descriptions of the manuscript, with the texts of some of the contents, are given in an article by E. Flügel and, particularly, in an EETS edition by R. Dyboski.[112] Variant readings from B are given in Brunner's edition.

4. THE INTERRELATIONSHIP OF THE MANUSCRIPTS

The Middle English *Seven Sages* is ultimately derived from the French version of *The Seven Sages of Rome* designated A by Gaston Paris, but referred to here as A*, to avoid confusion with the version of the *Seven Sages* in the Auchinleck mansucript, here designated A.[113] French Version A* is a prose *Seven Sages*, containing the same stories in the same order as the Middle English texts, and showing marked similarities of both content and, allowing for translation,

[107] Brunner, p. 1.

[108] Brunner, p. 192.

[109] Brunner, p. xiii.

[110] Mynors, *Catalogue*, p. 352.

[111] H. Varnhagen, ed., *Eine italienische Prosaversion der Sieben Weisen* (Berlin, 1881), p. xi. See also Varnhagen's review of Petras in *Englische Studien*, 10 (1887), 279–82 (p. 279).

[112] Ewald Flügel, ed., 'Liedersammlungen des XVI. Jahrhunderts, besonders aus der Zeit Heinrichs VIII: III', *Anglia*, 26 (1903), 94–285; Roman Dyboski, ed., *Songs, Carols, and Other Miscellaneous Poems, from the Balliol MS. 354, Richard Hill's Commonplace-Book*, EETS, ES 101 (1907), pp. xiii–vi, xxxiv–lix. A typed transcript of this manuscript by D. C. Browning is kept at Balliol College. See also Eamon Duffy, *The Stripping of the Altars: Traditional Religion in England c.1400–c.1580* (New Haven, CT, 1992), pp. 75–77.

[113] Gaston Paris, ed., *Deux rédactions du Roman des Sept Sages de Rome*, Société des Anciens Textes Français (Paris, 1876), p. xvi.

phrasing.[114] French Version A* probably dates to the twelfth century, and is likely to have been derived from a lost French metrical version—perhaps the parent version of the entire *Seven Sages*-group.[115] As Karl Brunner remarks in his edition of the *Seven Sages*, the search for a particular manuscript of French Version A* that is most closely related to the Middle English texts 'is seriously hampered by the fact that there are so many of them and that most show only insignificant variants'.[116] Of course, it is possible that the Middle English texts derive from a now lost French version, perhaps one in verse, but, as Brunner observes, if such a version once existed, 'with a work so widely spread as the *S.S.*, one might have expected traces of it'.[117] Killis Campbell put forward the hypothesis that French Version A* was originally translated into Middle English around 1275,[118] and that this translation was the parent version of all the extant Middle English manuscripts.[119] This proposition will be discussed in full later in this introduction.

Before Campbell's research, most critics believed that the majority of the Middle English manuscripts were independent translations from a common Old French source.[120] Thomas Wright, original editor of the *Seven Sages* in Dd.1.17, certainly saw no connection between his text and the other poems.[121] Campbell's close comparison of A, Ar, E, B, and C (R had not yet been identified) revealed a large number of identical lines and similar rhymes—so many that he concluded that these manuscripts must ultimately be derived from a common Middle English source, which he designated y (R was later included in this grouping).[122] He also found enough similarities between F and these manuscripts (particularly from *Roma* onwards) to assume that it too was derived from y. All these manuscripts,

[114] See Campbell, 'Study', p. 87–91, for a full discussion of this conclusion. As Brunner remarks, *Seven Sages*, pp. xiii–xv, the problem of the source of the Middle English poems was first tackled by Paris, *Deux rédactions*, p. xxvii, and his suggestion of French Version A* as the source was more fully established by Petras, *Über die mittelenglischen Fassungen*, pp. 31 ff., and by Campbell, 'Study', pp. 87–91.

[115] See Campbell, *Seven Sages*, pp. xxxiv–xxxv.

[116] Brunner, p. xv.

[117] Brunner, p. xvi.

[118] Campbell, 'Study', p. 85, *Seven Sages*, p. lix.

[119] Campbell, *Seven Sages*, pp. liv–lv.

[120] See, for example, Petras, *Über die mittelenglischen Fassungen*, p. 31.

[121] Wright, p. lxviii.

[122] Campbell first discussed the interrelationship of the Middle English manuscripts in 'Study', pp. 43–84, before R had been identified; see also his subsequent edition of the *Seven Sages*, pp. xl-lvii, which is based on C and R.

then, formed a group which was designated by Campbell as Y. No Y-group manuscript was derived from another: all showed certain fidelities to the Old French source that were in no other manuscript.

Campbell also compared D with the other Middle English manuscripts, and found sufficient similarities of phrasing and incident (with D agreeing with the Y-group against the Old French) to conclude that D was not an independent translation from the Old French, but was connected to the Y-group. D could not have been based on y, or any of the Y-group manuscripts, since it was often more faithful to the Old French than any of them. Nor could y have been based on D, because it, too, was sometimes more faithful to the Old French than was D. Hence Campbell concluded that D and y were related through a common original, which he designated x. Therefore x was the Middle English parent version. Since the earliest extant text of the *Seven Sages* dates to *ca.* 1331–40 (the Auchinleck manuscript), Campbell dated y to about 1300, and so x to 'about the year 1275', which he regarded as 'a conservative guess'.[123]

Looking at the interrelationship of the Y-group manuscripts, Campbell concluded that the texts formed the following sub-groups:

1) C and R, derived from a common original, designated cr. [Northern Version]
2) F, A, Ar, E, B. [Southern Version.] Within this sub-group, A, Ar, E, and B are further grouped together against F; and then A and Ar form a final grouping, as do E and B.[124]

In his edition of the *Seven Sages*, Karl Brunner largely accepted Campbell's conclusions, adducing supporting evidence of his own.[125] The stemma printed in his edition summarizes these conclusions (lower-case letters indicate hypothetical versions of which there are no known extant manuscripts):[126]

[123] Campbell, *Seven Sages*, p. lix.

[124] Brunner's edition used the subtitle 'Southern Version', presumably to distinguish it from Campbell's earlier edition of the Northern manuscripts C and R. The *Seven Sages* bibliography (Runte, Wilkeley, and Farrell), adopts 'Southern Version' along with 'Northern Version' for C and R, and 'Midland Version' for D, to classify the Middle English texts.

[125] Brunner, pp. xvii–xxi.

[126] Brunner, p. xxi.

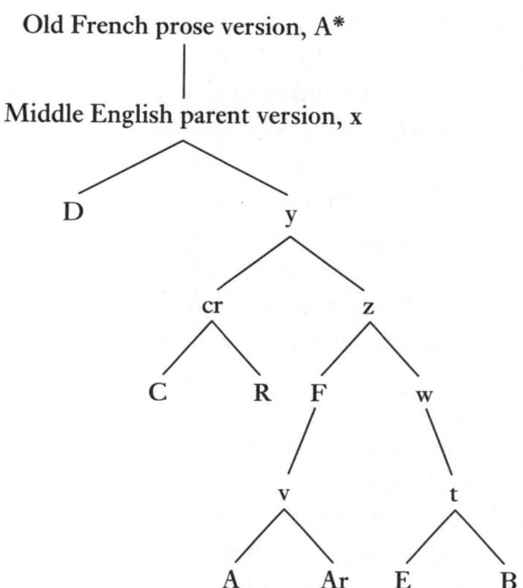

However, Brunner was still sceptical of Campbell's conjectured relationship between D and y, and hence of the existence of the Middle English parent version, x. Brunner showed that some of the supposed agreements of incident between D and the Y-group against the French could not be maintained in the light of a closer examination of the manuscripts of A* (Campbell had not had access to any of these, but had used the edition published by Le Roux de Lincy, which contains a slightly different prose version from that of A*). Of the textual parallels between D and the Y-group that Campbell cited as evidence, Brunner remarked that though these 'cannot be regarded as absolutely conclusive, they give his opinion a good deal of probability'.[127] So Brunner included an alternative stemma in his edition, showing D and y independently derived from the Old French.

Both Brunner and Campbell classified the texts according to shared readings and errors, and common additions and omissions. Such recensionism is perhaps not so fallible a system when applied to the Middle English *Seven Sages* as when used to classify other texts: because the poem is a translation, and because we have access to the Old French original (in manuscripts of A*), we can determine with

[127] Brunner, p. xx.

greater safety which is likely to be the correct reading, and which the error. Nevertheless, neither Brunner nor Campbell always paid due regard to the possibility of independent errors or omissions, except when such errors worked against their classifications.

The evidence for y, cr, z, and w, originally proposed by Campbell, and reformulated by Brunner in his edition of the *Seven Sages*,[128] seems reasonable enough. What is questionable, however, is the conclusion that A and Ar are derived from a common parent (v in Brunner's stemma). As evidence, Campbell says that the two often agree with each other against the Old French, and against all other Middle English manuscripts: he cites five examples.[129] However, in all these cases it could equally be argued that A and Ar are merely preserving the reading of x, which has been altered in the other extant texts. For all five examples, the other Y-group texts offer readings that differ from each other: if, as Campbell suggests, the common reading of A and Ar was dependent upon their unique parent, and so comprised a variant reading, then we might expect to find some agreement amongst the rest of the Y-group texts, some common preservation of the original reading of x, but this is not the case. Furthermore, one of Campbell's five examples is erroneous. Campbell claims that A and Ar alone include the following detail:

> Wiȝ riche baudekines ispredde (A l. 2734)
> Wiȝ riche cloþes all byspred (Ar l. 2734)[130]

F, however, has this too, and is in some respects closer to Ar than is A:

> In cloþys full ryche he was bespredd (F l. 1953)[131]

Campbell offers more substantial evidence in the form of a shared error. In the tale *Vidua*, both A and Ar say that the wife was cut in the *wombe*, instead of the thumb, as stated by the Old French, and by E and B (C and R say finger; F, hand; D does not specify). Yet this

[128] Brunner, pp. xvii–xxi.

[129] Campbell, 'Study', p. 55.

[130] Quotations are taken from the following editions: for A, Ar, E, B, and F, Brunner's edition; for C and R, Campbell's edition; for D, my edition; for A*, that of the CRAL. Unless otherwise specified, line numbers from Brunner's edition refer to his general numbers given to the right of the edited text, except for those quotations taken from after l. 2740, when they refer to the line numbers of the individual manuscripts.

[131] Campbell may have realized this himself later, since he omits this example in his edition of the *Seven Sages* (pp. xlv–xlvi).

common variant could well have arisen independently. He also observes that A and Ar alone preserve the Old French in *Senescalcus*, having the king offer twenty marks to procure himself a woman.[132] Nevertheless, E is very close: *Take xx pounde and spare nought* (l. 1579). *Pounde* could be a natural substitution for *marke*, and anyway, the fact that A and Ar best preserve the Old French here does not prove that they had a unique, common source, because, again, they could have done so independently.

Brunner lists a further shared error: in *Medicus*, l. 1070 of his edition, A reads *enderdai*, and Ar *oþer day*, while E and B have *othyr yere*, and F, *odur yere* (l. 1849), which are closer to *þe twe*[*l*]*ft ȝere* of C and R (l. 1168). Neither A* nor D specifies a time. The reading of A and Ar is likely to be the error because the speaker at this point in the tale is the Queen of Hungary, and she is telling of her extramarital affair, which resulted in pregnancy. Since her son is no longer a baby, it is certain that this event took place the *othyr yere* rather than the *oþer day*. Yet it is still possible that this common error, like the substitution of *wombe* for thumb in *Vidua*, could have arisen independently.

Campbell admits that Ar sometimes agrees with E and/or B against A (l. 56). For example, in *Senescalcus*, Ar and E (Campbell claims B, too, but is mistaken) have in common the error of saying that the king took delight in women. A, B, C, R, and D follow the Old French correctly and say that he hated women. However, Campbell concludes that these agreements do not contradict the classification of Ar with A, but 'merely indicate that in such cases, Ar best preserving the original, independence has been asserted by the poet of A'.[133] Such an explanation is hardly satisfactory for the example cited here, however, since A (and B) is most likely to be preserving the original reading rather than asserting independence: it is Ar and E that have a common variant. Of course, this could have arisen independently, but it is worth noting that both Campbell and Brunner readily dismiss the evidence of common variants when they work against their classifications, but accept them when they read in their favour (A and Ar's shared error of *wombe* instead of thumb in *Vidua*, for example). Having listed two such awkward variants, Brunner makes the claim that such variants, however, 'are likely to have arisen independently, just as all other variants which seem to disprove the above assumption'.[134]

[132] Study', p. 55. [133] 'Study', p. 56. [134] Brunner, p. xix.

There is perhaps a stronger case for the derivation of E and B from a common source, since this is based not only on shared errors (for example, both of these mistakenly name the clerk in *Roma* as *Junyus* (l. 2779) instead of Genus, but retain January as the month named after him), but also on common additions, or omissions of several couplets preserved in A and Ar, and in either C and R, or the Old French, or both.[135]

Nevertheless, there are other examples of common variants that can be cited against Campbell and Brunner's classification. In *Roma*, B agrees with C, R, F, and D in calling the besiegers of Rome *hethen kyng*es (l. 2826); A, Ar, and E call them sultans. The Old French reads *rois paiens* (39.001). This example questions the existence of the common parent w for A, Ar, E, and B. In the same tale, we are told that the besiegers *voloient avoir la chaiere saint pere* (39.001). A reflects this by saying that they wanted *to strwre seinte Petres sate* (l. 2746); but Ar and F have the common error *to fell seynte Pet*ers *gate* (Ar l. 1788), *to felle seynt Petur gate* (F l. 1971). None of the other texts has anything similar. This example works against the grouping of A and Ar against E and B.

A final example may be drawn from *Inclusa*. In this tale, the lady locked in the tower wishes to show the knight below that she loves him. In the Old French, and in D, Ar, and B, she throws some rushes, bound together, down towards him, holding on to one end herself: *tantost prist .I. gros jon crues dedanz, si le lanca si que le gros chief en coula jus* * et *le gresle desus* (43.007).[136] This is translated in Ar, for example, as:

Scho toke a rech and knyt it ryȝt
And þrewe it doune to þe knyȝt;
þe smaller ende vpwarde fold,
þe gretter to þe erþe smote. (ll. 2011–14)

However, in E, F, C, and R (A is wanting here), she throws down a love letter. For example:

Sho lokyd owte and saye hym sone,
And toke a letter jwretyn fulle ryght,
And caste hit downe before the knyght. (E ll. 2941–3)

[135] Brunner, p. xviii–xix; Campbell, *Seven Sages*, pp. xlvi–xlviii.
[136] An asterisk in A* transcribes a *punctus* in the manusript (CRAL, p. xii).

How can Ar and B, placed at the very bottom of Brunner's stemma, preserve the Old French and, since the same reading is in D, presumably the Middle English parent version x against their other Y-group companions? Furthermore, although E follows C, R, and F in having a letter instead of rushes, it actually matches Ar and B much better in terms of phrasing. Compare the following:

> Scho toke a rech and knyt it ryȝt
> And þrewe it doune to þe knyȝt (Ar ll. 2011–12)
>
> And toke a letter jwretyn full ryght,
> And caste hit downe before the knyght. (E ll. 2942–3)
>
> And to hym sche caste a lettyr
> For to spede all the bettur. (F ll. 2190–1)
>
> A lett*er* so̷ne sho kest hy*m* tyll,
> Wharby he might wit al hir will. (C ll. 3335–6)

This, and the other examples, must surely raise doubts about the simplicity of Campbell and Brunner's classification. The last instance in particular seems to raise the possibility of multiple exemplars, contaminated manuscripts, or oral contamination.[137] Campbell actually entertained this possibility for E, because he found several matches between E and Ar against the other manuscripts: 'it does not seem improbable—though I am unable to prove it—that the author of E has known and been partly influenced by Ar'.[138] The example we have just looked at, however, hints at much larger problems than the occasional agreement of E with Ar, against B. In this instance, E falls in line with C, R, and F in content, but Ar and B follow D and the Old French, thus defying Brunner's stemma and the idea of the common parent y. However, it could be argued that y in fact preserved the reading of x here, and had rushes as the device used by the lady, and not a letter, so that Ar and B are not defying the stemma at all. In this case, though, we have to say that the change to a letter must have arisen independently in C, R, F, and E if we want to preserve Brunner's stemma, and this hardly seems likely: C, R, and F have many agreements of

[137] I am grateful to Rosamund Allen for the suggestion of oral contamination: details such as the rush or the letter could have been easily memorized from hearing another manuscript read aloud.

[138] 'Study', p. 59.

phrasing and detail at this point. The answer to these problems may well lie in a history of multiple exemplars and contaminated texts, or oral contamination, but since there are no such manuscripts now extant, this remains conjectural. In any case, the situation is much more complicated and interesting than Brunner's stemma would allow. The extant manuscripts of the *Seven Sages* are noticeably scattered both chronologically and dialectally. Many must have been lost for each text that has survived, and so there is little hope of constructing a stemma on the basis of such slight evidence.

5. THE RELATIONSHIP OF DD.I.17 WITH THE OTHER MANUSCRIPTS

Turning to the Midland Version of D and its relationship with the other manuscripts, it will be remembered that Brunner was not completely satisfied by Campbell's evidence for a connection between D and y through the common Middle English parent x. Campbell listed some fifty-two parallel passages between D and A, or D and E, noting that 'Others might be cited, but these will suffice for the purpose'.[139] They do, indeed, form impressive evidence, but since Brunner's dissatisfaction may well be shared by others, it is possible to provide further proof. First, it should be noted that Campbell seems to have restricted his comparison to A, using E only when A is wanting. In fact, some of the parallel passages are even more convincing when D is compared with another manuscript: there is no reason to assume that A best represents y in every instance. In the following examples, D is quoted first, followed by the manuscript with the closer match, then A, as cited by Campbell (quotations and line numbers are taken from my own edition for D, and from Brunner's and Campbell's editions for the Y-group):

I schal saue thy lyf a daye. (D l. 381)
I schal saue the o dai (E l. 375)
I schal the waranti o dai. (A l. 389)

Thus thay were at on alle,
And wenten agayen into ˋþeˊ halle. (D l. 388–9)

[139] 'Study', p. 77.

Aft*er* þir wordes rase þai all
And went ogayn into þe hall (C ll. 467–8)
Wiȝ þis word þai ben alle
Departed and comen to halle. (A ll. 397–8)

To do thy wyl by anyght,
Yf I schal helle the aryght. (D ll. 1546–7)
Haue a womman to pleie w*ith* a nyȝt
Ȝef ȝe wil be hol aryȝt (Ar ll. 1567–8)
Haue womman to pleie ariȝt,
Ȝif ȝe wil be hol apliȝt. (A ll. 1567–8)

Bot sayed for non wordlys wyne
Schulde no man parte hom atwyne. (D ll. 2485–6)
þe lady swor for no wynne
Sche ne wolde neuer p*ar*t atwynne (Ar ll. 2571–2)
þe leuedi saide for no wenne
Sche ne wolde neuer wende þenne. (A ll. 2581–2)

These examples clearly show that D often matches another manuscript more closely than it matches A, and Campbell's evidence would have been more impressive if he had not restricted himself to A alone. Furthermore, comparison of D with all the other manuscripts reveals many other textual parallels not found in A that are as impressive as those cited by Campbell. The following examples cite the manuscript matching D's reading most closely. A's reading is also given where extant, for purposes of comparison.

That on a day in the \`h´alle
He disputide with ham alle (D ll. 167–8)
þat þe ferth ȝer*e* in þat hall
Dessputed he with his maist*ers* all (C ll. 209–10)
þe ferȝe ȝer, hit was no dout,
Wiȝ his maister he gan to despout (A ll. 179–80)

And hew adown this mykyl bowe,
And latte the branche haue rome ynow. (D ll. 614–15)
And hak oway þe grete bogh,
And lat þe ymp haue son inogh. (C ll. 653–4)
Hewe hi*m* to þe grounde doun riȝt,
Lat þe ȝonge tre atire, a pliȝt. (A ll. 607–8)

And the bore neghyd nee;
He clam vppon the tree on hyghe. (D ll. 950–1)

Into þe tre he clymbes on high,
And þe bare þan come him negh. (C ll. 985–6)
Vp to þe hawe tre he steghȝ,
þe bor hi*m* com swiȝe neghȝ. (A ll. 891–2)

That I bytook my sone teche,
And he hase loste hys speche,
And wolde haue lyne by my wyf.
He schal dee, by my lyf! (D ll. 1308–11)
For I toke ȝow mi son to teche,
And ȝe haue gert him lose his speche,
And also for to force my wife;
þarfore sal he lose his life. (C ll. 1487–90)

By Good that hys ful of myght,
Thow schal nowt come herein tonyght! (D ll. 1440–1)
Nay, sche seyde, be god allmyght,
Thou schalt not come here yn to nyȝt! (F ll. 611–12)

And yf thow leuest nought me,
Remou thi bed and thow mayst se. (D ll. 2349–50)
Yf that þou beleue not me,
Graue vp thy bedd *and* thou may see. (F ll. 1706–7)
þemp*er*our had wonder of þis,
And let remue his bed, iwis (A ll. 2457–8)

And thou wol holden that thow hase hyght. (D l. 3258)
If þou will hald þat þou has hyght (C l. 4023)

And kyst hym and hys modir in fere,
And made thaym swyth fayer chere (D ll. 3367–8)
Bot þe kyng kissed þam both in fere,
And said: 'Bese meri, *and* mase gude chere (C ll. 4231–2)

These are only a few examples out of many. Obviously, some agreements may simply be coincidences, drawn from words and phrases endemic to the formulaic romance style employed in these poems. Yet there is surely a weight of evidence in favour of a connection between D and the Y-group. It must be remembered that if there is no such connection, then these coincidences of phrasing are also coincidences of translation, and if we look at the Old French for the last parallel quoted above, for example, we find nothing about the son kissing or cheering up his parents. The writer ends the tale in this way: *Quant li peres l'oi, si fu moult esbahiz* et *pensis, * lors se tint moult à engignié* (A* 52.005). If this textual parallel between D and C and R is deemed coincidental, then the parallel of new content must also be a coincidence. That both redactors added exactly the same new detail in exactly the same words is very unlikely.

It seems reasonable to conclude that both the Midland Version of D and the Y-group texts had a common source in the Middle English parent version x. There is, however, one noticeable shared error in D, C, and R. In *Aper*, the swineherd fills his sleeves with fruit in the Old French, and in A and B: *Il s'abessa, si en comenca à cueillir tant qu'il en ot plain son giron. * En tant conme il emploit l'autre giron* . . . (12.007–8).[140] A translates this as:

> Ful he gaderede his barm,
> Ȝet ne þouȝt he of non harm.
> In his oþer lappe he gaderede some (ll. 885–7)

However, in D, C, and R the swineherd fills his hood instead of his sleeves:

> Hym thought that the fruyt was goode,
> And gadderd bretful hys hoode. (D ll. 944–5)
> In his hode he gederd þar*e* (C l. 981)[141]

Since the Old French and most of the Y-group texts have the swineherd fill his sleeves, or laps, it seems likely that this was the reading in the Middle English parent version x. Therefore either D and C, R changed this to 'hood' independently, or there is some connection between the two. Since this is the only shared error common to these texts, it seems easier to conclude that it arose independently.

6. THE MIDLAND VERSION

Although the Midland Version of D is related to the texts of the other Middle English *Seven Sages* group (the Y-group) through a common parent version, it differs from those texts in many ways,

[140] E (ll. 885, 887) and A (l. 885 only) have 'barme' instead, most probably arising from confusion over the double meaning of the word 'lappe' as both part of a garment and part of the body, since A reads 'lappe' at l. 887.

[141] It seems likely that A's *non harm* represents the reading in x, and at some stage was translated as 'good', either in copying or through memorial transmission. The new rhyme of 'hood' was then supplied, explaining the change from 'barm' as the object used to carry the fruit. I am grateful to Rosamund Allen for this suggestion.

and the uniqueness of this version of the *Seven Sages* has never been fully considered. Its original editor, Thomas Wright, devoted fewer than a couple of pages in his introduction to the text in question, preferring to offer a general discussion of the work's origin in *The Book of Sindbād*. Although Killis Campbell spent some time detailing the narrative and textual differences of D compared with the other Middle English versions, he did not offer any consideration of the reason for such changes, or their effectiveness. As intended editor of C, he was obviously much more concerned to promote his own text as 'the most perfect *poem*, holding, as it does, in language, style, and metre, the first place in the early English group'.[142]

It is only fair to observe that it is sometimes difficult to determine whether a particular feature of D is an original addition on the part of its redactor, or whether it was in the source text, the Middle English parent version known as x. Some of the features unique to D could also have been in x, but omitted in the Y-group texts. However, because such features are also absent from the Old French source, it is perhaps simpler, if not safer, to assume that they are genuine additions on the part of D's redactor. In any case, even if these seemingly genuine features of D were derived from x, D is still alone in preserving them, and so original in that respect. Other features are more obviously unique to D, such as textual abridgements. It should also be added that there may, of course, have been some intermediate stages between x and D as we now have it. So when we speak of the redactor of D, we may well be speaking of more than one person. All these points should be borne in mind throughout the following discussion.

Campbell was probably right to award to the text he edited the first place in terms of language, style, and metre. It is not in the area of language or style that D's uniqueness lies. D, like most of the other Middle English *Seven Sages*, has more than its fair share of formulaic phrases and metrical irregularities, and, due to scribal carelessness, D also has several missing lines. Rather, D distinguishes itself in terms of narrative manipulation and characterization, revealing a marked interest in plot and its logical coherence.

Whilst D often follows the Old French source more faithfully than the Y-group (for example, in specifying the tree in *Tentamina* as a

[142] Campbell, 'Study', p. 69. For Campbell's declaration of his intention to edit C, see 'Study', p. 42, n. 1.

pear tree, or in having the mirror set on a pillar in *Virgilius*), when it does diverge, it usually does so in a meaningful way. In contrast, the Y-group texts rarely make any major changes to the French. Additions are usually of a smaller nature, in the form of elaborations: for example, the Prince is named Florentine or the king in *Senescalcus* is said to rule Calabria in addition to Apulia. There are some more significant alterations: in *Medicus* we are told that Ypocras's illness was sent by God as a punishment; in B the steward in *Senescalcus* is put to death in the manner of Crassus in *Virgilius*; in F the wife in *Vidua* has to cut off some fingers from her husband's corpse in addition to the other mutilations, and in *Tentamina* there is a further test, in which the wife kills her husband's hawk.

Nevertheless, these are still largely additions. What characterizes D is its propensity for radical omission and alteration of its source. In D we have abundant evidence of a redactor thinking about the source material and making deliberate narrative choices. As a result, he makes the poem his own in many ways. The redactor of D makes the following significant omissions or alterations:

(1) The Prince's mother dies whilst he is at school, not before he goes.
(2) *Canis*—the knight drowns himself in a fish pond at the end of the tale. In the other versions he goes into self-imposed exile, or on a pilgrimage.
(3) *Medicus*—D omits the barrel episode.
(4) *Gaza*—D omits the discovery of the headless corpse, and the son's subsequent scheme to avoid detection.
(5) *Puteus*—the husband invents an elaborate excuse for having been out at night (he thought he heard his missing spaniel), and in D (and F) the husband is put to death at the end of the tale.
(6) *Tentamina*—in D the trials are thought up by the wife herself, not her mother.
(7) *Virgilius*—D omits the lengthy preamble to the main tale, in which we are told of Virgil's other images. Virgil is recast as Merlin.
(8) *Avis*—the wife escapes detection.
(9) *Sapientes*—D omits the lengthy description of the sages' search for Merlin.
(10) *Vidua*—in D we are told that the husband killed himself; the

knight does not repudiate the woman for mutilating her husband's corpse.

(11) *Inclusa*—D makes the wife the originator of the escape plan, not her lover. The earl kills himself at the end of the tale. D, however, omits the episode in which the earl marries his own wife to the knight.

All of these changes, and the many other minor alterations, are discussed further in the notes accompanying the text.

It is clear that in D any material extraneous to the workings of the plot has been pruned away. Narrative digressions, such as the search for Merlin in *Sapientes*, or the account of Virgil's other images in *Virgilius*, were of no interest to its redactor, whatever opportunities they might have afforded for entertainment or invention. When Gower retold the story of 'Virgil's Mirror' in Book V of the *Confessio Amantis*, he, too, cut the preamble. Although the episode is of local interest, it holds back the main story and detracts from the narrative drive of this *exemplum*. In D plots are made simple and functional: once the point of the tale has been made, the narrative ends. This is certainly the case in *Gaza*: the moral of this story, told by the Empress, is that the son dishonoured his father by not burying his severed head in a Christian grave, but casting it unceremoniously into a ditch. The Prince will serve the Emperor in a similarly disrespectful manner, she claims. However, one could argue that in this instance, at least, the redactor of D has ended the story too soon in that the reader still wants to know what happens when the headless corpse is discovered: the other texts tell us this at length. Functional plot lines and the audience's appetite for story do not always coincide. The omission of the barrel episode at the end of *Medicus* is much more successful, since this scene is by nature an elaboration: it does not further or complete the story in any meaningful way.

The redactor of D also has a propensity for making the fate of the female characters happy, but that of the men more unfortunate. In D the 'wicked women' of *Avis* and *Vidua* escape detection and repudiation respectively (in the other versions they are disowned by their men). In *Canis, Puteus,* and *Inclusa*, the husbands meet their death at the end of the tales (in the first and last they are driven to suicide): the other texts do not carry their misfortune quite this far. All these examples are from tales told by the Seven Sages, warning of the wiles of women. It could be argued that because the women tend to triumph and the men perish, the warning of the Sages gains more weight. In the other versions of the *Seven Sages*, the antifeminist stance of the Sages as narrators invades the tale itself, procuring punishment or humiliation for the women. In *Canis* and *Vidua*, at the end of the tales, the male character delivers a short speech condemning all women. For example:

> *þou* hast itawt me a newe ran,
> þat i schal neuer leue wimman.
> For þere þai make semblant fairest,
> þai wil bigile þe alþerformest! (A ll. 2713–16)

At the end of *Avis* in the other versions, the wife's deceit is discovered when her husband finds the tools of her trickery, and he chases her out of the house. This, in particular, does not ring true: it is unlikely that a woman clever enough to devise such an elaborate plan would be foolish enough to leave the evidence on show. The redactor of D resists the temptation to curb these wicked women in the tales themselves, allowing them free play with impunity.

Not only does the redactor alter the fate of the characters, he also adds to the process of characterization. In *Canis*, for example, in which two nurses leave a baby unattended in order to watch a tournament, D is unique in portraying the nurses' sense of duty and initial reluctance to abandon their charge: *Thay ne durst nowerware goo* (l. 755), and their subsequent seduction by the music of *tro[m]pe and taburne*, a fine stroke of characterization:

> Wen thay seen al ware goo,
> And no man leued bot thay two,
> And herdyn tro[m]pe and taburne,
> Thay forgate hare honoure;
> Thay left the childe anon tho,
> And dyde ham bothe forthgoo. (ll. 756–61)

The nurses are then said to climb a tower to watch the tournament *Pryuyliche tha no man see* (l. 763), so that they are further depicted as acting irresponsibly, and knowing that they are doing so. In the other versions, when the tournament is over we are told that all the people hasten home:

> When þe bourdice was broght til ende,
> þe knightes wald no lenger lende,

Bot ilka man his hernayse hent,
And hastily hame er þai went. (C ll. 847–50)

In contrast, D focuses on the nurses, and so consolidates its earlier characterization of them by revealing their guilt:

When the iustis were doon
The norise hiede ham in ful sone—
Thay ne durst no langer dwelle. (ll. 802–4)

Finally, when they discover the upturned cradle and believe the baby to have been attacked by their master's greyhound, the words of one of the nurses serve to epitomize the special emphasis that this text has placed on the nurses' behaviour and subsequent guilt:

Alas that stonde,' sayden schoe,
'That we ȝeden iustys to see!'
Thay were ful of sorow and wo,
And dyde thaym bothe forto goo. (ll. 818–21)

The redactor of D has transformed these nurses from simple agents of the plot into more fully realized characters by providing insight into their thoughts and reactions.

Similarly, D shows a definite preference for direct speech when compared with the other Middle English texts. The nurses's reaction to finding the upturned cradle is an example of this:

'Felaw,' scho sayed, 'be my blode,
Thys grewhond his waxyn woode,
And hase eten the childe therfore.
Alas that euer we were bore!'
The toþer noris sayed, 'Iwys,
Certis, felaw, sothe hit his . . .' (ll. 812–17)

This is followed by the lines quoted above (818–21). The other Middle English versions have no dialogue here at all, merely reporting, for example:

Þe norice was sori in hert
And ech of hem vnderstode
Þat þe greihond was wod,
And hadde þat faire child islawe (A ll. 776–9)

The Old French has some direct speech, but only a little: *ha, lasses! que ferons? que porrons nous devenir? fuions nous en!* (10.017). D's tendency towards dialogue is marked throughout, and adds a certain liveliness to the poem. In *Puteus*, when the hapless husband is caught out of his house at night by the watchmen, D is alone in having him try to talk his way out of his predicament with a comic speech in which he claims to be looking for his missing spaniel.

The finest example of the redactor's skill in both characterization and narrative manipulation is found in *Inclusa*. In this tale a knight falls in love with an unknown lady in a dream and sets off in search of her. Her finds her in another country, where she is kept locked in a tower by her husband. She reciprocates his love (she, too, has dreamt of him), the knight becomes her husband's steward, and eventually the lovers escape together. In D, the husband throws himself out of the tower, and breaks his neck.

D's treatment of this story shows how the *Seven Sages* as a tale collection could be responsive to the subtle shifts of perspective and narrative strategy that a skilful redactor could bring to bear. The redactor of D transforms the character of the wife, and the quality of the story, making her a shrewd, intelligent woman, responsible for planning her own escape. In the other versions, her lover is responsible, as the heading in B makes clear: *Maxius tale of an erle how a knyght disseyved hy*m *of his wiff* (p. 139). Hans R. Runte has pointed out that the knight's, rather than the wife's, responsibility lessens the impact of the tale as an *exemplum* against the wiles of women, and in the Latin *Historia Septem Sapientum*, the redactor solves this problem by making *Inclusa* a tale told by the Empress in which she highlights the knight's disloyalty to the earl, his master.[143] D solves the problem in a different way by making the wife responsible for the deception, and so, in terms of the logic of the frame, a 'wicked woman' suitable for such a tale.[144] However, in so doing the redactor of D has also rewritten *Inclusa* with a shrewd regard for narrative coherence, character, and motivation.

In D, the wife initiates her escape plan by giving her lover a ring,

[143] Hans R. Runte, 'From the Vernacular to Latin and Back: The Case of *The Seven Sages of Rome*', *Medieval Translators and Their Craft*, ed. Jeanette Beer, Studies in Medieval Culture, 25, Medieval Institute Publications (Kalamazoo, MI, 1989), pp. 93–133 (pp. 94–95).

[144] However, D omits a detail of the French original preserved in all the other Middle English poems: in these other texts, the knight murders the mason responsible for building the secret entrance into the wife's tower. So whilst the wife's culpability in D marks her as a 'wicked woman' in terms of the frame, this omission on the part of D's redactor would perhaps suggest that he did not want to blacken the character of the knight or, by extension, lessen our sympathy for the protagonist and his lover. Such a reading, of course, runs contrary to the prescriptions of the frame-tale *moralitas*.

telling him to make sure her husband sees him wearing it, and to return it to her that same evening. In the other texts she gives her lover the ring simply to remind him of her, and when the lord recognizes the ring on the knight's finger this causes an unforeseen complication: fortunately the knight perceives the lord's astonishment and is able to prevent discovery by reaching the lady in the tower before her husband, and returning the ring. In D, however, this is all part of the wife's plan. When the husband asks to see his wife's ring, and she is able to produce it, he concludes that one ring may easily resemble another: later we see that this conclusion is exactly what the wife anticipated and desired. The incident with the ring has all been an elaborate preparation for her real plan: her lover is to tell her husband that he is now able to return to his homeland, having been in exile for killing a man, and that his lady has brought the news. In the other versions it is the lover himself who thinks up this plot. The wife predicts that her husband will want to meet the lady, and she herself will pretend to be that woman, disguising herself in different clothes. When her lover objects that her husband will surely recognize her, the wife finally reveals the purpose of the ring: because the husband was led to believe that one ring resembled another, he will now accept that one woman may look like another:

> Therfore dout the nought,
> Thys schal been al hys thought:
> As a rynge was lyche anothyr,
> So may a womman be lyche anothir.
> There schal the knote of gyle be knyt—
> The rynge schal blynde hys wyt. (ll. 2989–94)

The plan works: the knight and his 'lady' are allowed to return to his homeland. It is a wonderful stroke on the part of the redactor of D to have the wife formulate a plot that hinges on her correct prediction of her husband's essentially antifeminist reaction in which he believes a ring and a woman to be equatable objects: the wife, locked up by her jealous husband, uses his very antifeminist tendencies to plan her escape. In the other versions the knight is extremely lucky to pull off his plan, for he is merely relying on having disguised the lady in some unusual clothes.[145] As it happens, the lord only believes that

[145] Catherine van Buuren-Veenenbos noted how in Version K the lady 'wore a "guimple ensafrenee / De soie qui fu desguisee," which makes it more credible that

the lady is not his wife because of the earlier incident with the ring, as in D; but in these other versions this was never part of the scheme, and is simply a very fortunate coincidence.

The voice of the lover, objecting to the planned disguise, could be seen as the voice of D's redactor, objecting to the flimsy plot mechanics of his source:

> Quod the stywarde, "That may nouȝt fye!
> And he se the with hys eye,
> Anon as he haues a syght
> He wyl knowe the anoonryghte." (ll. 2981–4)

The redactor of D has taken the detail of the ring, incidental in the other versions, and made it central to both the characterization of the wife and the functioning of her, and the story's, plot. He has transformed the wife from the passive creature of the other versions, dressed, disguised, and abducted from her husband by her lover-knight, into the shrewd heroine of her own story; and in doing so, he has also transformed the tale itself into one of special narrative drive and coherence. As mentioned above, by giving the wife an active role, the story more properly functions as an *exemplum* against the trickery of women. However, it might also be argued that by developing the wife's character in this way the redactor aligns our perspective more closely with that of the wife and her lover than with that of her husband. Moreover, D omits the lover's murder of the mason who constructed the secret entrance to the wife's tower, again suggesting a shift in sympathy towards the lovers. This story shows how individual tales could be shaped to work both within and against their narrative frame, and how the *Seven Sages* offered scope to an original redactor to play with the shifting perspectives inherent in the tale collection genre as a whole and *The Seven Sages of Rome* in particular.

7. DIALECT OF DD.I.17

An investigation of the dialect of the version of the *Seven Sages* in Dd.1.17 poses difficult and perhaps irresolvable problems. Though Dd.1.17 dates from around 1400, the *Seven Sages* text that it contains

her own husband should not recognize her' ('A Middle Scots Version of the *Seven Sages of Rome*', in Niedzielski, Runte, and Hendrickson, *Studies*, pp. 63–78 (p. 68)).

may have been in circulation for anything up to a century beforehand, and it is impossible to know how many episodes of copying lie behind the surviving text. The extent to which the text has been corrupted, as evidenced especially in the scribal mistreatment of many of the original rhyme-words, suggests that the process of transmission was not only long, but also geographically diverse. As a result, this version of the *Seven Sages* is best characterized, from the dialectal point of view, as a *Mischsprache*, a text which, through incomplete processes of scribal 'translation', exhibits features proper to more than one of the broadly recognized dialect areas of Middle English.[146]

The extreme difficulty of disentangling the dialectally mixed language written by a scribe such as that of Dd.1.17 was emphasized by M. L. Samuels, with reference to the copy of *Piers Plowman* that, together with *Mandeville's Travels* and *How Men þat Been in Heele Schulde Visite Seeke Folke*, accompanies the *Seven Sages* amongst the Middle English texts in the manuscript.[147] Strictly speaking, the scribe's linguistic profile should be investigated on the basis of an extended survey that would take account of all of these texts, and would also acknowledge that each of them would undoubtedly have had a different history of transmission. Such an investigation lies far beyond the scope of the present enquiry, and a linguistic profile drawn up on the basis of the *Seven Sages* alone serves to illustrate how extensively the linguistic forms favoured by the scribe have become mixed with those of his predecessors in the process of transmission.

The application of the standard Middle English dialect criteria established by Moore, Meech, and Whitehall,[148] and adopted in the *MED*[149] immediately reveals the dialect to be principally a mixture of

[146] Michael Benskin and Margaret Laing, 'Translations and *Mischsprachen* in Middle English Manuscripts', in *So Meny People Longages and Tonges: Philological Essays in Scots and Mediaeval English Presented to Angus McIntosh*, ed. Michael Benskin and M. L. Samuels (Edinburgh, 1981), pp. 55–106; *LALME*, I.9, 12–22, Appendix II, 32–33.

[147] M. L. Samuels, 'Scribes and Manuscript Traditions', *Regionalism in Late Medieval Manuscripts and Texts: Essays Celebrating the Publication of A Linguistic Atlas of Late Mediaeval English*, ed. Felicity Riddy, York Manuscripts Conferences: Proceedings, Series 2 (Cambridge, 1991), 1–7 (p. 1).

[148] Samuel Moore, Sanford Brown Meech, and Harold Whitehall, 'Middle English Dialect Characteristics and Dialect Boundaries: Preliminary Report of an Investigation Based Exclusively on Localized Texts and Documents', *Essays and Studies in English and Comparative Literature*, University of Michigan Publications: Language and Literature, 13 (Ann Arbor, 1935), 1–60.

[149] See Hans Kurath *et al.*, *Middle English Dictionary: Plan and Bibliography* (Ann Arbor and London, 1954).

northern and Midlands forms, the South being eliminated, for example, on the grounds that the plural of the present tense has endings in *s*, *-ys* (northern), and *-en* (Midlands), and 'foot' is represented by the form *fot* rather than *vot*. These tests, however, do not serve by themselves to narrow down the area where D might have been copied.

Using *LALME*'s criteria, one is confronted with an unusually large number of linguistic forms for many of the items, and these may to some extent be sorted into rough groups that probably reflect geographically discrete episodes in the transmission of this version of the *Seven Sages*. In addition to the orthographical framework of reference provided by *LALME*, a little help in locating the text may also be derived from Kaiser's study of Middle English word-geography.[150]

Although principally a mixture of northern and Midlands forms, the text shows signs of having been copied in several areas of the country. First, analysis of the rhyme-words shows that the northern forms in the extant version of the *Seven Sages* are undoubtedly of immediate scribal origin: on several occasions the rhyme has been corrupted by the scribe replacing unfamiliar forms with ones from his own dialect: for example, the northern *wars* is substituted for what was presumably *wurs* at l. 3365, rhyming with *curs*; *bathe* is rhymed with *twae* and *twaye* at ll. 1900 and 1925 respectively, presumably replacing some form of the very rare rhyme-word *beie*, providing an important diagnostic tool for the ultimate geographical origins of the text; and *a-mange* replaces what must have been *a-monge* at l. 571, rhyming with *wronge*. Secondly, the rhyme-words and certain internal forms suggest that the original dialect of the poem belonged to the south-west Midlands. Thirdly, there is evidence for the text at some stage having been copied in Lincolnshire and Norfolk, as well as having several other seemingly 'relict' forms that are difficult to associate with any single dialectal area in particular.

Dialect of Scribe

The dialect of the scribe is clearly defined as northern by comparison with the *LALME* dot maps for *twa*, *fra*, the *ba-* type of 'both', the

[150] Rolf Kaiser, *Zur Geographie des mittelenglischen Wortschatzes*, Palaestra, 205 (Leipzig, 1937).

-lk- type of 'such', and for the forms of 'much' ending in *-il(e)* or -*yl(e)*. Scotland is clearly excluded by the scribe's use of forms for 'which' with initial 'w-': this marks the northern boundary line, whilst the forms mentioned above determine the Humber-Ribble line as the lower cut-off point. Narrowing down this area any further through the 'fit-technique' has not proved successful,[151] due to the lack of consistently well-attested forms. However, it is possible to make a few observations about some items of the text's linguistic profile.[152]

(4) **SHE.**[153] *Scho* is by far the most frequent form in this text, being used over one hundred times; it is particularly well-attested in the West Riding of Yorkshire. Of the several minor variants in the text, *sho* (1) is also noticeably well-attested in the West Riding; *schoe* (1) is recorded only in the West Riding and Devon; and *so* (1) is found in Lincolnshire (questioned) and East Lothian.
(Other forms: *ho* (10), *he* (7), *sche* (2))

(10) **SUCH**. Of the minor variants, *swylke* (2) is found in Lancashire, Lincolnshire, and Yorkshire for the area in question; *sylke* (1) is found in Lincolnshire and the East Riding only.
(Other forms: *swylk* (4), *syche* (4 (2 rh)), *swilk* (2), *swilke* (2))

(11) **WHICH**. Of the forms found for this item, *wylk* (1) and *wilk* (1) are attested in Westmorland, Lancashire, Lincolnshire, and Yorkshire, and in Durham, Lancashire, Lincolnshire, and the North and West Ridings respectively.
(Other forms: *whilk* (2), *whilke* (1), *wych* (1))

(12) **EACH**. The most common form, *ilke* (15), is recorded in all areas in question except for Westmorland and Northumberland. Of the minor variants, *ilc* (2) is found only in Lincolnshire.
(Other forms: *ilce* (3), *ilk* (1), *ilk-a* (1), *hilk-a* (1))

151 Michael Benskin, 'The 'Fit'-Technique Explained', in Riddy, *Regionalism*, pp. 9–26.

152 These observations are drawn from vol. 4 of *LALME*, the 'County Dictionary'. This approach follows the one taken by Alexandra Barratt in her edition of *The Seven Psalms: A Commentary on the Penitential Psalms Translated from French into English by Dame Eleanor Hull*, EETS, 307 (1995), pp. xxxiii–xl.

153 The number is that of the *LALME* questionnaire. 'NOR' or 'SOU' after an item indicates that the item was collected by *LALME* for only the northern or southern part of the survey respectively (see I.552); 'rh' indicates that the form in question is a rhyme-word; the number given in brackets after an item indicates the number of times it is found in the text. Those items pertinent to the dialect area in question are discussed fully; other forms are listed at the end of each entry.

(13) **MUCH**. Of the two popular forms, *mykyl* (15) and *mykil* (11), neither is attested in Westmorland or Cumberland; *mykyl* is also unattested in Durham and north-west Yorkshire, and *mykil* is unattested in the East Riding. Of the minor variants, *mikil* (1) is recorded in Cambridgeshire, Cheshire, Durham, Ely, Lancashire, Lincolnshire, Norfolk, Peterborough, and the West Riding; *mykyle* (1) is recorded only in the West Riding and Shropshire; and *mykile* (1) is found only in Lincolnshire.
(Other forms: *myche* (11 (6 rh)))

(19) **IS**. The most common variant by far, *hys* (90 (18 rh)), occurs so often as to imply that it is a form at least accepted if not favoured by the Dd.1.17 scribe, but this spelling is not recorded as a main form for any northern county. It is listed however as a minor variant for Lincolnshire, Northumberland (questioned), and the East and West Ridings for the area in question.
(Other forms: *his* (27 (3 rh)), *is* (5), *ys* (1 rh))

(25) **WOULD** ***pl.*** *Wolde* (4) is most common, and is widespread, but *walden* (1) is attested only in Lancashire.

(34) **AS NOR**. The commonest form by far is *as*, but of the variants, *has* (7) is found only in Durham, Lincolnshire, and the West Riding for the area in question.
(Other forms: *als* (1), *alse* (1))

(71) **AMONG** ***adv*** **NOR**. The minor variant *a-mange* (1 rh), a scribal alteration of *a-monge* in rhyme, as mentioned above, occurs only in Lincolnshire and the West Riding for the area in question.
(Other forms: *a-mong* (1 (rh)), *a-monge* (1 (rh)))

(96) **CAST** ***pt*** **NOR**. Of the several forms, *kast* (4) is attested only in Lincolnshire and the West Riding for the area in question.
(Other forms: *kest* (7), *cast* (3 (1 rh)), *keste* (2 (1 rh)), *kaste* (1 rh), *caste* (1))

(100) **DAUGHTER NOR**. *Doug*t*er* (3) and *dog*t*er* (1) are found only in the East Riding; *dougter* (1) is found in Rutland; and *dog*h*t*er (1) occurs in Cheshire, Cumberland, Derbyshire, Lancashire, Lincolnshire, Northamptonshire, Nottinghamshire, Rutland, and Yorkshire.
(Other forms: *dogter* (2), *dout*er (1))

(188) **NEITHER + NO NOR**. Of the three forms, *nowthir* + *no* (2) and *nowthyr* + *no* (1) are both unrecorded, whereas *nouthir* + *no* (1) is found only in Durham and Lincolnshire.

(210) **SAY** *pt-sg* **NOR**. The commonest form by far, *sayed* (102 (2 rh)), is recorded only in Derbyshire, Lancashire, Lincolnshire, and Staffordshire. Of the minor variants, *sayede* (3) is attested only in Lancashire.
(Other forms: *sayd* (11), *sayde* (8), *sayden* (1))

(214) **SEVEN** *ord* **NOR**. Two forms are found: *seuent* (1) is widespread, but *seuenet* (1) is recorded only in Cheshire, Norfolk, and the West Riding.

(231) **THEE NOR**. The form *te* (1), found in the line *Tak me thy childe that is te leue* (l. 54), is attested only in the West Riding as a minor variant, which it also is in this text.
(Other forms: *the* (85 (22 rh)), *þe* (1), *thi* (1))

(244) **UPON NOR**. The most common form is *oppon* (35), recorded only in Lancashire, Lincolnshire, the East and West Riding, and the Isle of Man. The last of these places clearly falls outside the area in question, and the Lancashire attestation is below the southern boundary line.
(Other forms: *vppon* (10))

(247) **WELL** *adv* **NOR**. Of the minor variants, *wille* (5 (2 rh)) is recorded only in the West Riding; *wylle* (5 (1 rh)) is found in the West Riding and Norfolk; and *wile* (1) is recorded in Lincolnshire, the West Riding, and Berwickshire.
(Other forms: *wel* (26 (11 rh)), *wyl* (2), *wyle* (1), *wil* (1), *wele* (1 rh), *welle* (1 rh))

From this evidence, it seems probable that the scribe's spelling system (if it can be called that) reflects in general terms the usage of the southern part of the area indicated above, namely Lancashire, the East and West Ridings, and a small area of northern Lincolnshire. In particular, those occurrences of *oppon*, a well-attested form, are recorded very close to the southern boundary line. It is impossible to be more specific; the forms are often particularly well-attested in the West Riding: this is certainly the case for *scho*, *twa*, *fra*, *bath*, *bathe*, *swylk*, *swilk*, *swilke*, *whilk*, and *whilke*, but this does not account for all the variants, and there are some that are unrecorded in the West Riding.

It also seems likely that Lincolnshire can be eliminated for the scribal dialect, since only a very small part lies within the boundary lines and several of the forms recorded in the county fall south of this area. For example, the minor variant *mykile*, attested only in Lincolnshire, is entered on the maps below our boundary line, as is *nouthir* + *no* (attested elsewhere only in Durham, on the border with Northumberland, and so too far north). It may be the case, then, that these forms are evidence of the text having been copied in Lincolnshire at an earlier stage in its history. Additional evidence for this is the minor variant found once for the ending of the weak preterite, *-te*, which is recorded only in Lincolnshire and, again, falls below the northern area in question on the maps; and, perhaps, the minor variant *arre* for 'ere', found once, and recorded only in Lincolnshire and Oxfordshire.

Dialect of Original

Some of the poem's rhyme-words and corrupted rhymes provide notable evidence for the dialect of the original, although once again there are few well-attested or reliable forms.

(30) **THEN**. *Tho* (30 (24 rh)).
(Other forms: *than* (54), *thanne* (8), *thane* (3))

(85) **BOTH**. As mentioned above, there is evidence for some form of the very rare rhyme-word *beie* at ll. 1900 and 1925, rhyming with *twae* and *twaye* respectively; similarly, *bo* may originally have rhymed with *two* at l. 2067, now changed to *bothe*.
(Other forms: *bothe* (14 (1 rh)), *both* (13), *bathe* (2 (rh)), *bath* (1))

(227) **STEAD**. The form *stude* is found once, as a rhyme-word with *dude*, ll. 1738–9.
(Other forms: *stede* (2 rh))

(259) **WORSE**. As mentioned above, *wurs* may have been the original rhyme-word for *curs* at l. 3365, now changed to *wars*; however, of the other forms, *wors* rhymes with *curse* at l. 414, and *worse* with *cursse* at l. 2429.

These forms suggest that the original dialect belongs to the south-west Midlands. Also of interest is the rhyme at ll. 1284–5 of *lyste/nyght*: the original must have been *nyste*. The *MED* cites *niste* as a south-west Midlands form (the word is not mapped in *LALME*). This conclusion is supported by some of the forms within the line: *hare* for 'their' occurs twenty times, and is actually more frequent than the *th-* forms employed by the northern scribe (there is also one occurrence of *or* for 'their' at l. 1354, a rare Gloucestershire form); *fram* for 'from' occurs eleven times, again more frequent than the northern *fra*. Finally, *to* for the preterite singular of 'take' is found at l. 1432, and although not mapped in *LALME*, this form is listed as a south-west Midlands variant by the *MED*. The area narrowed down includes West Herefordshire, South Worcestershire, and parts of North Gloucestershire, Warwickshire, and a small area of Shropshire.

However, it has to be said that the picture so far given cannot account for all the forms in the linguistic profile, and must remain a tentative suggestion. Looking at these remaining forms, there is persuasive evidence for the text having been copied in East Anglia at some stage; Norfolk, in particular, seems likely.

East Anglian Forms

(32) **THOUGH**. The form *thau* (3) is recorded only in Suffolk.
(Other forms: *thow* (3), *tho* (2), *the* (1))

(45) **NOT**. Several forms are suggestive: *nowte* (1 rh, with *bythoute*, ll. 2879–80) is recorded in Norfolk and Suffolk; *nougt* (1) is found in Suffolk and Herefordshire; *nawt* (2) is recorded in Norfolk, Somerset, and Warwickshire. Of forms collected under *-ought*, there are four occurrences of *-oute* in rhyming position (*broute*, *wroute*, *thoute*, and *bythoute*), again suggestive of Norfolk.
(Other forms: *nouȝt* (41 (8 rh)), *nought* (28 (7 rh)), *nowt* (24 (8 rh)), *nout* (7 (2 rh)), *noght* (2 (1 rh)), *nowght* (2), *noughte* (1 rh))

(54) **THROUGH**. Of the minor variants, *thourth* (1) is recorded only in Norfolk and Devon.
(Other forms: *thorow* (14), *thourow* (8), *thorou* (1), *thourugt* (1), *thorug* (1), *thourgh* (1), *thorugh* (1))

67) **ADDER SOU**. The form *nadder* (2) is found only in Norfolk. Of the variants, *nedder* (1) is recorded in Norfolk, Gloucestershire, Shropshire, and Worcestershire, whilst *naddir* (3) is unrecorded.

(100) **DAUGHTER NOR**. The form *dout*er, found once, is attested only in Suffolk.
(Other forms: see above)

(130) **FOUR *ord* NOR**. The sole form *fyrde* (1) is recorded only in Norfolk.

(235) **THITHER**. The forms *thydir* (3) and *thydyr* (3 (1 rh)) are most frequent. The former is recorded only in Warwickshire, but the latter only in Norfolk, Suffolk, Buckinghamshire, and Surrey.
(Other forms: *thyder* (2), *thydyre* (1), *thider* (1))

(248) **WENT *pl* NOR**. The minor variant *wentyn* (1) is recorded only in Norfolk and Cheshire.
(Other forms: *went* (10 (1 rh)), *wente* (7 (1 rh)), *wenten* (7), *ȝede* (3 (2 rh)), *ȝeden* (2))

(277) **-LESS NOR**. The suffix *-lees* (1 rh, with *ches*, ll. 3306–7) is recorded only in Cambridgeshire, Ely, Huntingdonshire, Leicestershire, Norfolk, and Northamptonshire.

Of the remaining forms, the following are attested in counties not covered by the areas considered above:

(31) **THAN**. *thane* (2), recorded only in Essex, Leicestershire, and Northamptonshire.
(Other forms: *than* (9))

(32) **THOUGH**. *tho* (1), attested only in Leicestershire.
(Other forms: see above)

(47) **A, O NOR**. of note is *ae* in *araes* (misrhymed with *loos*, ll. 71–72), recorded only in Westmorland.

(54) **THROUGH**. *thourow* (8), attested only in Surrey.
(Other forms: see above)

(69) **AIR NOR**. *eeir* (1 rh, with *fayre*, ll. 133–4), the sole form, is attested only in Huntingdonshire.

(99) **COULD *pl.*** *couthe* (1 rh, with *mouthe*, ll. 2679–80), attested only in Leicestershire.
(Other forms: *couth* (1 rh))

(100) **DAUGHTER NOR**. *dougter* (1), recorded only in Rutland.
(Other forms: see above)

(211) **SEE *pt-sg*.** *saye* (1 rh, with *day*, ll. 1600–1), with a possible original occurrence a few lines earlier at l. 1534 (rh, with *lay*); recorded only in Middlesex, Northamptonshire, and Surrey; *syghe* (4 rh), only recorded in Middlesex.
(Other forms: *sawe* (14 (1 rh)), *see* (12 (11 rh)), *saw* (6), *sygh* (1 rh), *segh* (1))

***pt-pl*.** *seghe* (1 rh, with *hyghe*, ll. 3135–6), attested only in London and Nottinghamshire.
(Other forms: *sawe* (3), *seen* (3), *seyen* (2), *syghe* (1 rh))

(242) **TWO**. *twaye* (1 rh, with *bathe*, ll. 1924–5), attested only in Kent.
(Other forms: *twa* (12), *two* (8 (5 rh)), *twey* (3 rh), *tway* (3 rh), *twae* (3 rh))

(252) **WHITHER**. *wydir* (1) is recorded only in Hertfordshire.
(Other forms: *wydyr-* (1), unrecorded in *LALME*)

The following words occur in forms unrecorded in *LALME*:

(12) **EACH**. *ilce* (3).
(Other forms: see above)

(14) **MAN**. *maane* (1 rh, with *oon*, ll. 932–3).
(Other forms: *man* (73 (17 rh)), *mane* (10 (8 rh)))

(36) **AGAINST**. *agayens* (1).
(Other forms: *agayns* (1))

(37) **AGAIN**. *agayen* (4 (1 rh)).
(Other forms: *agayn* (10 (1 rh)), *agayne* (3 (2 rh)))

(57) ***Present participle***. *-en* (1).
(Other forms: *-yng* (4), *-yn* (1), *-ynge* (1), *-and* (1))

(67) **ADDER SOU**. *naddir* (3).
(Other forms: see above)

(77) **BE *ppl* NOR**. *by* (1).
(Other forms: *ben* (7), *been* (2), *be* (2))

(87) **BROTHER *pl* NOR**. *bryther* (1), the sole form.

(88) **BURN *pt* SOU**. *bernyd* (2), the sole form.
***ppl* SOU**. *brent* (1 rh, with *schent*, ll. 1144–5), the sole form.

(89) **BURY *pt* SOU**. *byrid* (1), the sole form.
***ppl* SOU**. *beryd* (1), the sole form.

(95) **CAN *pl* NOR**. *cune* (1 rh, with *bygyne*, ll. 67–68), *cane* (1 rh, with *bygyne*, ll. 77–78).
(Other forms: *conne* (2), *cunne* (1 rh))

(100) **DAUGHTER NOR**. *dogter* (1).
(Other forms: see above)

(103) **DIE**. *dede* (1 rh, with *sprede*, ll. 622–3), *deyen* (1 rh, with *eyen*, ll. 914–15).
(Other forms: *dee* (15 (10 rh)), *dye* (8 (5 rh)), *deye* (2 rh), *dey* (1 rh))

(110) **EITHER *pron***. *hayther* (1).
(Other forms: *ayther* (1))

(120) **FETCH SOU**. *fete* (1).
(Other forms: *fet* (1 rh), *feche* (1))

(142) **HAVE** ***3 sg*** **NOR**. *ase* (1).
(Other forms: *hase* (14), *haues* (4), *has* (1))
pt-sg **SOU**. *haddyn* (1).
(Other forms: *hadde* (92 (7 rh)), *hade* (3), *had* (3), *hadd* (1), *adde* (1), *hadden* (1))

(145) **HEAVEN NOR**. *euene* (1 rh, with *seuene*, ll. 374–5).
(Other forms: *heuene* (6 rh), *heuen* (2 rh))

(161) **LADY NOR**. *lauydy* (3).
(Other forms: *lady* (30), *leuedy* (9), *lauedy* (6))

(163) **LAUGH** ***pt*** **NOR**. *louhe* (1), *louke* (1), *loge* (1).
(Other forms: *loughe* (1 rh))

(165) **LEAD** ***pt*** **SOU**. *lede* (1 rh, with *byhede*, ll. 1294–5).
(Other forms: *ladde* (6 (1 rh)), *lad* (1), *lade* (1), *laddyn* (1))

(171) **LIVE** ***vb***. *leuene* (1 rh, with *gyuen*, ll. 3296–7).
(Other forms: *lyue* (4 (1 rh)), *leue* (3 (1 rh)))

(188) **NEITHER + NOR**. *nowthir* + *no* (1), *nowthyr* + *no* (1).
(Other forms: see above)

(203) **PEOPLE NOR**. *pepyle (2), pypyl* (1).
(Other forms: *pepyl* (1))

(210) **SAY** ***pt-sg*** **NOR**. *sayden* (1).
(Other forms: see above)
pt-pl **NOR**. *sayed* (5 (1 rh)), *sayeden* (1).
(Other forms: *sayden* (7 (1 rh)))

(211) **SEE** ***3 sg*** **NOR**. *syȝe* (1 rh, with *suythe*, ll. 780–1).
(Other forms: see above)
pt-pl. *syghe* (1 rh, with *hyghe*, ll. 3135–6).
(Other forms: *sawe* (3), *seen* (3), *seyen* (2), *seghe* (1 rh))

(231) **THEE NOR**. *thi* (1).
(Other forms: see above)

(242) **TWO**. *twae* (3 rh, with *bathe*, *playe*, and *play* at ll. 1900–1, 2149–50, and 2409–10 respectively).
(Other forms: see above)

(246) **WEEK** ***pl***. *wykkes* (1), the sole form.

(247) **WELL** ***adv*** **NOR**. *wyle* (1).
(Other forms: see above)

(255) **WHOSE SOU**. *who* (1), the sole form.

(257) **WITEN**. *wyet* (1).
(Other forms: *wyten* (2), *wet* (2), *wyt* (1), *wyte* (1), *wite* (1 rh), *wetyn* (1))

sg **NOR**. *wyt* (1), *wet* (1).
(Other forms: *woot* (1))

(271) **-ANK NOR**. *ay* (1).
(Other forms: *o* (8 (6 rh), *a* (4))

Some of this evidence may be accounted for simply by the fact that the items were collected by *LALME* only for either the northern or southern part of the survey. It is also possible that the northern scribe of D was much less accustomed to copying Middle English than he was Latin, which accounts for most of the manuscript's vast bulk, and this may explain some of the more unusual spellings. Investigation of his copies of *Piers Plowman*, *Mandeville's Travels*, and *How Men þat Been in Heele* would probably shed light on both this issue and the general complexion of his work in the *Seven Sages*, as detailed above.

Vocabulary

The following are listed as southern words in Kaiser's study of Middle English word-geography: *areryd* (l. 497), *beriel*, in the sense of a tomb, or burial-place (l. 2559), *copinyere* (l. 2172 rh), *mytte* (MS *myght* (*sic*), l. 1399 rh), *skere* (l. 3398 rh).[154] These forms, and particularly those that appear in rhyme, lend some weight to the suggestion made above that this version of the *Seven Sages* is likely to have originated in the south-west Midlands.

8. EDITORIAL PROCEDURE

With its long textual history and different versions of the text, the *Seven Sages of Rome* is like many other Middle English poems such as *Sir Orfeo*, *Guy of Warwick*, or *Bevis of Hampton*. Indeed the latter two were included with the *Seven Sages* both in the Auchinleck manuscript of *ca.* 1331–40, and in Cambridge, University Library,

[154] Kaiser, *Zur Geographie*, pp. 281, 283, 284, 287, 289.

MS Ff.2.38, dated to the end of the fifteenth century, or the beginning of the sixteenth. However, whilst scribal revision in the Midland Version has resulted in a narratively original version of the *Seven Sages,* the text has suffered somewhat at the hands of its most recent scribe, and the complex nature of the dialect of D raises interesting problems for its editor. As mentioned above, many of the rhyme-words have been corrupted as a result of repeated copying. Some of these would be easy to restore: for example *made* (l. 151) must have been *maked* in the original, to rhyme with *naked.* However, there are numerous less clear examples involving spelling rather than morphology: the text contains twelve variants for the common rhyme-word 'high', for instance, and whilst the rhyme itself may not be corrupted, some of these forms must be 'translations'. Nevertheless, many of these forms have such a widespread geographical distribution that there is insufficient information with which to determine which of them belong to the original dialect, and which are later introductions. Analysis of the dialect of the other Middle English texts in D could shed some light on this problem, but ultimately this would only enhance our knowledge of the scribe's repertoire and, as we have already seen, the *Seven Sages* text bears traces of copyings between the original and that of the scribe of D. Furthermore, there is evidence to suggest that some of the rhymes have undergone a more substantial 'translation'. For example:

> He went forth in mykil care,
> And left alle hys maysters thare (ll. 394–5).

Elsewhere, *thare* is mis-rhymed with *were* (ll. 1430–1, ll. 2700–1), indicating it to be part of the northern scribe's repertoire, rather than an original form. Indeed, *in mykil care* as a whole is most likely a northern rhyme-tag, as ll. 1420–1 suggest:

> He knokede and was in mykyl kare.
> The wyf askyd wo was there.

Here, however, the scribe has not bothered to change *there* into *thare*; but the corrupted rhyme implies that the original had some alternative tag to *in mykil kare* both here, and at l. 394, cited above. This is now lost to the modern editor.

Even if all the corruptions were as straightforward as *made/naked*, emendation would still be, in some ways, an artificial exercise, since the rest of the line would remain partially 'translated'. The text of the version of the *Seven Sages* in Dd.1.17 is such a thorough-going *Mischsprache*, of several geographically discrete components as to render recovery of the original impossible: and for the majority of the corrupted rhyme-words there is insufficient evidence with which to determine the correct reading with any real certainty. In view of these problems, the rhymes have been left as they stand in the manuscript. Morphological corruptions are discussed in the notes.

Emendations, therefore, are kept to a minimum, being offered only when the sense is clearly corrupt, or the scribe has made an obvious error. The more conjectural of these are discussed in the notes.[155] The text has not been emended on metrical grounds, since its status as a *Mischsprache* means it offers no reliable evidence for the metrical practice of the original.

Punctuation, capitalization, word-division, and paragraphing have been modernized.[156] All abbreviations have been silently expanded, including the scribe's practice of sometimes writing a single *E* for *Emperour* and, occasionally, *Emperes(se)*. Since the scribe uses two forms, *Emperes* and *Emperesse*, throughout the poem, the abbreviation has been expanded to match whichever form has been used closer to the point in the text where the abbreviation occurs.

The scribal distinction between *u/v*, and *y/i* has been preserved as in the manuscript. The scribal long *i*, frequently used at the

[155] Wright's emendations are also discussed. As mentioned in the 'Preface', Wright's edition contained a number of errors. Eugen Kölbing published a long list of corrections, 'Collationen', *Englische Studien*, 6 (1883), 448–50. However, there are still a number of errors or instances of manuscript corrections that have gone unnoticed (Wright's reading is given first, followed by that of the manuscript; it should also be noted that the line numbering in Wright is inaccurate in a number of places):

77 To] Tho 177 Was] Wa 235 of] ob 525 maydens] mayndens 685 syrtnlyche] syrculyche 701 Afte] Aste 707 As] And 767 An] And 952 byhyde] hyhyde 1131 hyt] hit 1284 lyfte] lyste 1355 fonde] fande 1574 syre] sire 1697 an] and 1826 aske] ask 1869 Emperour] Empour 1931 And] A (l. 1929 in my edition) 2018 take] toke (l. 2016 in my edition) 2234 ne] no (l. 2232 in my edition) 2337 Cawe] Gawe (l. 2335 in my edition) 2345 buyles] buylys 2376 walmys] walmes (l. 2374 in my edition) 2497 scille] stille (l. 2495 in my edition) 2640 kynge] kynge`s´ (s interlin.; l. 2638 in my edition) 2649 kynges] kyngys (l. 2647 in my edition) 2823 that (omitted by Wright) 2842 so (omitted by Wright) 2864 to] added by Wright 3396 answere] awswere.

[156] One idiosyncracy of the scribe is his tendency to divide, and misdivide, words wherever possible. In the opening lines of the poem, for example, he has written the Emperor's name as 'de occlicius' (l. 4), and also 'Bi twene' (l. 7), 'a nayer' (l. 7), 'for thoght' (l. 15), 'a non' (l. 18), 'by fore' (l. 20), and 'In to' (l. 21).

beginning of words, and for the personal pronoun 'I', has been printed as *i* and *I* respectively. The use of thorn and yogh has been preserved, except for one incident in l. 2725, when *ȝ* is used as a long-tailed *z* in *sarȝyns*, and so has been printed as *z*.

Missing lines are indicated by a line of dots in square brackets, and are not included in the numbering of the text.

The Latin names for the tales, first assigned by Karl Goedeke, are given in the margin.[157]

The following conventions are used in the edition and apparatus:

canc. cancelled
eras. erased
exp. expunged
foll. by followed by
interlin. interlineated
om. omitted in manuscript
over eras. over erasure
relin. relineated
rev. reversed in manuscript
written over indicates a correction by means of superimposition of one letter onto another letter, or part of a letter
] separates the *lemma* from the manuscript reading
⟨ ⟩ angle brackets enclose letters or words that are illegible in the manuscript as the result of physical damage.
[ ] square brackets enclose letters or words that are not in the manuscript, and are either emendations or words supplied conjecturally to make sense of the line, as indicated in the apparatus.
ˋ ˊ indicate interlineations.

[157] Karl Goedeke, '*Liber de Septem Sapientibus*', *Orient und Occident*, 3 (1866), 385–423.

SELECT BIBLIOGRAPHY

EDITIONS

Works within each sub-section are listed chronologically by date of publication.

1. *THE SEVEN SAGES OF ROME*

Middle English

Y-group

Weber, Henry, ed., *Metrical Romances of the Thirteenth, Fourteenth, and Fifteenth Centuries: Published from Ancient Manuscripts*, vols. 1 and 3 (Edinburgh and London, 1810) [A, with missing lines supplied from C]

Ellis, George, ed., *Specimens of Early English Metrical Romances, Chiefly Written During the Early Part of the Fourteenth Century*, 2nd ed., vol. 3 (London, 1811) [Abstract of A with extracts]

Halliwell, James Orchard, ed., *The Thornton Romances. The Early English Metrical Romances of Perceval, Isumbras, Egalmour, and Degrevant. Selected from Manuscripts at Lincoln and Cambridge*, Camden Society, 30 (London, 1844) [Extracts from F]

Campbell, Killis, ed., *The Seven Sages of Rome*, The Albion Series of Anglo-Saxon and Middle English Poetry (Boston, 1907) [C, with variants from R]

Brunner, Karl, ed., *The Seven Sages of Rome (Southern Version)*, EETS, 191 (1933) [A, with variants from Ar, B, E; F given in 'Appendix']

The Auchinleck Manuscript: National Library of Scotland Advocates' MS. 19.2.1, with an introduction by Derek Pearsall and I. C. Cunningham (London, 1977) [Facsimile of A]

Cambridge University Library MS Ff.2.38, with an introduction by Frances McSparran and P. R. Robinson (London, 1979) [Facsimile of F]

Burnley, David, and Alison Wiggins, eds., *The Auchinleck Manuscript*, National Library of Scotland, 5 July 2003, Version 1.1, http://www.nls.uk/auchinleck/ (accessed 12 June 2005)

Balliol College MS. 354, Early Manuscripts at Oxford University: Digital Facsimiles of Complete Manuscripts, Scanned Directly from the Originals, Oxford Digital Library, http://image.ox.ac.uk/show?collection=balliol&manuscript=ms354 (accessed 12 June 2005)

Midland Version

Wright, Thomas, ed., *The Seven Sages, in English Verse, Edited from a Manuscript in the Public Library of the University of Cambridge*, Percy Society: Early English Poetry, Ballads, and Popular Literature of the Middle Ages. Edited from Original Manuscripts and Scarce Publications, 16 (London, 1845)

Prose Version

Gomme, George Laurence, ed., *The History of The Seven Wise Masters of Rome: Printed from the Edition of Wynkyn de Worde, 1520*, Chap-Books and Folk-Lore Tracts, 1st ser., 2 (London, 1885)

Middle Scots

Van Buuren, Catherine, ed., *The Buke of the Sevyne Sagis: A Middle Scots Version of The Seven Sages of Rome Edited from the Asloan Manuscript (NLS Acc. 4233), c. 1515*, Germanic and Anglistic Studies of the University of Leiden, 20 (Leiden, 1982)

Welsh

Jones, G. Hartwell, trans., '*The Seven Wise Men of Rome*', *Selections from the Hengwrt MSS. Preserved in the Peniarth Library*, vol. II (London, 1892), 647–62

Williams, Robert, ed., '*Seith Doethion Ruvein*', *Selections from the Hengwrt MSS. Preserved in the Peniarth Library*, vol. II (London, 1892), 301–24

French

*Version A**

Section de traitement automatique des textes d'ancien français du CRAL, Université de Nancy II, ed., *Les Sept Sages de Rome: Roman en prose du XIIIe siècle d'après le manuscrit no 2137 de la B. N.*, Travaux du CRAL, 2 (Nancy, 1981)

Runte, Hans R., ed., 'An On-Line Edition of French Version A From All Manuscripts', Society of the Seven Sages, http://myweb.dal.ca/hrunte/FrenchA.html (accessed 12 June 2005)

Version C

Speer, Mary, ed., *Le roman des Sept Sages de Rome: A Critical Edition of the Two Verse Redactions of a Twelfth-Century Romance*, Edward C. Armstrong Monographs on Medieval Literature, 4 (Lexington, 1989) [Also includes Version K]

Versions D and H*

Paris, Gaston, ed., *Deux rédactions du Roman des Sept Sages de Rome*, Société des Anciens Textes Français (Paris, 1876)

Version K

Keller, Heinrich Adelbert, ed., *Li romans des Sept Sages* (Tübingen, 1836)

Misrahi, Jean, ed., *Le roman des Sept Sages* (Paris, 1933)

Speer, Mary, ed., *Le roman des Sept Sages de Rome: A Critical Edition of the Two Verse Redactions of a Twelfth-Century Romance*, Edward C. Armstrong Monographs on Medieval Literature, 4 (Lexington, 1989) [Also includes Version C]

Version L

Le Roux de Lincy, [A. J. V.], ed., *Roman des Sept Sages de Rome en prose: Publié, pour la première fois, d'après un manuscrit de la Bibliothèque Royale avec une analyse et des extraits du Dolopathos* (Paris, 1838)

Aïache, Mauricette. 'Les versions françaises en prose du *Roman des Sept Sages*', unpubl. thesis (Ecole Nationale des Chartes, 1966)

Version M

Runte, Hans R., ed., *Li ystoire de la male marastre: Version M of the Roman des Sept Sages de Rome*, Beihefte zur Zeitschrift für romanische Philologie (Tübingen, 1974)

Latin

Version S

Goedeke, Karl, ed., '*Liber de Septem Sapientibus*', *Orient und Occident*, III (1866), 385–423

Gobi, Jean, *La Scala coeli de Jean Gobi*, ed. Marie-Anne Polo de Beaulieu, Sources d'histoire médiévale (Paris, 1991)

II. *DOLOPATHOS*

Latin

Johannes de Alta Silva, *Dolopathos, sive De rege et Septem Sapientibus*, ed. Hermann Oesterley (Strassburg, 1873)

——, *Historia Septem Sapientum. II. Johannis de Alta Silva Dolopathos sive De rege et Septem Sapientibus*, ed. Alfons Hilka, Sammlung mittellateinischer Texte, 5 (Heidelberg, 1913)

——, *Dolopathos: or The King and the Seven Wise Men*, trans. Brady B. Gilleland, Medieval & Renaissance Texts & Studies, 2 (Binghamton, 1981)

French

Johannes de Alta Silva, *Li romans di Dolopathos*, ed. Charles Brunet and Anatole de Montaiglon (Paris, 1856)

III. *THE BOOK OF SINDBĀD*

Hebrew

Cassel, Paulus, ed., *Mischle Sindbad, Secundus, Syntipas* (Berlin, 1888)

Hilka, Alfons, ed., *Historia Septem Sapientum. I. Eine bisher unbekannte lateinische Übersetzung einer orientalischen Fassung der Sieben Weisen Meister (Mischle Sendabar)*, Sammlung mittellateinischer Texte, 4 (Heidelberg, 1912)

Epstein, Morris, ed. and trans., *Tales of Sendebar: An Edition and Translation of the Hebrew Version of the Seven Sages Based on Unpublished Manuscripts*, Judaica: Texts and Translations, 1st ser., 2 (Philadelphia, 1967)

Persian and Arabic

Clouston, W. A., *The Book of Sindibad or, The Story of the King, His Son, the Damsel, and the Seven Vazirs* (Privately printed, 1884)

Old Spanish

Keller, John Esten, trans., *The Book of the Wiles of Women*, University of North Carolina Studies in the Romance Languages and Literatures, 27, Translation Series of the Modern Language Association of America, 2 (Chapel Hill, 1956)

——, ed., *El libro de los engaños*, rev. ed., Textos antiguos españoles, 1, University of North Carolina Studies in the Romance Languages and Literatures, 20 (Valencia and Chapel Hill, 1959)

Syriac

Gollancz, Hermann, trans., '*The History of Sindban and the Seven Wise Masters*', *Folk-Lore*, 8 (1897), 99–130

Later Adaptations

Sheykh-zada, *The History of the Forty Vezirs or The Story of the Forty Morns and Eves*, trans. E. J. W. Gibb (London, 1886)

SECONDARY WORKS

Artola, George, 'The Nature of the *Book of Sindbad*', in Niedzielski, Runte, and Hendrickson, pp. 7–31

Barnes, Geraldine, *Counsel and Strategy in Middle English Romance* (Cambridge, 1993)

Belcher, Stephen, 'The Diffusion of the *Book of Sindbād*', *Fabula*, 28 (1987), 34–58

Benfey, Th., 'Beiträge zur Geschichte der Verbreitung der indischen Sammlungen von Fabeln und Erzählungen; ursprüngliche Grundlage der *Sieben Weisen Meister*', *Orient und Occident*, 3 (1866), 171–80

Boitani, Piero, *English Medieval Narrative in the Thirteenth and Fourteenth Centuries*, trans. Joan Krakover Hall (Cambridge, 1982)

Bordman, Gerald, *Motif-Index of the English Metrical Romances*, FF Communications, 190 (Helsinki, 1963)

Burton, Richard F., review of *The Book of Sindibad or, The Story of the King, His Son, the Damsel, and the Seven Vazirs*, by W. A. Clouston, *The Academy*, 26 (1884), 175–6

Campbell, Killis, 'The Source of the Story *Sapientes* in *The Seven Sages of Rome*', *Modern Language Notes*, 23.7 (1908), 202–4

——, 'A Study of the Romance of the *Seven Sages* with Special Reference to the Middle English Versions', *PMLA*, 14 (1899), 1–107

Chauvin, Victor, *Biblographie des ouvrages arabes ou relatifs aux arabes publiés dans l'Europe chrétienne de 1810 à 1888*, vol. VIII, *Syntipas* (Liège and Leipzig, 1904)

Clouston, W. A., *Popular Tales and Fictions: Their Migrations and Transformations*, 2 vols. (Edinburgh, 1887)

——, 'The Tell-Tale Bird: Latin Source, Other European Versions, and Asiatic Analogues of Chaucer's *Manciple's Tale*', *Originals and Analogues of Some of Chaucer's Canterbury Tales*, ed. F. J. Furnivall, Edmund Brock, and W. A. Clouston, Chaucer Society, 2nd ser., 20 (London, 1888), pp. 437–80

Comparetti, Domenico, *Researches Respecting the Book of Sindibad*, [trans. Henry Charles Coote], Publications of The Folk-Lore Society, 9 (London, 1882)

Cooper, Helen, *The Structure of The Canterbury Tales* (London, 1983)

Cox, Edward Godfrey, review of *The Seven Sages of Rome*, by Killis Campbell, *Modern Language Notes*, 24 (1909), 153–6

Crosland, Jessie, '*Dolopathos* and the *Seven Sages of Rome*', *Medium Ævum*, 25 (1956), 1–12

Denham, Jill, '*The Seven Sages of Rome*: A Source for Gower's *Confessio Amantis*; *The Seven Sages of Rome*: A Source for Chaucer's *The Manciple's Tale*; Some Critical Reflections on Gower, Chaucer, and *The Seven Sages of Rome*', unpubl. M.Phil. thesis (University of Cambridge, 1993)

Foehr-Janssens, Yasmina, *Le temps des fables: Le roman des Sept Sages, ou l'autre voie du roman*, Nouvelle bibliothèque du Moyen Âge, 27 (Paris, 1994)

Gittes, Katharine S., *Framing the Canterbury Tales: Chaucer and the Medieval Frame Narrative Tradition*, Contributions to the Study of World Literature, 41 (New York, 1991)

Hammer-Purgstall, [Joseph von], review of *Li romans des Sept Sages*, ed. Heinrich Adalbert Keller, *Jahrbücher der Litteratur*, 90 (1840), 36–124

Hartung, Albert E., gen. ed., *A Manual of the Writings in Middle English 1050–1500*, vol. 9 (New Haven, CT, 1993)

Heltveit, Trygve, 'Dialect Words in *The Seven Sages of Rome*', in *English Studies Presented to R. W. Zandvoort on the Occasion of His Seventieth Birthday*, Suppl. to *English Studies*, 45 (1964), 125–34

Hibbard, Laura A., *Mediaeval Romance in England: A Study of the Sources and Analogues of the Non-Cyclic Metrical Romances*, new ed., Burt Franklin Bibliographical and Reference Series, 17 (New York, 1963)

Hinckley, Henry Barrett, 'The Framing-Tale', *Modern Language Notes*, 49.2 (1934), 69–80

Jaunzems, John, 'Structure and Meaning in the *Seven Sages of Rome*', in Niedzielski, Runte, and Hendrickson, pp. 43–62

Johnson, James D., 'Walter W. Skeat's *Canterbury Tale*', *Chaucer Review*, 36 (2001), 16–27

Kane, George, *Middle English Literature: A Critical Study of the Romances, the Religious Lyrics, Piers Plowman*, Methuen's Old English Library (London, 1951)

Kelly, Douglas, '*Disjointure* and the Elaboration of Prose Romance: The Example of *The Seven Sages of Rome* Prose Cycle', in *The Spirit of the Court: Selected Proceedings of the Fourth Congress of the International Courtly Literature Society (Toronto 1983)*, ed. Glyn S. Burgess and Robert A. Taylor (Cambridge, 1985), pp. 208–16

——, 'Motif and Structure as Amplification of *Topoi* in the *Sept Sages de Rome* Prose Cycle', in Niedzielski, Runte, and Hendrickson, pp. 133–54

Kölbing, E., 'Collationen', *Englische Studien*, 6 (1883), 442–59

Lewis, Celia Milton, 'Framing Fiction with Death: *The Seven Sages of Rome*, Boccaccio's *Decameron*, and Chaucer's *Canterbury Tales*', unpubl. Ph.D. thesis (Baylor University, 2001)

Loiseleur-Deslongchamps, A., *Essai sur les fables indiennes et sur leur introduction en Europe* (Paris, 1838)

Lotfizadeh, Bonnie Diane Irwin, '*The Book of Sindibad* and *The Seven Sages of Rome*: Perspectives on the Frame and its Relationship to the Interpolated Tales in the Persian, Arabic, Latin, and Spanish Versions', unpubl. Ph.D. thesis (University of California, Berkeley, 1991)

Lumiansky, R. M., 'Thematic Antifeminism in the Middle English *Seven Sages of Rome*', *Tulane Studies in English*, 7 (1957), 5–16

Lundt, Bea, review of *Le temps de fables: Le roman des Sept Sages, ou l'autre voie du roman*, by Yasmina Foehr-Janssens, *Fabula*, 36 (1995), 335–8

Mehl, Dieter, *The Middle English Romances of the Thirteenth and Fourteenth Centuries* (London, 1968)

Metlitzki, Dorothee, *The Matter of Araby in Medieval England* (New Haven, CT, 1977)

Menocal, María Rosa, *The Arabic Role in Medieval Literary History: A Forgotten Heritage*, University of Pennsylvania Press: Middle Ages Series (Philadelphia, 1987)

Millersdaughter, Katherine Elizabeth, 'Incest and Imperial Politics in the Middle English and Middle Welsh *Seven Sages of Rome*', in 'The Geopolitics of Incest in the Age of Conquest: Gerald of Wales through Geoffrey Chaucer', unpubl. Ph.D. thesis, (University of Colorado at Boulder, 2003), pp. 187–221

Mussafia, Adolf, *Beiträge zur Litteratur der Sieben Weisen Meister* (Vienna, 1868)

Napier, Arthur S., 'A Hitherto Unnoticed Middle English Manuscript of the *Seven Sages*', *PMLA*, 14 (1899), 459–64

Niedzielski, Henri, 'La formation d'un cycle littéraire au Moyen Âge: Exemple des *Sept Sages de Rome*', in Niedzielski, Runte, and Hendrickson, pp. 119–32

Niedzielski, H., H. R. Runte, and W. L. Hendrickson, eds., *Studies on The Seven Sages of Rome and Other Essays in Medieval Literature Dedicated to the Memory of Jean Misrahi* (Honolulu, 1978)

Nöldeke, Th., review of *Sindbad oder die Sieben Weisen Meister: Syrisch und Deutsch*, ed. Friedrich Baethgen, *Zeitschrift der deutschen Morgenländischen Gesellschaft*, 33 (1879), 513–36

Palermo, Joseph, '*Roman des Sept Sages*', *Dictionnaire des lettres françaises: Le Moyen Âge*, ed. Robert Bossuat, Louis Pichard, Guy Raynaud de Lage (Paris, 1964), pp. 656–7

Paris, Gaston, review of *Dolopathos, sive De rege et Septem Sapientibus*, ed. Hermann Oesterley, *Romania*, 2 (1873), 481–503

Perry, B. E., 'The Origin of the *Book of Sindbad*', *Fabula*, 3 (1960), 1–94

Petras, Paul, *Über die mittelenglischen Fassungen der Sage von der Sieben Weisen Meistern* (Breslau, 1885)

Robbins, Mary, 'Medieval Astrology and *The Buke of the Sevyne Sagis*', *Forum for Modern Language Studies*, 38 (2002), 420–34

Runte, Hans R., 'From the Vernacular to Latin and Back: The Case of *The Seven Sages of Rome*', in *Medieval Translators and Their Craft*, ed. Jeanette Beer, Studies in Medieval Culture, 25, Medieval Institute Publications (Kalamazoo, MI, 1989), pp. 93–133

——, 'The *Matron of Ephesus*: The Growth of the Story in the *Roman des Sept Sages de Rome*', in Niedzielski, Runte, and Hendrickson, pp. 109–18

Runte, Hans R., J. Keith Wikeley, and Anthony J. Farrell, *The Seven Sages of Rome and The Book of Sindbad: An Analytical Bibliography*, Garland Reference Library of the Humanities, 387 (New York, 1984)

Runte, Hans R., Ralf-Henning Steinmetz, and other members of the Society of the Seven Sages, 'Supplement to *The Seven Sages of Rome and The Book of Sindbad: An Analytical Bibliography*', Society of the Seven Sages, http://myweb.dal.ca/hrunte/ABSupp.html#UP (accessed 12 June 2005)

Schmirgel, Carl, 'Typical Expressions and Repetitions in *Sir Beues of Hamtoun*', in *The Romance of Sir Beues of Hamtoun*, ed. Eugen Kölbing, EETS, ES 46, 48, 65 (1885, 1886, 1894)

Skow, Katherine Kent, 'The Whole is the Sum of its Parts: A Structural and Thematic Analysis of *Die Sieben Weisen Meister*', unpubl. Ph.D. thesis (University of Illinois at Urbana-Champaign, 1992)

Thorpe, Lewis, '*Les Sept Sages de Rome*: Un nouveau fragment de manuscrit', in *Mélanges d'histoire littéraire, de linguistique et de philologie romanes offerts à Charles Rostaing* (Liège, 1974), pp. 1143–7

Van Buuren-Veenenbos, Catherine, 'A Middle Scots Version of the *Seven Sages of Rome*', in Niedzielski, Runte, and Hendrickson, pp. 63–78

Varnhagen, H., review of *Über die mittelenglischen Fassungen der Sage von der Sieben Weisen Meistern*, by Paul Petras, *Englische Studien*, 10 (1887), 279–82

Whitelock, Jill, '*The Seven Sages of Rome* and Orientalism in Middle English Literature, With an Edition of the Poem from Cambridge, University Library, Dd.1.17', unpubl. Ph.D. thesis (University of Cambridge, 1998)

Yohannan, John D., ed., *Joseph and Potiphar's Wife in World Literature: An Anthology of the Story of the Chaste Youth and the Lustful Stepmother* (New York, 1968)

THE SEVEN SAGES OF ROME

In Rome was an Emperour, f. 54ra
A man of swyth mikil honur,
As þe book tellys vs,
Is name was Deocclicius;
Al the londe hadde to gye,
And hadd a wyfe that hight Helie.
Bitwene thaym twa come an ayer,
A good child and a faire;
The Emperour and is wif
Loueden the child as hare lyf.
The Emperour wax an old man,
And on a day thynke he gan
Vppon his sone that was so bolde,
And was bot seuene wynter olde.
The Emperour forthoght sore
Tha the child ware sette to lore;
After the Seuen Sages he sent,
And messangers anon thare went,
And broghten the clerkes of honour
Ryght byfore the Emperour.
Into a chambir out of the halle
He toke thaym, and refreynde alle
Whilk of thaym he myght take
Hys sone a wyes man to make.
The heldest answerde the Emperour,
That whas a man of mykil honour;
A lene oor man he was,
Kyd was callid Bancillas.
He sayed to the Emperour,
'Woldestow do me that honour
To bytake thy sone to me,
Thow scholdest bath here and see
Er thys seuen ȝer ware agoon
He sholde conne hymself alon,
By God Almyghty that is in heuen,
Also mykyl as we seuene.'
The secunde mayster was nawt so holde
Ase [B]ancillas, no nawt so bolde;

10 Loueden] Louenden 27 oor] r *written over* ȝ 28 Bancillas] B *written over another letter, perhaps* C 38 Bancillas] Cancillas

A man he was that loued pees,
And whas callid Ancillees.
'Sire Emperoure, ȝif it so bee
Thow wille bytake thy sone to me,
For thy loue I wille hym teche
Into is hert fort reche
Al the clergy vndir sonne
That we seuen clerkes cunne.
This I wile sikere the
Gyf he schal byleue with me.'
  The thirde a lene man was,
And couthe mykil solas,
And was callid Lentulus.
Hee sayed to the Emperour thus:
'Sire Emperour, take nowt agreef;
Tak me thy childe that is te leue,
And er ther passe thre and fyue—
Yf he haue wyt, and his on lyue—
He schal conne hymself alone
As mykil wit as we ilkone.'
  The fyrde mayster he roos and spake.
He was nowthir whyit no blake—
An inred man he was,
f. 54rb And was callid Maladas.
'Sire,' he sayde, 'take me thyn heire
That his bothe good and faire.
Bote, forsothe, I wile forsake
That my felawes hase vndirtake—
A wondir thyng that were bygyne,
To teche hym that my felawes cune—
Bot I walde teche hym, as I am a man,
Also mykil good as I can.'
  The fyfte mayster vparaes,
That of wisdom bare grete loos;
He was boren in Rome toune,
And was callid Mayster Caton.
He sayd, 'Sire Emperour, iwys,
The sothe tale that his this:

45 sonne] *2nd minim of 2nd* n *written over another letter* 49 Thyrde *in left margin*
59 ffirde *in left margin* 61 An] And

To teche hym that my felawes cane,
A grete foly it were bygyne;
Bote yf thow wilt bitake hym me,
I wille, for honour of the,
As I am trewe mane,
Hym teche the clergy that I can.'
The sexte was a ȝong man
That no berd non bygane,
And sayed, 'Sire, bythoght fening,
Take thy sone in my kypyng,
And that wole do so, by myn attente,
That ȝe no schal nouȝt repente.'
In this manere answerde he,
And was callid Maystir Iesse.
The seuent mayister answerd thus,
And was hoten Marcius:
'Sire, I haue seruyd the ȝare
Sythen I couthe first of lare;
Fram that day hidyr to,
Al that euere I haue done
I queth ȝou, Sire Emperoure,
Woltow do me that honour
To take me thy childe to ȝeme,
And I wille teche hym the to geme.'
The Emperour with wordis stille
Thaynked thaym with good wille.
'By the deth that I schal dee,
I nylle party ȝoure company.
I nylle take my sone to one:
I bytake hym ȝow ilkone
To teche hym in chambyr and in halle,
That I be holden to ȝou alle.'
Thay thanked alle the Emperour
That grauntyd hem that honour
To haue in hare kepyng
That he loued thorou al thyng.
Thay token leue at the Emperour,
And ladde the childe with honour—

77 To] Tho   84 berd] d *written over another letter*

The seuene mayster alle yfere—
Ther the childe schulde lere.
Than sayd Maystir Catone,
'Yf he dwelle here in the toune,
Certes it may nought be
That he [ne] schal here or see
Wylen to don or speke with mouthe,
And that nolde we nought that he couth.
Sykyrly forto telle, f.54rc
There most he nouȝt dwelle.'
The seuen maysteres thay hym nome
I note how mykil out of Rome
Forto ordayne and dyuise,
Or the childe ware sette aprise,
Ware thay myȝte a stude make,
A real for the childes sake,
Whare he myght of wit lere,
And none vileny heere.
A studie thay fonden swyth fayre,
And a stude of good eeir;
Fayre welles there wellyde fast,
And fayre trees schadow tokast.
In the fayrest place of alle
Thay lete reren a halle;
Nought as anothir halle it nas,
Euen four-cornarde it was.
Thay late rere in ilce-a syde
Fayre chambirs, many and wyde;
Euery mayster hadde oone
In to lygge and to goon.
Than al togydir was wrought
Er the childe wer thydir brought,
Fyrst gamen to bygynne—
The seuene sciens payent therin.
Whan al togydyr was wrought,
The childe tharin was brought.
Amyd the halle hys bede was made;
When he lay therin naked,

120 ne] *om.* 123–4 *on same line* 127 dyuise] y *written over 2 minims*
141 syde] y *written over another letter* 148 payent] e *written over minim*

Hon ilce half he myȝt byholde
At ilke tyme whane he wolde;
Vppon the wallis he myght see
What hys lesson schulde bee.
Alle hys maystirs were about
To teche hym, for hys fadir dout;
Euermore wil he wooke,
When on leuede, anothir tooke,
That or the seuen ȝere were goon,
Of seuen artis nastir noon
That he no couthe good skil inne;
Wastir noon to bygynne.
Whan his maystirs taught ⟨noght⟩,
He lernede of his owen thoght,
That on a day in the `h´alle
He disputide with ham alle,
And thay were glad of that he couthe,
And sayed ilcon [to] othir [with] mouthe,
'The childe wax a wyes man;
Proue we more what he can.'
Thay were bythout in a wile
Forto do the childe a gyle,
Forto proue of hym more
How depe he was in lore.
The childes bede wa[s] maked in stage
Of four postis as a kage;
Vndir ilc post thay layden—
Aste the clercus hemseluen sayden—
Four yuen-leues togydir knyt
Forto prouen of his wit.
  Vppon morwen tho it was day
The childe awakid there he lay.
He loked low, he loked hee, f. 54va
And kast wildeliche his hye;
He loked in ilce half of his bede
As a man that ware adrad.
Than come the maystir Bancillas,
And askyde the childe wat him was:

170 to . . . with] *rev.* 177 was] wa 186 kast] a *written over* e

'Wy lokesttow so aboute thy bede?
Artou of enythyng adrade?'
The childe answerde in his bede,
'I am of no man adrade,
Bote a lytil I merueyle me
Of a thyng that I see.
This house that is so strange dyʒt,
The rofe hys sonkon tonyght,
Or the flore his resyn on hye
Sythen I last the rofe see.'
'Certys,' quod Maladas,
'That ware a wondir kas,
For in noonekynne wyse
The flore ne may nouʒt aryse.
The post been grete and nouʒt smal—
How myʒte the rofe awale?
Hyt ne may on non wys be,
Thyng that thou tellyst me.'
'By God, maister, I am noght dronken!
Yf the rofe his nouʒt sonken,
Ne the flore rysyn on hye
Sithen I last the rofe see,
Than his my bede vndirlayede;
That no may nouʒt bee wytsed.'
Thay nolden no langer with hym ʒede,
Ne suffry langer lygge in bede,
Bote while he wente in solas
Maden the bedde as hit was.
Ilkon sayed to oþer thus:
'He his a wyse man, ywys.'
Wyl the childe at scole was,
Hym byfel a harde caes:
Hys modir deyde that hatte Elye,
As we schalle alle dye.
Sone aftir that scho was dede,
Hys fadir hadde anothir rede.
Grete lordis of honour
Come anone to the Emperour,

214 may] y *written over* n 216 lygge] y *written over 2 minims* 218 bedde] *2nd* d *written over* e 221 scole] o *written over* e

And sayden, 'Thow hase londis ynow—
Hit were tyme forto wouwe,
And to haue anothir wyf
Forto ledde with thy lyf.
Thou no hauest no childe bot hon,
And mygtyst susteyne many oon.'
The Emperour was iolyf ob blode,
And hare councel vndirstood,
And to thaym alle sayede hee,
'Lordyngs, thanne aspye ȝe
A womman worthy to be my make,
And with ȝoure consel I wil hire take.'
Tho thay seen he wolde acente,
Forto seche anon thay wente
Of hye lynage and faire manere
A lady forto be his feere.
Alle the lordis soghten fast,
And fande a lady at the last. f. 54[vb]
At schorte wordis forto telle,
The Emperour ne wolde nouȝt dwel;
Hee wedded hirre ase the law was,
And lyueden togydir in solas.
Bot it lastid bot a while—
The wyf fordide hit with a gyle.
  The Emperasse was sone tolde
Of that child that was so bolde,
That was the Emperour eir,
A good childe and a faire.
He that tolde hire that tale
Broght hir in mykil bael,
For euermore scho was in thoght
That the childe were to deth broght.
  In a myry morny[n]g of May
The Emperour in his bedde lay,
And the Emperesse in feere.
'What we saye now non schal here,
Sire,' scho sayed. 'Hit is me tolde
That thou hase a sone bolde,

232 ledde] *2nd* d *written over* e 235 blode] l *written over another letter*
246 fande] *foll. by* the *exp.* 261 mornyng] mornyg

A good childe and a faire,
That sal be oure bothe ayere.
Forsothe, sire, I hold hym myn
Also wel as thou dost thyn;
Therfore I besyche the,
For loue thou ouwest to me,
Send after hym yf it his thy wylle,
And late me spek with hym my fylle.
Graunt my bone and make me glade;
Hyt his the first that euer I badde.'
The Emperour lay al stille,
And lete hyre saye al hire wille.
Of falsnesse non heed he nam,
Bot at the last out hit kame.
The Emperour answerde tho,
'Certis, dame, I haue no mo,
No child bot hym, iwis,
And now I wet how hit his
That thow desyres hym to see,
He schal come hom to the.'
The lady sayed thare [scho laye],
'Leue sire, this ilke daye
Lat dyght messangers ȝare
Aftir hym forto fare.'
Quod the Emperour and swor þerto,
'Forsoth, dame, hit sal be doon.'
Bot the Emperour wist nought
What was hire wikkyd thought.
On euyl deth mot scho dey!
Scho purchasede thourugt nigremancye
That seuen dayes and seuen nyght
He no schold spek with no wyght.
Yf ony word hym hadde sprong,
That men myght here of his tong,
Anon hys hert scholde tobreke,
Ne scholde he neuer eft more spek.
This hadde the wikkid womman wrout
For brynge the childe to nowt.

287 scho laye] *om.*

Than messangers were ȝare
After the childe forto fare.
He sayed to the messangeres f. 54vc
That ware bolde and feres,
'To the Seuen Sages ȝe sal wynde,
And saye that I ham gretyng sende,
And bidde thaym withouten delay
Come withinne the thyrdde day,
And bryng with thaym my sone dere
That thay haue forto lere.'
Thay nolden there longe dwelle,
The messangers were ful snelle;
Hastilich the way thay nomen,
To the Seuen Sages thay comen,
And sayden, 'Clerkis of honour,
Wylle ȝow gretis the Emperour,
And byddis ȝow within this thrid day
Come to hym without delay,
And bryng with ȝow his sone dere
That he betauȝt ȝou to lere.'
Thay were resayued with gret honour
For loue of the Emperour.
The childe and his maisters alle
Went dowen out of halle
Into a herber to make solas,
And there sawe a wondir kas.
Hit neght fast toward nyght,
And the mone schone wil bryght,
And thay byhelden towarde the scky
Vppon the mone that [was] so hyȝe,
And on sternes there bysyde,
Of thyng that affter wolde bytyde.
Than byspake Maystir Caton:
'Felaus, I see in the mone
[. . . . .]
We haue made vs alle todon!
The Emperour hase send vs sonde
That we schal brynge his sone alle to honde,

315 longe] l *written over minim* 334 was] *om.* 338 *see note*

And when he comes his fadir byfore,
And he speke, he his lore.
His stepmodir hase thorug nigrimancye
So demed how the child schal dye:
Yf he speke, he his ylore,
And we schal by schend therfore.
The Emperour, by swete Ihesus,
Alle he wille wyten vs.'
The childe kast hys heyn ahey,
And sawe alle that Caton see.
'Maystir,' he sayde, 'asee ȝe
Anothir thyng that I se?
In a stere I see me lyche:
And I myghte forbere speche
Seuen dayes and seuen nyght,
I scholde couere agayn my [m]yght,
And my woo turne to game,
And ȝe alle out of blame.'
Than sayd Mayster Bancillas,
'Forsoth, this his [a] wondir cas!
Tharefore take counsel sone
What his best to don,
How we myghte ouercome this wyf
Forto saue oure al[l]er lyf;
For bettir be auisemend,
Certenlych we be schent.'
f. 55ra The childe answerd ther he stood,
'I wyle gyf ȝou counsel good:
Seuen dayes I mot forbere
That I ne gyf no answere,
And yf I speke loude or stille,
With the forme word I sal deye,
And ȝe both, ȝe maistires seuene,
The wysesde I holde vndir euene.
Fondys ilkon, yf ȝe may,
Forto holde my lyf a day
With qweyntys of clergye,

342 he] he *written over* b 353 thyng] *written twice* 356 nyght] y *written over minim* 357 myght] syght 359 alle] *foll. by* turne *exp.* of] *written twice* 361 a] *om.* 365 aller] aler

For ȝe be schent yf I deye.'
Bancillas sayed, 'If I may,
I schal saue thy lyf a daye.'
And alle the othir sayed, iwys,
That ilkon wolde be for hys,
And ilc mayster toke hys day
To kepe hit withouten delay.
Sonenday hadde Bancillas,
And ilkon wyst wylk his was.
Thus thay were at on alle,
And wenten agayen into ˋþeˊ halle,
And maden the messangers solas,
And ȝede to bede wan tym was.
  O morwe when the day was lyght
Thay hyeden that the childe were diȝt.
He went forth in mykil care,
And left alle hys maysters thare;
With hym toke he neuere oon
Bot Maistir Bancillas aloon,
And anon are the no[m]e
Ryght to the cite of Rome.
The childe into palayes kame,
And into halle the way he name,
And hys fadir he gan lowte,
And the lordyngs al abowt.
Hys fadir askyd how he ferde,
And the child nowt answerde,
Bot lowtid to his fadir anon,
And stod stille as a stoon.
The Emperour than wroth was,
Spake to þe maystir Bancillas:
'Mayster, how his this game goone
That my sone speke wordis none?
And tho I hym bytoke to ȝow
He spake langage good inowe,
And now ne spekys he bettir no wors—
Therefore haue Godys curse!'
'Sire,' quod Maystir Bancillas,

392 when] h *written over* e 397 Bancillas] B *written over another letter*
398 nome] none 403 lordyngs] s *written over another letter*

'Forsoth, hit his a wondir cas!
Ȝysterday he spak as wel
As ony of vs, by Saynt Myghel.'
  Wyle the Emperour and Bancillas
Spake of that wondir cas,
To the Emperesse the worde was broght
That the child ne spake nought.
Scho come adoun into the halle,
And hyre maydens with hire alle,
And welkomede the childe anone,
And he stod stille as a ston,
And fayre he gan the lauydy loute,
f. 55rb And hir mayden alle aboute.
He stod stille and spake noughte;
He wist ful wille hir wikyd thouȝt.
The lauedy sayed to the Emperour,
'Y grette thy sone for gret honour,
And hys mouth whas fast stoke;
He wolde neuer a word speke.'
Thanne sayede the Emperour,
'Dame, by Saynt Sauiour,
He wolde nothyng spek with me;
How scholde he, dam, spek wit the?'
The lauedy sayd, that thouȝt gile,
'Sire, lete vs twayne bee a wyle
In a chambir togidir steke,
And certis yf he sal euer speke,
I sal make hym speke, iwys,
Yf anny speche in hym ys.
Forsoth, I shal bee his leche
Yf euermore shal haue speche.'
The Emperour of alle the londe
Tok hys sone by the honde,
And sayed, 'Dame, take hym here,
And wende wydir ȝe wille ifere.
I vowch hym wylle saue on the
To do what thy wylle bee.'
  The Emperesse of alle the londe

422 the] t *written over another letter*   451 wydir] r *written over minim*

Tok the childe by the honde,
And wente into a chambyr ifere,
And ful euyly, as ȝe mowe hyre,
Ful sone scho hadde a lesyng wrouȝt
Forto bryng the childe to nouȝt.
When scho into þe chambur cam
The childe by the honde scho nam,
And sayed to hym, 'Lemman dere,
Men wenes I be thy faderes fere.
By hym that made sone and mone,
He ne hade neuer with me done,
No neuermore he ne schal.
My body, maydenhod and alle,
I haue lokyn hit to the
To do with what thy wille bee.'
The childe stod and spake nought,
And was in swyth gret thought.
Aboute hys neke hyre armees ho layed,
And with hir fals tonge sayed,
'Kys me, yf thy wylle bee;
Alle my lyfe hys longe on the.'
The childe thouȝt on heuene blys;
He nolde nought the lauedy kys,
And no nothir thynge do
Bot crepe out of hire armes two.
Anon as the lady see
Out of hire armes that he flee,
Al that on hir hed was layed
Scho brayd hit adon at on brayd,
Torente hyre clothes, and foule ferde,
And cryde at þe Emperour herde.
For men scholde tak hed,
Scho made hyre vysages forto bled.
Than the Emperour herde hyr crye,
Into the chambir he gan hye,
And anon has he cam f. 55[rc]
A grete scryke vp ho nam,
And sayde, 'My Lord Syre Emperour,

455 childe] d *written over* l
472 armees] m *written over another letter*
491 scryke] y *written over 2 minims*
492 sayde] *foll. by* sir *exp.*

Lo hyre what a grete honour
Thy sone walde haue done the!
Here he walde haue strangyl me,
Or he walde haue lyen my by
Bot I hadde areryd cry.
Forsoth, he nys nouȝt thy blode;
Hit his a deuel, and his wode.
Forsothe, bot he be bondon anon,
He wil schende vs ilcoon.'
The Emperour was nere wode
When he sawe hys wyfys bloode,
Hire heued bare, hire clothes rente.
He swore anon, 'By Saynt Vyncent,
I schal neuere hete brede
Here the thyfe traytour be dede!'
   Anonryght the Emperour
Callid to hym a tormentour,
And anothir, and the thyrde,
And sayde, 'I ȝow hote and byde,
Take thys thyf and bynde hym fast
Whyle the cordis wyle laste,
And ledys ȝe hym thare thyfys hyng
Anon that he haue hys endyng,
And loke that he no tarye nouȝt
Er he be [t]o deth brought.'
None durste withsytte hys heste,
Nouthir the lest no the moste.
Thay tokyn hym and bandyn hym fast
Whyle the cordis wolde laste.
Thourth the Emperours commandement
Thay laddyn hym toward iuggement.
Knyghtys and leuedys in the halle,
Squyers and maydens alle,
Hadde wondire in hir thouth
What wo was in the chambir wrought.
   Erlys and barrons in the halle
Wenten to the Emperour alle,

496 lyen] *foll. by* by *exp.* 514 hyng] y *written over 2 minims* 517 to deth] do deth *over eras.* 525 maydens] mayndens 526 thouth] *2nd* t *written over another letter*

And sayed, 'Lord Syr Emperour,
Thow doost thyselfe lytil honour
Forto suffyre thy sone by slawe
Withouten any proses of lawe.
Lat hym leue al this nyght
Til tomorwe that day by lyght,
And than yf he schal by schent,
Lat hym passe thourgh iuggement.'
Than answerde the Emperour
To the lordis of honour,
'Lordyngs, I wil ȝow telle,
For ȝoure loue he schal dwelle
On lyue tyl tomorwe day,
And by than as hit may.'
Thay thankit al the Emperour
That hadde don ham that honour,
That he grauntit ham that bone,
And that thay hadden hit so sone.
The Emperour comandede anone
Afftir the childe forto goon,
And thay brought hym into the halle
Among the gret lordis alle. f. 55va
The Emperour comanded anone
That he scholde to prison goon,
And in prison he lay ale nyght
Til on the morwen the day lyȝt.
Now his the childe t[o] prison brouȝt;
Mykile sorowe was in hys thout.
God that sytys in mageste,
Delyuere hym whan his wil bee.
The Emperes was sory in thout
That the childe agayn was brogt.
Scho morned and made mykil wo
Til the day was ago.
Than thay were in bed brought,
Forto change hir lordis thouht
When thay were in bede ifere,

539 honour] h *written over another letter* 544 thankit] thank hit 554 nyght] y *written over 2 minims* 556 to] the 565 thouht] *2nd* h *written over another letter*

What scho sayed ȝe schulle here,
How ho brought hire lorde in wille
Er hit was daye the childe to spille.
Scho wippe and hir hondis wronge,
And ofte syked sore amange.
The Emperour laye and herde,
And asked hyre why ho so ferde,
And sayed, 'Tel me anon
Why thow makyst al this mon.'
'Sire,' quod the lady tho,
'Hit his no wondir tho me be wo!
Thow were bettir to be dede
Than wyrke eftyr sory rede.
Thou brewest thyself mykil bale
To leue ilke mans tale.
Also mote bytide the
As dyde the fyne appul-tre:
For a branche that sprange biside
The grettir les alle hir pride.'
'Certis, dame,' quod Emperour,
'I woot thow louyste my honour,
And tharefore, dame, I the bydde
Tel me how that bytydde,
And latte vs studye tharevppon
What his best forto doon.'

Fyrst Talle [*Arbor*]

Anon the lauedy hire tale bygan,
And sayd, 'Sire, hit was a man,
As men sayen, hit was a knyȝt,
And hadde a herber fayr dyght.
Now schaltou here how hit bytyde.
In the herber ryght amyde
Oppon the appul-tre thare stoode
A fayre tre and a goode.
Bothe harlyche and latte
The lorde was of tyme thareatte,
And grette daynte he hadde

The tree see fayre spradde.
Withinne a wylle, hit is nouȝt longe,
A branche `out´ of the tre spronge,
And the knyght dayenteth hadde
How hit wax and fayre spradde.
'Oppon a day kam the knyght,
And sawe hym crokyn a lytil wyght;
A bou of the grette tre
Lettyde hym that he myȝt nout the.
Quod the lorde to his gardinere, f. 55vb
"Go feche an ax wil I ham here,
And hew adown this mykyl bowe,
And latte the branche haue rome ynow."
The gardiner was sone went
To do the lordis commaundement.
Thus he lette norische the ȝong
That was out of the holde sprong,
And of hold he lete hewe
Many bowes and nowght fewe.
Thay lette the ȝonge branche sprede,
And the holde tre bygan to dede.
The gardiner sawe alle the rote.
"Forsothe, sir, thare his no bote;
Al the virtu ther scholde bee
Is lopon into the lytyl tre."
"Parfay," quod the lorde tho,
"Gardyner, when hit hys sooe,
Ther nyl bee no noþer botte
Bot dyggyt vp by the rote."
Thus was the tre bodun wronge
For the braunche that of hym spronge.
Than the mykil tree wax al badde,
And the lytil the maystre he hadde.
'Thus sal the branche that of the spronge
Fondon forto do the wronge,
And hewes thy bowys in ilke-a syde
That hys thy power that spredis so wide.
Thus when he bygynnys to bolde

603 spradde] a *written over* e 607 fayre] y *written over* r 628 tho] o *written over* e

He wille brynge the adown in olde.'
  Thus whas the wykkyd womman tale
Forto browe the childes bale.
'Dame,' quod the Emperour,
'By lorde Saynt Sauour,
For alle the men that beres brethe
He sal tomorwen thole dethe.'
  On the morwen tho hit was day bryȝt
The Emperour clepid a knyght.
'To my pryson thou schalt goon,
And say my tormentours anoon
Thay do my sone to tormentrie.
Certis this day he schal dee.'
The knyght was sory in hys thought,
Bote withsaye hym dorst he nought,
Bote bade the tourmentours ilkon
Doe the childe to dethe anoone.
Anoon the childe was lade to spyle
To doo the Emperours wille.
Toward the deth as he was
He mette with Mayster Bancillas.
The childe was aferde to dee,
A kast on hym a ruful hye.
He rade forth and sayed nought;
He wyst wylle the childis thought.
Forto saue the childes honour
He come wille sone to the Emperour.
  'Sire,' quod Maystir Bancillas,
'Certis this his a wondir cas,
That thow art in wille pytte
To sle thy sone withouten gylte.'
Thanne sayed the Emperour anoon,
f. 55[vc] 'I haue enchesone mo than oon.
Ȝe seuene haue haddyn in ȝoure powere
My sone al this seuen ȝere
To teche nortyre and wyt,
And ȝe haue hys tonge cnyt;
Whan I prayd hym for charite,
He walde nought speke a worde with me.
And anothir cheson I haue goode:

The fule thefe, the vnky[n]de blode,
He was aboute my wyf to spyle
For he no most nought haue hys wille
To by hyr flesche lygge.
He schal dee, sy[cur]lyche,
And ȝe also, by Good in heuene,
Ȝe schal dee, al seuene!'
Than sayde Bancillas,
'A, Sire Emperour, alas
That thow greuest the so sore
Or thow haddyst queryd more.
Certys I dare lygge my lyf,
Of that thow tellis of thy wyf
The childe ne thought nought bot gode—
Wymman been of wundyr mode.'
The [Emperour] that wroth was
Answerde Bancillas,
'Bancillas, lat be thy fare.
I see my wyfys hed bare,
And hir clothes al torent
Aste the thef wold hir haue schent.'
Bancillas answerd tho—
For the childe hym wa[s] wo—
And sayed, 'Sire, for thy lyf,
Bynym nought thy sonnys lyf.
And yf thow dost, so mot byfalle
A[s] fel the knyght in hys halle
That byname hys growhund lyf
That hadde sauyd hys sonnys lyfe;
And for the dule he made therfore
The knyght hymseluen he was forlore.'
Quod Emperour than to Bancillas,
'Tel me how that tale was.'
'Sire,' quod Bancillas, 'werto?
Wat awantage were that to do?
Er the tale were [t]olde
The childes blode wolde bee colde.'

681 vnkynde] vnkyde 685 sycurlyche] syrculyche 696–7 *on same line* 696 Emperour] *om.* 703 was] wa 704–5 *relin.* 705 Bynym] y *written over 2 minims* 707 As] And 716 tolde] colde

The Emperour commande tho
Afftir the childe forto goo.
The childe that glad was of sokur
Was brought byfore the Emperour.
Thourow the Emperour commandement
Agayn to prison he was sende.
Anoon as the childe was agoon
The mayster bygan hys tale anoon.

A Tale of þe Mayster [*Canis*]

He sayed how ther was a knyght,
A ryche man of gret myghte,
And had a good womman to wyf,
And a womman of good lyf.
Bytwen thaym thare cam a ayer,
A good child and a fayre;
And ȝonge hagge hit was,
A twelmowth holde it was.
Ther was nothing sycurliche
f. 56ra That the knyght louyd so myche.
The knyght hadde anoþer iuel
That he louyd swyth wel:
A grewhond that was good and snel,
And the knyght louyde hit wel,
And was swyth good of dede
To alle bestis that he toȝode,
And for his godnesse he was lore,
And the knyght was sory therfore.
Knyght ordaynde a day
In a tyme, hit was in May,
Elcon with othir wolde play,
And fond to breke a schaft or twey.
The knyght of hit [herde] telle
In his felde thay wolde dwelle;
Ryght a lytil fram his halle,
Ther thay were asembild alle.

734 sycurliche] syrcurliche 748 herde] *om.*

Al that in the court was
Wente to see the solas,
Saue the childes norises two;
Thay ne durst nowerware goo.
Wen thay seen al ware goo,
And no man leued bot thay two,
And herdyn tro[m]pe and taburne,
Thay forgate hare honoure;
Thay left the childe anon tho,
And dyde ham bothe forthgoo.
In a toure thay clymbyd on hyghe,
Pryuyliche tha no man see.
Thare thay stode both stille,
And seen the gam al at wille.
  In the court ther was wrowt
An olde toure that seruyd of nouȝt,
And in a creuas there was brede
A nedder and hadde therein a bedde.
Tho the nadder wok and herde
Al the pepyl, how hit ferde—
Trumpe, tabur, and melodye,
And heraudis loude crye—
The nadder sowt way overalle
Til scho come out of the walle.
Out of the walle scho came;
Into the halle the way scho name,
And drow hym toward the credile þerbyne
To sle the child that was therinne.
Toward the credyl as he suythe
The good grewhond lay and syȝe,
And was swythe wrothe withalle
That he cam into the [h]alle.
The grewhond stood vppe anon,
And to the naddir he gan goon.
Ther thay faugthen togydir long,
And ayther wondid othyr strong.
As thay foghten, here ȝe moun,
The credyl went vppesodoun.

758 trompe] tronpe 767 An] And 783 halle] alle 785 he] h *over eras.*

The credyl vppon the pomels stoode;
The child hadde nought bote goode.
Hyt no woke, no hyt no wyppe,
Bote [lay] alle stille and sleppe.
The grewhond ȝede the worme so nyghe
That into the ȝerd the worme flyghe.
f. 56rb The grewhonde sewed hym so faste
That he slew hym at the last.
Tho the naddir was falle
The greuhonde layde hym in the halle,
Euelle wondyd oueralle,
And forsothe he lay and ȝal.
  When the iustis were doon
The norise hiede ham in ful sone—
Thay ne durst no langer dwelle.
Thay fande the grewhond lye and ȝelle,
And ferd as he were wodde,
And hys hed al bybledde.
Thay two norise was were and seghe
The credyl bothume turnyd on hyghe,
And sawe the grewhond al bybled;
Thay war both sore adrede.
'Felaw,' scho sayed, 'be my blode,
Thys grewhond his waxyn woode,
And hase eten the childe therfore.
Alas that euer we were bore!'
The toþer noris sayed, 'Iwys,
Certis, felaw, sothe hit his.
Alas that stonde,' sayden schoe,
'That we ȝeden iustys to see!'
Thay were ful of sorow and wo,
And dyde thaym bothe forto goo.
  As thay flowen toward the felde
The lauydy lay and byhelde,
And hyre herte bygane to colde—
As womman herte sone wolde—
And wondird wat hit myght bee
Tho he segh hir noris flee,

793 lay] *om.*   809 credyl] y *written over 2 minims*   814 eten] heten (h *exp.*)

And clepid hir anoon a swayn,
And badde hym faste fete the noris ag`a´yne.
Byfore the lady thay were brought.
The lauydy was sory in hire thoght,
And askid ware the childe was,
And thay veppe and sayed, 'Alas!'
'Certis, dam,' quod that oon,
'As wel mow we telle anoon,
My lordis grewhond his wexen wode,
And hase etten hym flesche and blode!'
The lady swyth sory was,
And bygan to cry, 'Alas!'
The lord herde the lady crye,
And thydirward he gan hye,
And sayed, 'Dam, wat his this fare?
Tel me anoon; nought no spare.'
The lady that was so woo
Sayed to hyre lorde tho,
'Sire,' ho sayed, 'sycurlyche,
The childe that thou louedest so myche,
Thy grewhond has waxen woode,
And hase eten hym flesche and blood!'

Than was the lorde sory inowe;
In towarde the halle he hym drowe,
And the lady with hym nam;
Into the halle sone he kam.
The grewhond hys lorde syghe,
And sete bothe hys fete on hyghe
Oppon hys brest to make solas—
And the more harme was. f. 56rc
The knyght drow out hys swerd anoon,
And smot out the rygge-boon.
The knyght comanded anoonryght
Bere the cradyl out of hys syght.
Ther stood a man that was glad
To do that the knyght bade,
And bare the credyl out in hys arme,
And sawe the childe hadde no harme.

832 ware] w *written over* t 846 ho] o *written over* e 847 myche] y *written over* *2 minims*

In hys arme the childe he hent,
And into the halle he went,
And sayed, 'Alas, thy good grewhond!
Hire isti sone hole and sounde.'
Tho that weren in the halle
Hadden grette wondyr alle
That the chylde on lyue was,
And sayden hit was a wondir cas.
At the last thay fanden alle
How the cas was byfalle,
How the naddir was yslawe
That the grewhond hadde todrawe.
'Alas!' quod the knyght tho,
'My good grewhond hys agoo.'
The knyght was sory therfore
That hys grewhond was forlore.
Into hys horchard th[e] way he nome,
And to a fische pole he come,
And for dule of hys hounde
He lepe in and sanke to gronde.
'Sire,' quod Maystir Bancillas,
'Now thow hauest herde this cas,
Yf thow wolt thy sone spille
Forto suffyre thy wyues wylle,
Also mote the byfalle
As dyde the knyght in hys halle
That slew hys hounde and lyse hys lyfe
For a worde of hyse wyfe.'
Tho the Emperour herde
Of that tale how hit ferde
He sayed, 'Maystir Bancillas,
Me ne schal nouȝt bytyde that cas
For no word of my wyf.
Today ne schal he lyse hys lyfe,
No nouȝt he ne schal by boundon so sore
Arre I haue inqueryd more.'
Thus thorow the Maystir Bancillas
That day the childe sauyd was.

882 the] thay 890 byfalle] *foll. by* as dyde the *canc.* 901 Arre] *2nd* r *written over another letter*

Myghte no man the lady glade;
Scho syghyd and sory semlant made,
And was sory in hyre thought
That the childe agayne was brought,
And bythought hire agayens nyght,
And dyd thareto alle hyre myghte,
To brynge the Emperour in wille
Vppon morwen the childe to spylle.
In bede than thay were brought,
'Sire,' scho sayed, 'wat haue ȝe thoght?
Ne see thou nouȝt with thyn eyen
Were I was in poynt to deyen
As thy sone me wolde aschent
That hys agayn to prison sente?
Also mote bytyde the f. 56va
As dyde the bore vndyr the tre
That was clauyd and thought hit gode,
And lese therfore hys hert blode.'
Quod the Emperour to hys wyfe,
'Dame, lete be thy stryf,
And tel me nowe, I the byde,
Of the bore how hit bytydde.'
And [. . . . .]
Anoon hire tale bygane.

A Tale [*Aper*]

And sayed, 'Syre, hit was a bore,
And woned in a holde hor.
Ther was a tre in the forest
That the bore loued best
To ete the fruyte that thare was oon;
Euery day that cam to maane
He come thydyraboute vndiren
To ete the fruyte that laye thervndur.
A h[e]rdeman hadde a best lore,
And mykyl dule made therfore.

926 And] *rest of line blank* 928 bore] o *written over* e 936 herdeman] hrde man

Longe nolde he nought abyde;
He soughte hys best in hilka syde.
Into the forest the way he nam,
And byfore the tre he cam
There the bore was wont by fede,
And her he ȝede he was adrede.
Hym thought that the fruyt was goode,
And gadderd bretful hys hoode.
'The bore come rennyng towarde þe tree
There hys mete was wount to bee.
Tho the knaue hadde a syȝt
Of the bore he hadde a [fr]yȝt,
And the bore neghyd nee;
He clam vppon the tree on hyghe.
The bore hyhyde hym thydyr faste,
And vuele spede at the laste,
And has he come ful wyle he syghe
How the knaue clam on hyghe,
And bygan tothes to wette,
And to the tre byre he fette,
And layden as he were wode
Til hys mouthe famed of blode;
And thau the tree were rote-fast,
Ȝyt was the knaue agaste.
Of the fruyt that was browne
The knaue kast the bore adoune,
And he was forvngrid sore,
And ete and nolde hew no more.
Vndir the tre he stode ful stille,
And of the fruyt ete hys fylle.
The knaue stode vppon a bowghe,
And kest adowne fruyt inoughe.
'When the bore hase eten hys fylle,
Vndir the tree he stode ful stille.
That knaue kest hym fruyt ynowe,
And clam adoune fra bough to boghe,
And with hys on hond at the laste,

938 he] h *written over minim* 943 he(1)] h *written over* ȝ he was] *foll. by* he wa *canc. and exp.* 949 fryȝt] syȝt 967 fruyt] *foll. by* hit *exp.* 970 fylle] y *written over* u 973 boghe] h *written over* e

And with hys legges held hym fast;
The tohir honde he lete doun glidde,
And claude the bore vndir the syde.
The bore lykyde the clavyng wele, f. 56vb
And anoon to grounde felle,
And lay slepyng stille as stoon.
The knaue drowe out a knyf anoon,
And rent hys wombe with the knyf,
And bynam the bore hys lyf.
'Thus schaltou be clouyd also
With fykyl wordis and with false,
An thy sone the traytur
Schal be madde a Emperour.
Thorugh thy false clerkis seuene
Thow wylt by gyllyd, by Good in heuen!'
Quod the Emperour, 'By Saynt Brydde,
That no sal me nouȝt bytydde!
He ne sal do no more sorowe;
Certis he sal dee tomorne.'
Oppon the morwen wen hit was day
The Eemperour made grete ray,
And commaunde hys men anoon
To slee the childe thay schuld gone.
Thay took the childe out of prison,
And ladde hym withouten toun.
As thay ladde hym by the strete,
On of hys maystirs he gan mete;
Toward the Emperour he rode,
And welne al to longe he bode.
When he hadde the child mette,
The maystir made hys hors go bete
Forto saue the childe fram schame—
Ancillas was hys name.
Ful hastylich the way he nam;
Byfore the Emperour he cam.
A clerk he was of grete honour,
And gret anoon the Emperour.
The Emperour answerde with ire,

978 wele] w *written over minim* 981 anoon] *2nd* o *written over* n 1003 he] h *written over another letter* 1005 maystir] maystirs

'Maugre haue thow, bone sire!
I ȝow took my sone to teche,
And ȝe haue raft hym hys speche.
By Ihesu Crist that hys in heuene,
Ȝe sal to prison al seuene.'
'A, sire,' quod Mayster Ancilles,
'God Almyghty send vs pees.
Sire, ne make ȝow nouȝt so wroth;
Thow wost nowght alle how hit goth.
And yf thy sone lyse hys lyfe
For the talys of thy wyfe,
I bysyke God in heuene,
For hys dyrworth mannys seuene,
That ȝe bytyde swilk a cas
As bytyde Ypocras
That slow hys cosyn withouten gylt,
And hymseluen þerfore was spylt.'
Quod the Emperour to Ancilles,
'Certis thow schalt neuer haue pees
Er I wyt of that cas
That bytyde Ypocras.'
Quod Ancillas, 'Sire, wereto?
Wat avantage were that ydo?
Er my tale wer tolde
The childys blode wolde be colde.
f. 56^{vc} Bote yf I mote hys lyf borowe
Al thys nyght tyl tomorwen,
Gyf he myght on lyf dwelle,
Of Ypocras I wylle telle.'
Anon the childe was aftir sent
Thorow the Emperours commandement.
Than was the mayster a glad man,
And anon hys tale bygane.

1026 bytyde] *2nd* y *written over 2 minims* 1038 yf] y *written over* 3

A Talle [*Medicus*]

'A nobile fysysian thar was,
And was callid Ypocras.
He hadde a cosyn of hys blode
That longe walde leren no goode.
Of the world lytyl he thought,
Bote at the laste he hym bythought
How and in what manere
He myghte any goodys lere.
Hys emys bokis he vnselde,
And ilka day on thaym byhelde,
And bycam a fysysian
Also good as anny mane.
'The kynge sone of Hungrye
Hadde a woundir maladye.
The kynge sent aftir Ypocras
Forto wyten wat hym was.
Ypocras was ale olde,
And hys blode wax ale colde;
He let atyre wile a fyne
And sent thydyre hys cosyne.
Anon as he was comen,
By the hande he was nome,
And he was ladde anoon
Also stille as a ston
Ther the kynge sone laye
That hadde by syke many day.
The childe couthe of fysenamye,
That he saw wyl with hys eye
When he hade a wyle syttyne
That the childe was mysgettyne.
Syche wyse clerkys were goo—
Now no by ther non of tho;
Thay late be al the clergye,
And tornys to pryde and lycherye.

1049 That] a *written over* e 1054 emys] y *written over 2 minims* 1068 anoon] a *written over* o 1072 fysenamye] *1st* e *written over minim* 1074 When] Wh *written over other letters*

'Thane the childe were gode of lore,
Ȝyt he wolde aqwere more.
Fram hyre maydens ten or twelue
He took the quene by hyreseluene,
And sayde, "Madame, be nought wroth;
To telle ȝe me, thynke nowt lothe.
Yf thou wilt haue thy sone on lyue,
Forsothe, dame, tho[u] most the schryue.
Tel me how thow hauest wroght,
Forsothe, the kynge ne gat hym nouȝt!
And bot thow telle how hit hys
I may nought hel thy sone, iwys.
Of hys hele he ase ne swat
Bot thow telle wo hym bygate."
The qwen that was the kyngys wyf
Was lothe to lesyn hyre sone lyfe,
And sayd to hym priuyliche
Bytwen thaym two, specialiche,
f. 57ra "Thare was a prince hire bysyde,
And oft sythes he wolde ryde
With my lorde forto play,
And loue wax bytwen vs twey,
And so he [was] getyn, iwys—
Now thow wost how hit hys."
'When he wyst al the cas,
He tornyd hit al [to] solas,
And the childe vndirtoke
As taught hym Ypocras booke,
And he helyd the childe ol and sound,
And hadde therfore many a pound,
And of the quene many gyftis fele
For he schulde hire counsel hele,
And went hom to Ypocras,
And told hym al how hit was.
Ypocras was welny wode
That hys cosin couthe so mykyl good,
And thout anoon a wy[k]kyd thout
Forto bryng hys cosyn to nowt.

1082 maydens] mayndens 1087 thou] thom 1102 was] *om.* 1105 to] *om.* 1116 wykkyd] wylkyd

'Oppon a day thay went to pleye,
He and hys cosyn thay twey,
Into a swyth fayre mede
There fayre floure gan sprede.
Ipocras stille stood,
And saw a gras that was god.
"Bon cosyn," quod Ypocras,
"I se a gras of grete solas;
Were hit dyggyd vppe by the rote,
Of many thyngs hit myght be bote."
Than sayd the childe to Ypocras,
"Leue syre, were hys that gras?"
Quod Ypocras, euer uorthym wo,
"Loe were hit stondis at my too.
Knele adoun oppon thy knee
And dyggy[t] vppe and bryng hit me,
And I wyl the telle, iwys,
Wat vertu therinne hys."
The childe knelid anoon adoun;
Ypocras drow anoon fauchon
And slow hys cosyn, the more arme was,
Wyle he dyggyd aftyr the gras.
'Tho went he hom anoon,
And bernyd hys bokys ilkon
In wrat as a man that were wode,
For no man schuld lerne of ham good.
When he hadde hys bokys brent,
And hys cosyn was schent,
He fel in a maladye
That he was in poynt to dye.
Than was ale hys bokys lore,
And he ne couthe ne medycyne þerfore.
Tho hadde he slane hys cosyne
That couthe wel of medycyne.
For faut of helpe he ferde amys,
And at the laste he deyde, iwys.
'Thus was Ypocras dede,
And, sire, therfore take thy rede.

1126 dyggyd] *1st* y *written over* u   1133 dyggyt] dyggyd

Thow no hauest no sone bote oon;
Yf thow lattist hym to deth gon,
Whan helde byndys thy bones stoute
f. 57rb Thare hys bote fewe that wyle þe doute.
And yf thow hauest thy sone bolde,
Forsoth, were thow neuer so holde,
For thy sone men wyle the drede—
Let hym lyue, I wylle the rede.'
Quod the Emperour, 'By myn hede,
Tonyght no schal he nought be dede,
Bytwene thys and tomorwen day;
Be thanne as hit be may.'
   Al that in the palas was
Maden myrth and solas,
Bothe more and the lesse,
Saue the wykkyd Emperesse.
Scho [ofte] syghyd [sore] amonge;
'Ala, alas!' was hyre songge.
The Emperour herd hyre say 'Alas!'
And askyd hyre wat hyre was.
'Sire,' scho sayed, 'wo hys me,
And altogydyr hit hys for the!
Thare thow art both lorde and sire,
And maystir ouer al the empire,
Thow arte abowte thyseluen to spylle,
Yf thy clerkys haue thare wylle;
Thay wille make hym Emperour,
That thyf that lyes in the tour,
And yf thou louest hym more thane me,
Also mote bytyde the
As hym that in the lym was dede
That made hys sone smyt of hys hede.'
Quod the Emperour, 'I the byde,
Telle me how that bytydde.'

1172 ofte] *om.* sore] and swore   1179 empire] emp*e*rire   1181 wylle] y *written over* e

A Tale [*Gaza*]

The Emperesse hire tale bygane,
And sayd, 'Sire, hit was a mane,
Emperour of Rome he was,
And nowt louyd no solas,
Bot was about to fylle a toure
Ful of golde and ryche tresour.
Swylke seuen clerkys hadde hee
Vndir hym as haue ȝe.
The seuen clerkis that with hym were,
Alle at hom nouȝt thay were;
Thorow the Emperour comandement
The fyue were out wente,
And the twa at home thay by[d]eth
Forto do that he thaym bydeth.
[. . . . .]
The othir ladde myry lyf,
And haddyn both childryn a wyf.
Hit was a man withouten kare,
And ryclych he wolde fare;
What he spendid he nouȝt rought,
And that hys nek sore abought.
When hys catel bygan to slake,
And he ne myght no fest make,
There felle a wyel in hys thoute,
And therthourow he wente to nowt,
And bitidde a wondir kas,
And ȝe schal here how hit was.
'He adde a sone that was heyre,
A good childe and a fayre.
Thay wente and breken that tour,
And bare away mykyl tresoure,
And mad hym myry and spendid faste, f.57rc
Al the wylle that hit wolde laste.
He that lokyd the tresour

1190 hire] r *written over another letter* 1197 haue] aue *over eras.* 1202 bydeth] byeth 1203] *see note* 1205 haddyn] h *written over another letter* 1215 here] *foll. by* a *exp.* 1218 and] a *written over minim*

Come a day into the tour,
And oueral he keste hys syght
To loke whehir hit ferde ryght.
He was freche, he was nought dronke;
He saw the tresour was sonke.
He lette remue the tresour anone,
And fand ware the thyf was goon.
Byfore thare the hole was
He sette a deppe caudron of bras.
A manere of glowe he dyde thareinne
To halden alle that com thareinne,
And helyd thare the cawdron stode
As thare were nought bot gode.

'He that the tresour stale
Hadde spendid hit and wastyd alle.
He sayed, "Sone, by Godys hore,
Of the tresour we wylle haue more!"
He and hys sone were at on,
And thydyrward thay gan goon
In the wanyng of the mone—
The fadir was desauyde sone.
In at the hole the fadir crepe,
And in the caudron sone he lepe,
And anoon he styked faste;
Than was hys sone sore agaste.
"Sone," he sayed, "I ham hent!
Fle anoon ar thow art schent."
"A, fadir," he sayde, "alas!
Certys thys hys a wondyr cas.
Forsoth I can no rede nowe;
Leue fadir, how reddyst thow?"
"Certis," he sayd, "hit his no rede
Bot hastilich smyt of my hede,
And god laysyr when thou myght haue,
Byrye hit in Cristyne graue."
The childe was in grete thought;
To helpe his fadir he myght nouȝt,
And saw thare was no nothir rede,

1230 Byfore] B *written over another letter* 1238 Godys hore] *scribbled over by later hand* 1239 more] *also scribbled over* 1240 were] *written twice*

Bote smote of his fadir hede,
And knyt hit in hys lappe onoon,
And dyde hym hastilyche to goon.
And anoon has he ham came,
Out of hys lape the hede he name,
And in a forme he let hit fale,
And dyde a wykkyd torne withalle.
Thane he hadde hys fadir gode,
Thane wax he hote of blode;
No sorow in hert he ne hadde
How foul deth hys fadyr hadde.
Than he had that hys fadir gate,
Hys fadir deth he al forgat.
'Certis, sire, thus woltu fare;
Therfore hys al my kare.
Thou schalt lese thyn honour,
And thy sone be Emperour.
As othir haue doon thou schalt als,
Thorow talys of thy clerkys fals.'
Quod the Emperour to the Emperesse,
'So I euer here mas, f. 57va
My sone ne schale neuer do me that sorowe;
Certys he schal dee tomorowen!'
Thus hys wyf, that cursyd lyste,
Brewed the childys deth that nyght.
Vppe o[n] the morwen lange are prime
The Emperour ros bytyme,
And thys was hys commandement,
That the childe anoon where schent.
The tormentours wer ful rade
To do tha the Emperour bade;
Thay ne made noon delay,
Bot took the child and went hare way,
And toward the stude thay hym lede
There men schulde the chylde byhede.
Ryght as thay come atte the ȝate,
Hys o maystir hym mette thareatte.
In hys hert was no game—

1264 came] a *written over* o 1286 on] of 1292 ne] e *written over* o
1294 stude] studye

Lentulus was hys name.
Oppon the childe he cast hys eie;
Hym thought for sorow he myght dee.
Anoon the way he nam,
And byfore the Emperour cam,
And sayed, 'My lord, Syr Emperour,
God the saue and thyn honour.'
The Emperour answerde anoon,
'A, tratour, thow art that oon
That I bytook my sone teche,
And he hase loste hys speche,
And wolde haue lyne by my wyf.
He schal dee, by my lyf!'
'Syre,' quod Maystir Lentulus,
[. . . . .]
'I ne leue hit nouȝt, by my lyf,
To do vylany by thy wyf.
Bot yf thou brewyst thy childis bale
For hys stepmodir tale,
So mote the bytyde in thy lyfe
As dyd the olde man in hys lyf.'
Quod the Emperour, 'I the byde,
Tel me how that cas bytyde.'
'Sire,' quod Maystir Lentulus,
'I nylle, by swet Ihesus,
Bot thy chylde deth by let
That he ben agayen fet,
And mot lyue al this nyght
Til tomorwen til day be bryght.'
The Emperour comaunde anoon
Aftyr the childe forto goon.
Thorow commaundement of the Emperour
The childe was ladde into the tour.
Lentulus was a glad man,
And anoon hys tale bygane.

1312 *see note* 1318 *see note* 1320 how] h *written over another letter*

A Tale [*Puteus*]

'Hyt was a man and hadde a wyfe,
And loued hyre as hy[s] owen lyf.
Scho was both ȝong and bolde,
And the housband whas holde;
Hys myrth in bede bygan to slake,
And scho tooke anoþer make.
In bed as thay lay in fere
The wyf aros, as ȝe moun here,
Fram hire hosbonde thare he lay,
A lytyl wyl byfore daye. f. 57vb
Witouten dore at the ȝate
Scho mete hyre lemman thareatte.
The godman withinne a while
Myssyd hys wyf and thout gyle.
He ros vppe as stille as stone,
And to the dore he gane goone,
And bygan ful stille to spye,
And herde of hyre putrye,
And went hym stille as stoone,
And steke to the dore anoone.
'When thay hadde done thayre wyle,
And spoken togydir or fylle,
The wyf fande the dore faste;
Than whas scho sore agaste.
Scho pute at the dore in hye,
And bygan loud to crye,
And badde the delue hys neke tobreke
That the dore hadde steke.
The syly man lay and herde,
And hys wyf answerd.
"Dame," he sayed, "go thy way!
Thow hauest bygonne a sory play.
Tomorwen sal oppon the goune
As many men as been in toune."
"Walaway!" [sch]o gan to synge,

1334 hys] hyre 1347 as(2)] *foll. by* a *exp.* 1358 crye] c *over eras.*
1367 scho] to

And hyr hondis forto wryng,
"Mercy, sire, I am thy spouse!
For Goddys loue, lat me to house."
Quod the godman anoon,
"Goo thare thow hast to goon!
So God Almyghty gyf me wyne,
Thou ne schalt to come hyreine
Ar alle our frendys ilkon
Haue gounde oppon thy body alon."
Quod the wyf, "So moti thryue,
I wylle nought so lange be alyue."
'Hastilich within a wylle
Scho was bythought oppon a gylle.
Byfore the dore, as I ȝow telle,
Thare was a mykyl deppe welle,
And a stoon lay thareby
As mykil as a manys the.
As hit tellys in the booke,
In hyr armes scho hit tooke;
In the wel ho lette hit falle.
The godman herd it into the halle
And hadde reuthe of hys wenche,
And wende ho wold hyreself adrynge,
And ros vppe in hys serke anoon,
And to the wel he gan goon
As man that was in good lyf,
And thout forto saue hys wyf.
The wyf was ful wyly,
And stod the dore swyth nee;
Into the halle scho gan goon,
And stek to the dore anoon.
The godman was ful vuele my[t]t[e];
He sowt hys wyf in the pytte,
And hurt hym and hent harme,
And scho lay in hyr bede warme.
f. 57vc On euyl deth mote scho dee—
So bleryd the sely manys ee,
And loue hir so myche—

1370 lat] a *written over* e 1377 moti] *foll. by* I *interlin.* 1384 the] *underlined and foll. by* thye *to right of line in later hand* 1399 mytte] myght

Ful falle alle syche!
When he fandir nouȝt in the welle
He walde ther no langer dwelle.
At hys dore he wolde inne,
And hit was stoken with a pyne.
He schof theronne and bade vndo;
Scho lay stille and let hym doo.
'The lawe was than so harde bounden,
Yf a housbond were in hurdom fonden
He schuld haue a iuggement
Were thorow he schuld be schent,
And armyd men by nyght thare ȝede
[. . . . .]
The godman was ful sore agaste
That he fande the dore faste;
He knokede and was in mykyl kare.
The wyf askyd wo was there.
The goodman was ful sore adrade
That herd hys wyf in hys bede,
And sayed, "Dame, I ham here,
Thy spouse and thy trewe fere.
Arys vppe and draw oute the pyne
Goode lef, and let me inne."
"A, traytour" quod scho tho,
"Ga bylyue were thou hauest to go!
To thyn hore, there tho were,
Go agayn and herborowe the thare."
To speke fayre he to hede,
For he saw hit was ned.
"Dame, lete me into my bede,
And now be thow nought adrede,
For by the lorde Saynt Nycolas,
I wyl forgyue the thy trespas."
"Nay, traytour," quod scho tho,
"Certis also wel thow myght goo.
By Good that hys ful of myght,
Thow schal nowt come herein tonyght!"
'As thay spoken lowde togyder,

1417 *see note* 1429 bylyue] *2nd* y *written over* u 1430 there] t *written over another letter*

The wakmen herde and come thydyr.
The toon sayed, "Wat art thow
That standys here thys tyme nowe?"
"A, sire," he sayed, "mercy!
And I wille ȝow telle resoune why.
I hadde a spangel good of plyght;
I haue hit mysde al thys seuennyght,
And I not how hit ferde.
Me thought hereout I hym herde,
And cam out to clepyn hym inne,
And my wyf hase put in the pyne
In the dore oppon hyre game.
Go forth, a Godys name!"
"Certis he lyes," quod hys wyf,
"Hyt hys a man of wykkyd lyfe!
I haue helyd for I wende
That he wolde somtyme amende.
Therfore now ȝe haue hym hent,
Lat hym passe by iuggement."
The wakmen nolde no langer abyde;
Thay token hym in ilke-a syde,
f. 58ra And lad hym into the toune,
And put hym in prisone,
And lay alle nyght in mykyl sorowe,
And hadde hys iuggement amorwen.
Thus he hadde hys iuggement,
And thorow hys wyf he was schent.
'So wyltou, Sire Emperour,
Certis lese thyn honour
To bynym thy sonys lyf
For a tale of thy wyffe.'
Quod the Emperour, 'By swet Ihesus,
For thy tale, Sire Lentulus,
Today `ne´ schal he lese the lyffe
For no tale of my wyf.'
Than commande the Emperour
Do hys sone into the tour.
Thay dyden anoon as he bade;

1466 nyght] y *written over 2 minims*

Tho was Lentulus glad.
When the Emperes that vndirstode,
For wrat scho was welne wode
That the Emperours thout was went,
And the childe to prison sent.
Al that day scho fonded hyre flyght,
How scho myght agayens nyght
Fonden a tale al newe
The childe deth forto brewe.
Scho was alredy bythout
Wen scho was to bede brogt.
Of sythes scho sygkyd sore,
And stilly scho sayed, 'Lord, thy ȝore!'
The Emperour lay and herde,
And askyd hyre why scho so ferde.
'Sire,' quod Emperesse tho,
'It his no wondir tho me be wo!
Now hys my wo to bygyne,
Now we sal parten in twynne;
I nylle no langer hyre abyde
To se the wo that ȝe sal bytyde.
By God Almyghty that hys in heuene,
Thy sonne and thy clerkys seuene,
Thay ben alle at on asent—
Certys, syre, thow worst schent!
And syre, bot thow leue me,
Also mote bytyde the
As dyde the styward of hy[s] lyf
That gret gyng hys wyf.'
'Dame,' quod the Emperour,
'I bysyke the, paramour,
Tel me now of that kas,
Whilk maner and how hyt was.'
'Certis,' quod the Emperes,
'Thow schalt here of wykkydnesse.

1508 hys] hy   1511 bysyke] *2nd* y *written over* o   1514 A Talle *in left margin*

A Talle [*Senescalcus*]

'In Pule was somtyme a kynge
That hatyd wymmen of alle thyng;
Neuer ȝyt in alle hys lyf
He nolde neuer haue no wyf.
In Romauns hyt tellys in a booke
That a grete ivel hym tooke.
The ivel passyd oueralle
That hys body al toswal,
That hys body was al toblaw;
f. 58rb No man myght hys membris know.
Into Salner he sent a man
Aftyr a nobile fesisian.
Anoon has he was come,
By the honde he was nome;
Into the chambyr he was lade
Forto make the kynge glade.
When he saw the kyng pyne
He askyd anoon hys vryne.
Anoon as he the vryne sawe
He wyst were hys ivel lay,
And sayed, "Sire, ne amay the nouȝt,
Forsoth thy bote hys broght."
When herde thys thythyng,
Thane comfordede the kyng.
The mayster was wys and snel,
And made hys medicyne wille,
And anoon gaf he hit the kynge,
And abatyd the swellyng.
"Syre," quod the fysisian,
"The behoues haue a womman
To do thy wyl by anyght
Yf I schal helle the aryght."
Quod the kyng, "So mot I the,
Astow wylt, hyt schal bee."
'The kyng callyd hys senescal,

1526 sent] *foll. by* a *exp.*

That `hadde´ hys hows to kepe alle,
And sayed to hym, "Thow moste aspye,
And hastylich thou most hye,
A fayr lady of colour bryght
Forto lygge by me anyght,
And at scho be of he lynage,
And a lady of ȝong age."
"Sire," quod the stiwarde anoon,
"Albyssi schal I fynde oon—
For los of thy malyd[y]e
Thay wille be aferd to dye."
Quod the kynge, "Thow sayest thi wille.
With gold and siluer thow schal thaym tylle;
Gyf thaym golde and siluyr inowe—
I am ryche man inowhe."
Than the styward vndirstood
The kyng wald gyue so mykyl good,
He took hys lyue and hom he cam,
And by the hond hys wyf name,
And sayed, "By Sayent Benedyght,
Tho schalt ly by the kyng tonyght!
Golde and syluer thow schalt wynne,
And ben asolyd of thy synne."
"Certis, sire," quod hys wyfe,
"Now thow louest lytil my lyf."
  'For couetyse that he hadde,
To the kynge hys wyf he ladde.
He went vnto the kynges bedde,
And sayed, "Syre, I haue spede.
I haue a lady of hegh bloode,
Bot scho wyl haue mykyl good,
And dyrke scho wolde that hit bee,
Scho nylle that no man hyre see."
"Parfay," quod the kyng anoon,
"Lette quenche the torches ilkon."
He lette quenche the torche ilkone, f.58[rc]
And took hys wyf by honde anoon,

1560 malydye] malyde *written over* o   1583 nylle] y *written over 2 minims*   1587 anoon] a

And dyde hyre to bed with kynge,
That couetous gadlyng.
Al the nyght thare scho lay
Til a myl byfor the day.
Al nyght scho sykkyd and sorow made;
The kyng no myghte hyre nothyng glade.
'The styward was of day adrede,
And kam to the kynges bede,
And sayed, "Syre, on al wys,
Thow most that lady ryse."
Quod the kyng, "By Saynt Ion,
Ȝyt no schal scho nouȝt gon!"
He heldyr thare tyl hit wa`s´ day,
And anoon as he saye
Hyt was the stiward wyf,
There bygan to ryse stryfe.
Than sayed the kynge,
That was wrothe somthyng,
"Styward, so God the rede,
Who made the do thys dyde?
Be thow in my court founde
Whanne the sonne gos to grounde,
Withouten ony othyr lawe
Thow schalt be angyd and todrawe!
Loke withouten ony delay
That I see the neuer aftyr thys day."
The senescal drade thys wordys sore;
He ne durst dwel ther no more.
Out of the court the way he name—
Wyste thay neuer were he bycam.
'Lo, my Lord Syre Emperour,
How he lese hys honour!
The styward for hys couetyse
Hys wyf he lost and hys seruys.
Certis, sire, so saltow alse
For couetyse of thy tales false
That thy fals clerkys tellen.
Forsoth, I nylle nouȝt longe dwellen,

1592 nyght] y *written over 2 minims* 1608 in] *foll. by* thy founde] nd *over eras.*
1625 nylle] y *written over 2 minims*

That thou nult lese thyn honour,
And thyn sone ben Emperour.
I the telle as hit his—
Do now what thy wille hys.'
Quod the Emperour to the Emperesse,
'By hym that made matyns and messe,
I nyll tomorwen ete no brede
Er the thef traytour be ded.'
O morwen commande the Emperour
Tak hys sone out of the tour,
And leden hym to hys iuggement
Anon that he were schent.
Withoutyn ony more chest
Thay dyden the Emperour hest.
Without the palas tho he was
He mete with hys maystyr Maladas.
Into the halle the way he nam;
Byfore the Emperour he cam,
And sayd, 'Alas, Sir Emperour,
Thou dost thyself lytyl honour
That thy sone schal be slawe
Withouten [any] proses of lawe.' f. 58va
'Certys,' quod the Emperour,
'[I] bade men sle the wykkyd tratour;
[Thow and] thy felaws, ȝe ben fals—
Thay schal ben hangede and thow alse!'
'Certys, syre,' quod Maladas,
'Thys hys a wondyr cas,
To bynym thy sones lyf
For a tale of thy wyf.
And yf thow dost, Syre Emperour,
God leue the falle swilk honour
As the olde man hadde welne hent
Ne hadde hys wyf haue had chastement,
That hadde mynt without respyte
Haue doon hire a ful despyte.'
Quod the Emperour to Maladas,

1647 any] *om.* 1648 quod] q *marked with brevigraph though written in full*
1649 I] *om.* 1650 Thow and] *rev.* 1657 swilk] s *written over 1st stroke of* w
1658 the] h *written over another letter*

'Thow sal tel me of that cas,
For I ne herde neuer in my lyue
Old man chasty ȝong wyf.'
'Sire,' quod Mayster Maladas,
'Yf thow wylt here of that cas,
By Ihesu Cryst omnypotent,
The chylde schal ben aftyr sent.'
Thorow commandement of the Emperour
The childe was lade into the toure;
Therfore gladdyd many a man,
And Maladas hys tale bygane.

A Tale [*Tentamina*]

'Sire,' quod Maystir Maladas,
'Herkyn how fel that cas.
Hyt was a man of olde lyfe,
And hadde a ȝong womman to wyfe,
And hys blode bygan to colde,
And the wenche bygane to bolde;
Than he slakyd of hys werke
Sche bygan to loue a clerke.
O day to the kyrke scho came,
And hyr modyr in councel nam,
And sayed to hyr modyr anoon,
"My lordys merryghe hys welne gone.
Now he slakys to lygge aboue,
I wyl haue anoþer loue."
"Dougter," quod the moder tho,
"I ne rede nouȝt thow do soe.
Thow an old man holde hym stille,
Dougter, thow wost nought al hys wille.
Ar thou do swylk a dede,
Proue hym first I wyle the rede."
The douter took hire leue anoon,
And dyde hyre hastylych to gon,
And thout hyr lorde forto proue
[. . . . .]

1665 No*ta* be*ne* *in left margin* 1685 merryghe] *1st* e *written over minim*
1690 an] and holde] h *written over* ȝ 1696 *see note*

'The lorde hadde an hympe gode
Tha in a fayr herber stood,
And the lorde loued hit myche
For in his orcher nere non syche
So nobil pers as hyt bare;
Thareof the wyf [was] ware.
On of hyr men with hyr he nam,
And to the hymp sone he cam,
And dyde anoon as a schrewe—
On the tre gobettys lete hewe,
And in the halle let hit lygge
To loke what he wolde sygge. f. 58vb
When the lord in cam,
Of the tre hed he nam.
"Dame," he sayd, "were grew this tre
That lyes thus hewen in t[hr]e?"
"Sire," scho sayed, "in thyn erber
Hyt grewe, nowthir fer no ner."
"Depardus, dame," quod he tho,
"Now hit hewen hys, let hit go."
In hys hert he was wroth,
Bote to contak he was loth;
He ne sayed nouȝt al that he thout.
'The dougter anoon the way nam,
And to the modir sone he cam,
And sayed, "Modir, so mot I the,
I haue doon as thow bade me.
Hys fayre hympe that thow see,
That sprade so brood and so heye,
I lete hewyt by the more,
And ȝyt was he nowt wroth þerfore."
"Dogter," quod the moder tho,
"I walde red the, as I mot go,
Proue hym ȝyt anothir stound
Are loue thow haue to ard bound.
Thow he were stille and spake nouȝt,
Thou wost neuer what [was] hys thout."

1697 an] and 1702 was] *om.* 1710 hed] h *written over another letter over eras.*
1712 thre] trhe 1719 *see note* 1733 was] *om.*

ȝyt [he] sewyd hyr modyr wylle,
And went hom al ston-stille,
And bythout hire al by the way
Oppon a schrewydschyp or tway,
And anoon in the stude
A gret schrewnes he dude.
'The lord a lytyl kenet hadde,
He loued hit wel the hit were bad.
Hyt byfelle that ilke day
The kenet on hir lappe lay.
God gyfe hyre iuel happe,
Scho slowe the kenet oppon hire lappe.
"Dame," quod he, "why dustou soo?
That was nouȝt wyl doo."
"Sire," scho sayed, "be nouȝt wroth.
Lo, he hase byfoulyd my clothes."
"Dame," he sayed, "by Saynt Rycher,
Thou myghtyst drawe thy clothes nere,
And late my hondis on lyf go.
I pray the, dame, sle no mo,
Thow thay lyge oppon thy clothe.
Yf thou dost I wylle be wrothe."
Scho thout tho, "[He] that wil sp[e]re,
To haue a lemman for hys f[e]re."
'That ilke day scho the way nam,
And to hir modir sone he cam.
"Dam," scho sayed, "so God my rede,
I haue doun asstow me bede.
Mi lord hade a kenet fel
That he loued swyth wel.
So God gyf me good happe,
I hym slow on my lappe,
And made hym lese ys hert blode,
And he sayed nouȝt bot good.
I nylle wounde nowt, iwys,
f. 58vc To loue were my wille hys.
Forsothe, dame, I may wel—
I haue spyde he hys nouȝt fel."

1734 he] *om.* 1741 He] The 1752 late] l *written over another letter* hondis] h *written over another letter* 1756 He] thay spere] spare 1757 fere] fare

"Dougter," quod the modir tho,
"I reed that thow do nouȝt soo.
Old men wille thole mykil wronge,
Bot, forsoth, hys wreche hys stronge.
Therfor my rede hys thys:
Proue thrys ar thou doo amys."
"Dame," quod the doghter tho,
"Gladlych, so mot I goo.
Bot thau he wrothe hym neuer so sore,
Forsothe, I nylle proue hym no more."
And at hir moder leue he nam;
Toward hyr oune house ho cam,
And by the way as scho ȝede
Scho thout oppon a schreud dede.
'Sone aftyr hit bytydde
That the godman lete byde
A swythe fayre companye,
And made a fayre maungerye.
As thay sytten and mad ham glade,
The goodman faire semlant made.
The wyf fast hyre keyes wrothe
In the ende of the borde-clothe.
Scho roos vppe and dyde hyre to gone,
And drow doun coppys and dyschys ilkone,
And schent robys of riche grene,
And broght al the gestis in tene.
The goodman was ful wroth,
And let castyn anothir cloth,
And made hare clothes be wypit and dyȝt,
And solace thaym as wel as he myght.
'When alle hys gestys were agoo,
Than bygan to wakken wo
Bytwen the goodman and hys wyf;
Than bygan to ryse a stryfe.
"Dame," he sayed, "so mot I the,
Thou hauest don me despites thre.
So mak me God good man,
Thou schalt be chasted yf I cane.

1781 Forsothe] F *written over another letter* 1784 ȝede] e *written over another letter*
1800 clothes] o *written over another letter* 1801 thaym] *foll. by* made *exp.*

Dame, thow hauest ben thryes wode;
Forsoth thou shalt by latyn blode."
He ladde hyr into a chambyr,
He and hys brothyr,
And lete the on arm blood [ther],
And aftyr the thothyr.
He leued no blode in hys wyf
Bot a lytil to holde hyre lyf.
When sche hadde so blede,
He layed hyre in a fayre bede.
When scho wok out of a swoune,
He gaf hyre met and drynk anoone,
And "Dame," sayed, "ly al stille;
Thou schalt haue met and drynke at wile.
And euer when thou waxist wode,
Thou schalt be latyn blood.
"Sire," scho sayed, "mercy, I ask ȝore,
And I wylle wrathe the no more."
"Parfay, dame," quod he tho,
"Forwhy that thou doo no moo
f.59ra Swilke trespas whil I leue,
This thre schal be forgyuen."
Than walde [sc]he no more
Leuen of the clerkis lore
For fere to be lat bloode,
Bot heldir algat trew and good.
'Sir,' quod Maystir Maladas,
'Lo, swilke a woundir kas
Hadde welne bytyde the olde wise;
Ne hadde he lerned to chatyse
Hys wyf at hys comaundement,
How williche he hadde ben schent.
Sertis, Sire Emperour,
Thus schaltou lese thyn honour,
And thow suffry thy wywys wille,
That thow wilt thy sone spille;
Aftir that mysdyde scho wile do mo,

1814 ther] *supplied by later hand* 1824 when] h *written over* e 1831 forgyuen] f *written over 1st stroke of another letter* 1832 sche] the 1838 olde] holde (h *exp.*) 1842 Sertis] *foll. by* Emperour *exp.*

And bryng the into more wo.'
Quod the Emperour, 'By Saynt Martyn,
That schal scho nowt, wyf hys scho myn!
So I euer broke myn hede,
Today ne schal my sone be dede.'
  Than the Emperes herde this,
Scho was swith sori, iwys.
Scho syghyd and sory chere made;
Myght hyr that day no man glade.
When scho was to bede broght,
Scho syghyd sore and sayed noght.
The Emperour that lay fol softe
Herde hys wyf syghen ofte,
And sayed, 'Dame, saye me thy wylle,
Why mornes thou and syghys so stille?'
Quod the Emperes to the Emperour,
'Certys, sire, for thyn honour.
Thow art smytyn in couatyse,
Whareof thy sorowe wylle aryse;
Thou couetes in alle manere
Thyn seuen clerkis forto here.
Thou schalt lese thyn honour
As dyde Crassus the Emp[er]our
That for couetyse was slawe
Withouten any proses of lawe.'
Quod the Emperour, 'By Saynt Ion,
Thou schalt telle me anon
How Crassus lese thourow couetyse
Is lyf, and on wilk wyse.'

A Talle [*Virgilius*]

  The Emperes hire tale bygane,
And sayde, 'Sire, hit was a mane,
Merlyn he hatte, and was a clerke,
And bygan a wondir werke.

1859 syghen] e *written over minim* 1861 Why] h *written over* y 1865 Whareof] h *written over another letter* 1869 dyde] *foll. by* the Emperour] Empour

He made in Rome thourow clergyse
A piler that stode fol heyghe,
Heyer wel than ony tour,
And theroppon a myrrour
That schon ouer al the toun by nyght
As hyt were daylyght,
That the wayetys myght see;
Yf any man come to cite
Any harme forto doon,
The cite was warnyd soone.
 'Thare was contek ofte and lome
f. 59rb Bytwen Pule and the cite of Rome.
The kynge of Pule hadde no myght
To stele oppon the town by nyght
For the myrrour was so clere
That kest lyght fer and nere.
Twa clerkys was in hys londe,
Twa bryther, that token on honde
Forto kast the myrour down
That lyght ouer al Rome toune.
The kyng asked the clerk bathe
What he scholde gyf hem twae.
That oon clerk sayed to the kynge,
"Certis, sire, we wylle nothynge
Er the myrrour be broght adoune,
And than gyf vs oure warryson."
Quod the kyng, "So mot I the,
I graunt wel at hit so be."
Thanne sayed the heldest brothir,
"Sire kynge, thou most do anothyr:
Ale priuyliche and stille,
Twa coffyns thou most fylle
Of golde and of preciouse stonnys.
Let make the coffynys for the nones,
Hye that thay were dyght,
And the myrour schal lese hys lyght."
The kynge hadde [thaym] redy dyght,

1884 nyght] y *written over 2 minims* 1890 ofte] o *written over* e 1900 clerk] lclerk (*1st* l *exp.*) 1911 coffyns] n *orig.* m, s *written over 3rd minim* 1913 coffynys] *2nd* y *written over* u 1916 thaym] E

And fylde thaym fulle that ilk nyght.
'Oppon the morne the way the nome
Ryght to the cite of Rome.
On morwen thay wenten messe to here,
And after went to play ifere.
Into the felde the way thay nome,
And lokyd that no man come,
And maden lytyl pyttys twaye,
And byrid the coffyns bathe,
And setten redy markys there
Wydyrout the coffyns were,
And went forth as stille a ston.
A comen to the Emperour anon,
And sayed, "We wyte, Sire Emperour,
About this cite gret tresour;
Vndyr the erth hit hys hyde,
And yf thou wylt hyt schal be kyde,
For a sweuen vs come tonyght
Were the tresour hys vndir erth dyght."
Quod the Emperour, "By Saynt Martyn,
And I wole do we[r]for of myn."
Atte the Emperour thay toke leue,
Ant wenten hom tho hyt was euen.
'On the morwen wen the day wa[s] bryȝt,
To the Emperour thay come ful ryȝt,
And sayden, "Certis, Syr Emperour,
We haue aspyed wher hys þe tresour.
Therfore, sire, tak with ous a man
That be wys man, ant can
Stond by ous a lytil stounde
To saue the tresour whan hit hys founde."
The Emperour toke with thaym a man anon,
And thay dydden ham to goon,
And doluen a lytyl withinne þe grounde,
And the tresour was sone founde.
Thay wenten anoon to the Emperour, f.59[rc]
And schewden hym that nobil tresour.
The Emperour was payed ful wel,

1937 werfor] we for 1940 was] wa

And wende hit were al gospel
That the clerkys dyden hym to wite,
And al was fals, euery smyte.
Tho hyt neghyt toward euen,
The twa clerkys token leue,
And went toward hare in agayen,
Thare thay haddyn al nyght layen.
Wyth myche myrthe to bede thay ȝede,
For thay hoppen forto spede.
'Amorwen when the day spronge,
In thayr bede thay thought longe.
To the Emperour thay gune hye
Forto blere more hys eye.
That on clerke sayed anoon,
"Parfay, syre, we moten goon
That the tresour were fete,
That we haue of tonyȝt mete.
Let senden a man the tresour to bede,
As he that iustay with ous ȝede."
Ham tolywryd a man anon,
And thider fast thay gone gone.
Thay ne dyggyd bot a lytil stounde—
The coffyn was ful sone founde.
Hyt was no need depe to delue—
He may wel fynde that hyde hymseluen.
Thay brogten anoon the tresour
Ryght byfore the Emp[er]our.
The Emperour was glad tho
That he hadde sylke clerkys two
That wyste ware to fynde so euene
Ware were tresour hyd so euene.
Tho the Emperour herde thaym lye,
And wend hit were al profecye,
And grete loue to ham kaste,
And al was lorne at the laste.
Tho hyt neghit toward heuene,
The clerkys token anoon hare leue,
Ant went hom with myche honour,

1963 hoppen] h *written over another letter* 1972 the] *over eras.*
1981 Emperour] Empour

And louhe to scorne the Emperour,
And made ham at ese that nyght
Til on morwen the day bryght.
'On the morwen tho the day sprong
Thaym thought in hare bed ful longe.
Alle both thay goon goon
To the Emperour anoon.
The ton sayed, "Sire Emperour,
Vndir the pyler that berys merour
Ther hys a goldehord bygune,
One the noblest vndir sone."
"Certis," quod `þe´ Emperour,
"I wolde nought for half the tresour
That the myrrour fel adown—
Hyt helpis forto saue the toun."
"Sire," quod that on clerke,
"We conne ordeyn so our werke
Of the tresour to haue oure wille,
And late the myrrour stande stille."
Quod the Emperour, "By Sayent Myghel,
To swylke a forwarde I graunt wel. f. 59va
Go, and God Almyghty ȝoue spede,
And to the myrrour take hede."
The clerkys toke mynours anoon,
And to the piler thay goon.
Thay bygune to dygge faste,
Than thay seyen at the laste
How the piler stode in bras,
And with sowdyng sowdyt faste.
Than sayed the tone clerke,
"Mynours, lat be ȝoure werke."
When the mynours were goon,
The clerkys made a fyre anoon
The pylar fot al about,
And closyd the fyere al witout.
'When thay hadden thus doon,
Tha[y] wentyn hom, and hyt was non.
Byfore the Emperoure thay come,

1997 Thaym] T *written over another letter* 2014 Almyghty] h *written over* t
2017 piler] er *written over* o *and small* r 2029 Thay] That

And anoon lef thay nome
To whend hom into thayr in
To ordayn and dyuyse a gyne
Forto holde the piler vpryght,
And the myrrour that was so lyȝt.
The Emperour gaf thaym leue,
And thay wolde no langer byleue;
To hare in son thay come,
And at thayre ostage leue thay nome.
The fyere was hote and bernyd faste,
And malt the soudyng at the last.
Thay were bot a lytil withouten toun
That the pyler fel adoun.
'Alle the lordys of the cite
Were ful sory, and myghte wel be.
Thay wente anoon to the Emperour,
And asked of the myrour,
Why he let kast adoun
That help forto saue the toune.
Non answere couth the Emperour
Bot for couetyse of tresoure,
Forto wyte of the wundyre,
Wat tresour was hyd thervndyre.
Al that in Rome was,
Riche and pore, none ther nas
That thay nere al at on
To sle the Emperour anoon,
And a wyle yf ȝe wille dwelle,
How he was slawe I wyl ȝow telle.
For he let falle the myrour
For couetyse of tresour,
Thay were al at on red—
Thourow tresour he scholde be dede.
Thay token gold, a grete bal,
And letten grynde hyt ryght smal,
And puttyn out hys eyen two,
And fylden the hollys folle bothe,
Hys eyen, hys nose, and hys throte—

2058 And] *foll. by* yf *exp.*

Thay fylden wit golde euery grote.
Thus thay were at on acent
Forto gyfe hym that iuggement.'
Quod the Emperesse to the Emperour,
'Thus for golde and tresour
The Emperour was slawe f. 59vb
Withouten any proses of lawe.
Thus ar thou falle in couetyse also,
Thorow thy clerkys tales false.
Thou wylt be schent, by swyte Ihesus,
As was the Emperour Crassus.'
Quod the Emperour, 'By Sayent Colas,
I ne schal nouȝt bytyde that cas
For no lesyng that thay mou telle!
My sone, iwys, schal nouȝt dwelle
On lyue lengur than tomorwen,
So Gode schilde me fra sorowe.'
And anon has hyt was day,
The Emperour made non delay.
To sla the childe he was ful rade;
He ferde as man that were made.
He badde hys tormentours ilchon,
'Doe thys childe to deth anoon.'
[. . . . .]
Thay dyden as the Emperour bade.
When the childe schulde dee,
Thare was many a wyppyng hee.
Ryght withouten the palyes ȝate
Thay mete Mayster Caton thareate.
The childe lette hys [eyen] glyede
Oppon hys maystyr al asyde.
Mayistyr Caton, that was wyse,
Lokyd on hys prentyse.
He loutyd to hym, and lete hym goon,
Ant went to the Emperour anoon,
And gret hym with gret honour
As men schulde an Emperour,
And he answerd ryght in the place,

2091 *see note* 2097 eyen] *om.*

'Maugre haue thou, and male grace!'
'A, sire,' quod he,
'Mercy, per Saynt Charite!
For Goddis loue, Syre Emperoure,
Hyre me speke, for thyn honour.'
'Haue doo, traytour,' quod he,
'Late see what thy resoon schal be.'
'Sire,' quod Mayster Caton,
'Hyt hys al agayen reson
That a dome man schal bere iuggement,
And for lesyngs been schent.
Yf thy sone today hys slawe
Withouten any prossesse of lawe,
Also mote the befalle
As dyde the burgees in hys halle
That bynam hys byrdys lyf
For the tale of hys wyfe.'
Quod the Emperour, 'By Seynt Colas,
Thou schalt telle me of that cas
That thou sayest that was bytyde,
Of the burges and hys berde.'
'Sire,' quod Mayster Caton tho,
'Thy sone that hys to dethe go,
Lete a knyght or a swayn
Anon brynge the chylde agayne,
And lete hym on lyfe dwelle
Whille that I my talle telle,
Or, by Good that alle wrought,
I nylle telle the ryght nowt
f. 59vc Bot the childe be eftyr sent
That hys toward hys deth went.'
The Emperour comande anoon
Aftyr the childe forto goon.
Than gladdyd many a man,
And Mayster Caton hys tale bygane.

2132 I] *foll. by* telle *exp.* 2137 comande] a *written over another letter*

A Tale [*Avis*]

'Hit was a burgeis and hadde a wyf,
And loue hyre as hys ouen lyfe,
And hadde a popyniay at spake,
And wyst by hys wyf a lake,
And tolde hym when he ham cam
Anothyr lotby scho nam,
And than bygane to wax stryfe
Bytwen the godman and hys wyfe.
The godman went a day to playe,
Out on iornay or twae
To frendys that he sawe nowt ȝore,
No wyste when he schulde more.
Whent the goodman was went,
Than was the lemman after sent,
And madyn myrth and melodye
Ryght byfore the bryddys eie.
'The wyf [sc]h[o] thout oppon a wylle
Forto do the birde a gyle,
And ful sone scho was thought
How that gyle myght be wrought.
Scho hadde a knaue al at hyr wile
That wyst hyr priuete loude and stille.
Scho madde hym sette a leddy[r] on hygh,
And oppon the laddyr he styghe;
A piger of watyr he fete,
And oppon the rof he hyt sette.
Oppon the rof he made an hole;
He went don a bare vppe a cole,
And a torche vp thermyde,
And as the wyf hym badde he dyde.
When thay were abede yfere,
The wyf and hyre copinyere,
The knaue hadde al hys thynge dyȝt.
He lokyd `in´ and sawe lyght,
And bygan onnoon hys rage,

2146 Anothyr] And nothyr 2152 When] h *written over* e 2157 scho] the
2163 leddyr] leddy

And cast watyr oppon the kage.
When he hadde caste twyes or thrye,
He dyde anothyr maystrie:
Grete blowen bladdyrs he brake,
And thay gaue a gret crake.
He tende hys torche at a cole,
And putte in ate the hole.
'The wyf sat oppon hire bede,
And made has scho were adrede,
Bote ofte sayed, "Benedicite!
What thynge may thys be?"
Quod hire horlyng in the bede,
"Ly stille, a be nought adrede.
Hyt hys lyghtyn, thondyr, and rayne—
Ly doun in thy bede agayn."
The byrde stode and sawe and herde
Al that gile, hou hyt ferde,
And whende hyt were soth that ho sayed,
And bylle vndyr wynge layede,
And toke rest tyl hyt was daye,
f. 60ra And the horlynge went hys way.
'When the godman hame cam,
To the cage the waye he nam,
And askyd the byrde how hyt ferde,
And the byrde answerde,
And sayed, "Sythyn I sawe the laste,
I haue been ful sore agaste."
Quod the goodman to hys birde,
"Tel me what was the bytydde."
"Sire," he sayed, "when thou wer gon,
Oure dame lemman cam anoon;
He was sent aftyr fol sone,
And dyde as was to done.
And the nyght that was,
There byfel a wondyr cas:
Hyt raynyd, and lygnyd, and thonryd fast,
And alle we were sore agaste."
The godman went to hys wyf,

2209 was] *foll. by* there by *exp.*

And abrayder of hyr lyf
That scho hadde don wil he was oute,
And callyd hys wyf foule scout.
"Alas, sire," quod the wyf,
"Why schul we lede thys lyf?
Thou louest to myche thy byrdys lore,
And al he lyees, by Goddy[s] hore!"
"Dame," he sayed, "by my hals,
Now thow schalt be proued fals.
While I was out he was here,
And in my chambyr ȝe lay ifere,
And that nyght the wedyr was strong—
Hyt laytyd, thondred, and reynned among.
Al that nyght til hyt was day
Thyn horlyng in that bede lay!"
"A, sire," quod scho, and was bolde,
"He þat that lesyng hase tolde,
He lyed, by Good that alle hase wroght—
Hyt raynyd, ne thondryd, no layt nout
Sythen thou wentyst out of thys toune,
And by neghbours proue ȝe moune."
"Certis," quod the godman,
"I wil foundyn yf I can
Proue the fals ryght anoon."
'He clepyd hys neghburs ilkon.
When thay were al come,
In concel thay were al nome
Whethyr anny rayn, thondyr, or lyȝt
Hadde be of al that seuennyght.
Than the neghbours answerd anoon,
"Swylk wedyr wastyr noon
Of al thys seuennyght and more."
Than forthout the burges sore
That he hadde hys wyf myssayde,
And dyde anoon a lyther brayed:
Ryght in that ilke selue rage
He slowe the byrde in the cage.

2215 don wil] don w *over eras.* he] h *written over another letter* 2220 by Goddys hore] by Goddy hore (*scribbled over by later hand*) 2230 lesyng] y *written over another letter*

'Thus the burges thourow hys wyf
Bynam hys good byrd hys lyfe.
So woltou, Sire Emperour,
Do thyself lytyl honour
For the wordys of thy wyf
To bynyme thy sonne lyfe.'
f. 60rb Quod the [Emperour], 'Maystyr Caton,
For loue of hym, by Saynt Symon,
That was so foule bleryd hy[s] eye,
Today no schal my sone dee.'
Tho the Emperes herde telle
That he scholde on lyf dwel,
Al that nyght tyl on morwen
Than madde scho mykyl sorowe;
Al that day to nyght come,
'Alas!' was ofte oppe ynome.
When thay comen to bede yfere,
The lady made sory chere.
Quod the Emperour, 'Hou may this be?
Dame, what hys wyth the?'
'Sire,' scho sayed, 'nothyng goode.
Forsoth, thou makest me welny wode!
Thou art about thyselue to greue
For thou wyl no concel leue,
No good concel vndir heuene
Bot of thyn fals clerkis seuene.
Therfore I ware the, sykirlich,
Thou wylt loue ham so myche
That thou wilt [lese] thyn honour
As dyde Herode the Emperour
That leuyd concel agayn hys prowe
Of seuen clerkis, as dostou.'
Quod the Emperour, 'By Goddis belle,
Of that cas thou most me telle.'
'Gladlich,' sayed scho,
'The bettyr yf hyt wylle bee.'
Anon scho bygan hyr tale
Forto brew the childes bale.

2257 Emperour] *om.* 2259 hys] hy 2279 lese] *om.* 2283 By Goddis belle] *scribbled over by later hand* 2287–8 *relin.*

A Tale [*Sapientes*]

Scho sayed, 'Hit was an Emperour,
A man of ful mykil honour,
And hadde seuen clerkys wyse
[. . . . .]
And brogten vp a vsage
Thad dyde swyth gret damage:
Whoso anny sweuene by nyght,
O morne when the day was bryght
[. . . . .]
And rych gyftis with hym nam
For the clerkis schuld telle
Of the sweuen that walde byfalle,
And wannyn riches to hare byhoue,
And broghten men in mysbyleue.
And the Emperour for wynne
May[n]tend hom in synne,
A[n]t lete ham haue al hare wille,
And ate the last speddyn ille.
'The Emperour hadde a maladye,
A wondyrful for the maystry:
Whan he wolde by any way
Out of Rome wende to play,
Withouten toun as he come
Anon hys syght hym was bynom.
Tharefore he was sore agremed,
And oft sythes sore aschamed.
Of hys clerkis cautel he toke,
And badde ham loke in hyr booke
Yf thay myghten with ony clergye
Hele hym of that maladye,
Bot thare was non of ham þat couthe
Telle hym nothyng with mouthe f.60rc
How he myghte hele wyne
Of that maladye that he was inne.
'At the last hyt was hym tolde

2291 *see note* 2295 *see note* 2302 mayntend] maytend 2303 Ant] At

Of a wys clerke and a bolde
That was hotyn Merlyn,
That couthe many a medicyn,
And anon he was sought,
And byfore the Emperour broght.
Merlyn onon with gret honour
Gret anon the Emperour.
Ate schortys wordys forto telle,
The Emperour wolde no langer dwel,
Bot tolde Merlyn al hys cas,
Wych maner and how hit was.
"Sire," quod Merlyn that was bolde,
"Of thynges that thou haues tolde,
Gawe into thy chambyr yfere,
And in skyle ʒe schal here
Why and wharefore hyt hys
That ʒoure syght fares amys."
'The Emperour and Merlyn anoon
Into the chambyr thay gonne gone.
When thay were in chambyr brought,
Merlyn told hym of hys thought,
And sayed, "Syre Emperour, iwys,
Vndyr thy bede a caudron hys
That buylys both day and nyght,
And that reuys the thy syght,
And thy lyf therefore hys worthy forlore
Bot any medicyne ben don therfore.
And yf thow leuest nought me,
Remou thi bed and thow mayst se."
The bed was remoude sone,
Bot thare was more fyrst to doon
Er the caudron wer founde—
Hyt was depe withinne the grounde.
The Emperour sawe atte the laste
That the caudron boylyd faste,
And anoon vndirstood
Merlyn was trew and couthe gode,
And sayed, "Merlyn, per charite,

2323 hotyn] y *written over* ʒ   2338 amys] a *written over another letter*
2345 buylys] uyly *over eras.* nyght] y *written over 2 minims*

What meruyle may thys bee?"
"Sire," quod Merlyn, "iwys,
I wyle telle the how hyt hys.
Thys seuene walmes sygnyfye
Seuen deuels in thy companye,
That ben thy seuen clerkys
That wyssys the to wykkyd werkys.
Thay been rycher of tresour
Than artou, Sire Emperour.
Thou hauest maynted thaym therine,
And God hys wroth for that synne."
"Maystyr," quod the Emperour,
"Myght we wet with ony tresour,
With any concel arly or late,
Thys seuene walmes forto abate?"
"Ȝe, sire," quod Merlyn,
"Thou myght don hyt wylle a fyne.
Thyn seuene clerkys in the halle,
Sende aftyr the grestest mayster of alle,
And smyte of hys hede, f. 60va
And anoon when he hys dede,
Thow schalt fynde abatynge adone
The gretyst walme of the caudrone."
The Emperour taryd nowt,
The grettest mayster in was broght,
And fulfylde Merlyns rede,
And lete smytte of hys hede,
And went to the caudron anoon—
Than was the maystyr walme agoon.
'Quod Emperour, "By Saynt Martyne,
I fynde the trewe, Mayster Merlyn.
For oght that man kan saye thareto,
As thou concels I wole doe."
Quod Merlyn, "Sire, so mot I waxe,
Thane most thou slae thy clerkys,
For by the deth that I schal dee,
Thou schal neuer see with eye

2367 tresour] *foll. by* than *exp.* 2378 of] *foll. by* the *exp.* 2392 wole] *foll. by* say *exp.* 2394 Thane] a *written over another letter*

Withoute Rome toune, iwys,
Wille ony of ham on lyue hys."
Quod the Emperour, "So mot I thryue,
Thare schal none leue on lyue."
He clepyd hys tormentours anoon,
And lete gyrde of the hedes ilkon,
And went to the caudron tho—
Than were the walmes agoo.
When thay were alle slawe,
Than the caudron was vpdrawe.
'Quod Merlyn to the Emperour,
"Sire, take knyghtes of honour,
And leppe to hors, and wend to play
Out of this cite a iorne or twae,
And say anonryght
Hou lykkys the nou thy syght."
The Emperour wolde no langer abyde;
He dyde hym anoon to ryde,
And lopyn to hors ilkon,
And wente out of the cite anoon.
Tho the Emperour come without þe ȝate;
Til he was lyght hym thought to late
To knele and thanke the kynge of myght
That he hadde hys eyensyght.
Than hadde Merlyn grete honour,
And lafte with the Emperour.
'Lo, sire,' quod the Emperesse,
'Wylke a mykyl wykkednes
The seuene clerkys hadde welne do,
Ne hadde Merlyne take hede þerto.
By God Almyghty that hys in heuene,
Thus wil thy clerkys seuene
Do by the, or ellys worse;
Yf thou lyuest thow schal haue cursse.'
Quod the Emperour, 'By Goddys hore,
He schal neuer tene me more,
He that makes al thys sorowe—
Certys he schal be dede tomorwen.'

2405 slawe] a *written over* o 2431 Goddys hore] *scribbled over by later hand*

The day was comen and nyght gon;
The Emperour raes onnoon.
There ne most be no lete—
Anon hys sone was forthe fete,
And ladde ther he schulde dee;
There was many a wepyng heye. f.60[vb]
As the childe was forthladde,
Ryght als God Almyghty bade,
The sexte maystir than come he,
That was hoten Maystir Iesse,
And sayed anoon, 'Sire Emperour,
Certys thou dost lytil honour
For word of a womman
To do [to] deth swylk a man
A[s] thy sone scholde bee,
And he leue langer than ȝe.
And yf thou lattys hym lese the lyfe
For tales of thy wyf,
Also mot the bytyde
As dyde the knyght in hys pryde
That deyed for dole of hys wyfe
Was woundyt wyth a lytyl knyfe.'
Quod the Emperour, 'By Goddys belle,
That tale thou schalt me telle.'
'By God,' quod Mayster Iesse,
'Thou schalt nout here a worde of me
Bot thy sone be after sent
That hys went to iuggement.'
The Emperour comaunded anoon
After the childe forto goon.
Than waster many a glad man,
And Mayster Iesse hys talle bygane.

2437 most] *3rd minim of* m *and 1st stroke of* o *written over* o 2439 schulde dee] de *of* schulde *and* d *of* dee *over eras.* 2448 to] *om.* 2449 As] And 2457 By Goddys belle] *scibbled over by later hand*

A Tale [*Vidua*]

He sayed, 'Sire Emperour, iwys,
Hyt hys nowt lese, soth hyt hys,
Hyt was a knyght, a riche schyreue,
That was lot hys wyf to greue.
He sate a daye by hys wyf,
And in hys honde helde a knyf.
At schort wordis forto telle,
In gamen bothe as thay felle,
With a lytil croume knyfe
The schyref woundyt hys wyf,
And took to hym so myche sorowe
That he deyd oppon the morowen.
For also mykyl as he slew hymseluen,
In kyrkeȝarde men wolde hym nout delue;
He was beryd bon and fel
Withouten the toun at a chapel.
'When he was in erth broght
Hys wyf wolde goo thyn nouȝt,
Bot sayed for non wordlys wyne
Schulde no man parte hom atwyne.
Of hyre frendys that were thare,
Baden hire lat be hyre fare.
At schort wordys, hyt was nought:
Myghte no mane torne hyre thoght,
Bote thare scho wolde be sykyrlyche
With hym that louyd hyr so myche.
Quod on of thaym that was thare,
"Lete we been al thys fare.
Lete hyr dwel al hyer stille
[. . . . .]
And when thys hete passid hys,
Scho wille come hom hireselue, iwys."
After clothes scho sent a knaue,
And made hyre bede bysyde the graue.
At schort wordys forto telle,

2474 thay] a *written over* e 2488 be hyre] *written twice* 2491 sykyrlyche] k *written over* r 2495 *see note*

There moste no man with hir dwelle. f. 60vc
The nyght was comen and day gon,
Scho made a good fyer anoon,
And sete hir doun thare bysyde
For hyt was colde wyntirtyde.
Scho wype and hyr hondys wronge
[. . . . .]
  'Fram the chappel a lytil wyght
Ther houyd a ȝong knyght.
Bysyde galows were thare strange;
Ther were thre thefys anhangede.
That was hys rent for hys londe,
Forto take theues on honde
To sauen thaym with al hys myght
That no man stelle ham the forme nyȝt.
Thau the knyght was both ȝonge and bolde,
He was swith sore acolde,
And ate the chappel fyer he sawe lyght,
And rode thyderward ful ryght.
He lyght adoun of hys stede,
And into the chappel ȝede,
And the lauedy anoon he grete,
And by the fyre he hym sete,
And sayed, "Dame, by the leue,
To warme me a wylle I mot haue leue."
The lauedy than sayed, "Ȝae,
Sire, welcome mot thou bee
Yf thou thynkyst no nothyr harme
Bot to syt and make the warme."
Than the knyght in hys atyre
Was warm of that fyere,
Hym thout hyt was a fayer leef,
And he was withouten a wyf,
And bygan onnoon to wowe,
And hyr hert bygane to bowe,
And knew wel hym by syght,
And wyst wel he was a knyght,
And anoon the lady bygane

2501 There] *foll. by* were *exp.* dwelle] *in right margin in later hand* 2506 *see note*
2530 that] a *written over another letter*

To haue loue toward the mane.
Er hyt was passyd myddenyght,
The lady was kast vpperyght,
And the knyght laye aboue,
And thus he wan the lady loue.
 'The knyght leppe vppon hys stede
Forto wende and take hede
Whethir the thefys hange stille
Wylle he was aboute hys wylle.
Wylle he was aboute hys playe,
The ton thef was awaye.
To the chappel he pryked anoon,
And to the lady he made hys mone,
And sayed, "Dame, me hys wo,
Myn on thef hys agoo!
I am ful sore agast tharefore,
Lest myn landys been lore."
"Sire," quod the lady tho,
"Therfore be nought wo,
Ne make thou dole therfore—
Ne schal nouȝt thy lond be lore.
To thys beriel we wyl goone,
And dyggyn vppe the cors anoone,
And hangge hym in hys stede
f. 61ra As fayer as the othyr dyde."
"Dame," quod he tho,
"On ilke half me hys wo:
There the thefys was funde,
The toon hadde a myche wounde.
He was woundyd and no mo,
And that body hys agoo,
And yf he were founde,
And he ne hadde no syche wounde,
Thanne were my londys lore,
And I were schent therefore."
"Sire," quod scho, "lat be thy stryfe;
Now hauest thou bothe swerd and knyf—
Tak the toon or the tothir,

2539 myddenyght] *2nd* y *written over 2 minims* 2545 Whethir] t *written over another letter* 2559 goone] e *written over another letter* 2566 toon] *foll. by* a *exp.*

And gyf hym swylk anothir."
"Certis, dame," quod he tho,
"Erst me schulde be ful wo
Er I wolde been ate the rede
To smyt a man that hys dede."
"Sire," quod scho tho, "therof al
[. . . . .
. . . .]
And drew a knyf out of hire schete,
That was kenne and scharpe grounde,
And made in hys hed a wounde,
And put vp hyr knyf anoon,
And sayed, "Sire, wel we goon."
'"Dame," quod he, "verrament,
ȝit myght I be schent:
In a countek he hadde lore
Twa of hys teth byfore."
"Sire," quod scho tho, "by myn hede,
Thareto goos a good rede.
He schal be markyd as was he—
Tak and bete out two or thre."
"Dame," quod he, "by Saynt Ioon,
I nyl bet out neuer on."
"Sire," quod scho, "by Sayent Marie,
Yf thou ne wolt nowt, than schal I."
In hyr hoond scho took a stoon,
And knockyd out twa teth anoon.
"Sire," scho sayed, "this char hys heued!
Hye that we hadden ysped
That he ware vpdrawe
Er any day bygan to dawe."
Thay token the cors anoon,
And to the galowes gone goone,
And hanged hym in that ilke stede,
Ryght thare that othyr dyde.
'Lo, sire,' quod Maystir Iesse,
'Was nowt thys grete pyte

2581 *see note* 2582 shete] h *written over* l 2585 hyr] *foll. by* a 2596 nyl] y *written over 2 minims* 2602 ysped] y *written over* I 2604 any] y *written over 2 minims*

That he was schent thus for hys wyf,
That for hir loue lese hyse lyfe?
Thus wol thou, Sir Emperour,
Certes lese thyn honour
And thou bynym thyn sone the lyf
For the tales of thy wyf.'
Quod the Emperour to Mayster Iesse,
'That cas no schal nouȝt betyd me.
So euer I broke my hede,
Today ne schal my sone be dede.'
 The Emperesse when scho hit wyste,
f. 61rb Wat scho myght do, sho no wyst.
So wo and so wroth scho was,
Myght hyr glade no solas.
To bede a euen when scho cam,
A gret sygh vp scho nam,
And sayed, 'Alas that harde stounde,
That euere I was to man bounde!'
The Emperour lay and herde,
And askyd hyr why scho so ferde.
Quod the Emperesse, 'So mot I the,
Altogyder hyt hys for the.
I see the wounde, hyt hys so wente,
Thourow thyn clerkys thow wil be schent.
Thay wylle gyle the wyth hare werke
As dyde Geneuer the clerke
That wyth qweyntyes and with bost
Schend the kynge`s´ and h[are] hoste.'
Quod the Emperour, 'By Saynt Colas,
Thou schalt telle me of that cas.
Hyt hys the wonderest that euer I herde—
I wylle wetyn how that ferde.'
The Emperesse bygan hyr tale
Forto brew the childes bale.

2621 when] h *written over* e 2625 euen] *1st* e *written over minim* 2630 askyd] s *written over another letter* 2636 Geneuer the] uer the *over eras.* 2638 hare] hys

A Tale [*Roma*]

The Emperesse, as ȝe mowe here,
Bygane hyre tale in thys manere,
And sayed, 'Thre haythyn kyngys thay come
Somtyme to besege Rome,
And the Pope thay walden haue slawe,
And agyed Rome aftyr thayr lawe,
And haue been maystyrs of the toun,
And broght Crystondom adon.
The haythyn men was ful strange,
And segyde the town lange.
Seuen clerkys were in Rome,
And holpen forto take game
Both day and the nyght
That the cite were lokyd aryght.
On ther was that was holde,
And of speche he was bolde,
And sayed, "We been in thys cite
Seuen clerkys of grete bounte;
Ilkon fonde yf he may
Fram harm saue the cite a day.
Lete ilkon do what he can,
And for I am an old man,
Lete me haue the laste daye,
And fonde to do what I may."
The hold man bythout hym faste
How he myght at the laste
Anythynge dyuyse
To make the haythyn kyngys to gryse,
And dyuysyde at the laste
A gyn that made ham alle agaste,
And alle was of hys oune thouȝt,
And woundyrlych hyt was wroght.
'When hys day was come,
Hys concel was soune nome;

2652 Crystondom] d *written over minim* 2663 yf] y *written over another letter*
2665 what] h *written over another letter*

He comaunded alle with mouthe
Arme thaym a[s] wel as thay couthe.
Alle that in the cite were
f. 61rc Dyden as the olde mane gan lere,
And hymself anoon he styghe
Into the heyghest tour on hyghe,
And dyde oppon hym a wondir tyre—
Alle hyt glowyd as fyere.
In the othyr honde a swerde he tooke,
As tellys the Romauns booke,
And turnyd toward that syde
There the Sarsyns were strawyd wyde,
And bygane to skyrme bylyue
As al the worlde schul todryue.
[. . . . .]
With a qweyntyse fyere he keste
Ryght bytwene hys swyrdys in lenkthe
As tho he smytte hyt out with strenthe.
'The Sarsyns byhelde faste,
And many were ful sore agaste
For nowt on of thaym thare wase
That couthe dyuyse wat hyt was.
The heythyn kyngys that there were
Forthought sore that thay com thare,
For al thay were sore afryght
When thay seyen that woundir syght.
Ilkon askyd othyr tho
What thynge hyt was that ferde soe.
Tha oon kynge was an olde mane,
And hys reson thus bygane:
"Lordys, ȝe schul here, ywys,
What me thynke that hyt hys.
The Crysten men hase non myght
Agayens vs forto fyght,
And hare gode hys of grete myght,
And hys into erth lyght—
Certynlyche that hys he.
Forsothe, I rede that we fle,

2680 as] al 2692 *see note* 2695 smytte] *2nd* t *written over* e 2711 fyght] y *written over another letter*

For certis and he come adoune,
He wylle sle Syre Mahoune
And oure othyr goddys ilkon,
And leue of vs on lyue nought on.”
When the kynge hadde thus tolde,
Thare was non of hem so bolde
That durst langer abyde syghte,
And anon turnyd to flyght.
When thay of Rome sawe that syght,
That [the] Sarzyns turnyd to flyght,
Thay wenten out harmyd ilkon,
Al that myghten ryde or goon,
And withinne a lytyl stounde
The Sarsyns ʒeden al to grounde.
'Thys Gyneuer the clerke,
With hys wylys and hys werke,
Made to fle with hys boste
Thre kyngys and hare hoste.
Thus wyle thyn clerkys false
With hare wylys schende the alse,
And thou schalt lese thyn empyre,
And thy sone be lorde and sire.
Thus hys thy concel wrought
Forto brynge the to nought.'
Quod the Emperour, 'So mot I the,
Emperour schal he nought bee,
Na schal hym no man lenger borowe— f. 61va
Certys he schal be dede tomorowen!'
Than hadde the Emperes hire wylle,
Thay felle on slepe and lay stille.
O morwen he ne forgat hyt nouʒt—
The childe was outen of the toun brouʒt.
Toward the deth he was lade;
Than was the Emperes glade.
The seuenet mayster rode bylyue
Forto holden hym on lyue,
And was hoten Marcius,
And sayed to the Emperour thus:

2725 the] *om.* 2736 empyre] emp*er*yre

'Syre, ryghtwys Emperour,
Thou dost thyseluen lytyl honour;
Thou leuest wykked concel, iwys,
That makes the fare amys.
And yf thy sone hys don to dede,
And slane for thy wyfvys rede,
Gode that tholyd deth on tree
Leue so bytyde the
As dyde hym that leuyd more
The falnesse of hys wyfvis lore
Thane that hymseluen sawe and herde,
And therfore he mysferde.'
Quod Emperour, 'By Sayent Geruas,
Thou schalt telle me of that cas.'
Quod Marcius to the Emperour,
'Nowt a word, by Sayent Saueour,
Bot thow slake thy sonnys sorowe,
And late hym lybbe tyl tomorwen.'
Quod the Emperour, 'By sone and mone,
I not what hys best to doone!
Ȝe be about to saue my sonys lyffe,
And yf hit hys sothe þat sayes my wyf,
Certes, mayster, ȝe were worthe
To by sete qwyke in erthe!'
'Sire, sire,' quod Marcius,
'Hyt hys nowt so, by swet Ihesus;
That thou schalt wet bytyme,
Tomorwen, lange or pryme.'
The Emperour comandyd anon
After the childe forto goon.
Than gladdyd Maystyr Marcius,
And bygan hys tale thus
To the Emperour anoonryght.

2786 To] Tho A Tale *in left margin by this line*

A Tale [*Inclusa*]

And sayed, 'In Hungerye was a knyght,
And mete a sweuen byfore the daye
That a leuedy by hym laye.
Bot hyt was a wondir cas—
He wyst neuer what the lady was.
When he wok, hyt was so faste,
Hys loue oppon that lady caste,
Tha hym thout withine a [þ]rowe,
And he see hyr, he couth hir knowe.
And the leuedy that self nyght
Mete ryght so of the knyght.
  'The knyght tok hors and armes anon,
And tok hys leue and dyde hym to gon
To loke were he myght hir fet,
The leuedy that he of met.
He rode hys way thre wykkes and more,
And oft sythes syghyde sore, f. 61vb
And hys way forth he name;
Into Puyle than he came.
As he rode in the londe,
O day a toun he fande,
And a castel was therinne
That was iuel forto wynne.
The lorde of the castel
Hadde [a swythe] fayere iuwel,
On the fayerest womman to wyfe
That euer myght bere lyfe;
And the godman was gelous,
And in a tour mad hyr a hous,
And therin most no lyfe
Bot a mayden and hys wyfe,
And for he wolde of gyle beware
Hys owen body the keye he bare,
And neuermore was the dore vndo
Bot when wolde comen hyr to.

2794 þrowe] prowe   2811 a swythe] *rev. mark for correction in left margin, see note*   2819 owen] w *written over minim*

'The knyght that met that sweuen at nyght
Of þat lady that was so bryght,
Thorow the toun as he rode
A whyle he houede and abode
Ryght a lytyl fram the toure
Thare was the lady of honour
That mete the sweuen of the knyght
In bede thare scho lay al nyght.
The knyght kest hys hee on hyghe,
And ate the wyndow the lady he see,
And by the syght he wyst hir thoght
That was the lady þat he hadde sowt.
And in the leuedy hert hyt felle
That was the knyght that ho loued wel.
Bothe thare hertys were ful lyghte
That hayther hadde of othyr syght.
'The knyght wente into the toune,
And took hys ine, and lyght adoune.
[. . . . .]
Hys hoste he in councel nam,
And sayed, "Who[s] hys thys castel
That hys touryde and kernelde so wel?"
"Sire," quod he, "by Saynt Symyoun,
Hyt hys the lordes of thys toun,
A swythe godman, ywys,
And in mykyle tene hys.
In thys contre hys a knyght
That werys on hym day and nyght,
And hase done twa ȝere and more,
And that greues hym ful sore.
He man[nes] hym wel ate the knyght
Al the daye and al the nyght."
'On morwen tho the day came,
Towarde the castel the waye he nam,
And wyth the lorde sone he mete,
And ful hendlych hym grete,
And sayed, "Syre, I am comen

2832 the] *foll. by* lady *exp.* 2839 *see note* 2841 Whos] who 2851 mannes] mande *mark for correction in left margin, see note* 2853 came] a *written over* o

For were that thou hauest vndirnome,
Forto helpe the[r]for of thyne,
Thy werre forto hende and fine."
Quod the lorde, "So mot I the,
Thou art ful welcome to me."
Atte schorte wordis forto telle,
He made the knyght with hym dwelle, f. 61vc
And he was good werrour and wyes,
And conquerd al hys enmys.
The lord louyd hym as hys lyfe,
And al hys good so hys wyfe
He bytoke vndyr hys hond,
And made hym stywarde of al hys londe.
'Oppon a day he went to playe;
Vndir the tour he made hys waye.
The lady loked oute on heygh,
And in the face the knyghte scho see,
And kende anoon that was hee
That scho desired so mykyl to see.
The knyght kest vpe hys hee
To the lady that sat so hye.
The leuedy durst speke nowte,
Bot of a qweyntys scho was bythoute.
There were in hyr chambyr ynowe
Fayer reschys and longe growe;
With that on and with that othir
Scho putte ilke resche in other,
And made a karole in a stounde.
The ton hende touched to grounde,
And the othir scho helde an heygh,
And the knyght byhelde and see,
And wyst wylle in hys thowt
Why that nicote was ywroght.
The knyght priuelyche and stylle
Asayed alle the lordys wille,
And thout wydyrout and were
That he wolde a toure rere,
Lenand to the mykyl toure,

2859 therfor] the for 2888 see] *1st* e *written over minim*

To do in hys tresour—
Thorow a qweyntyse he thout to wyne
The lady that was loke thereinne.
Quod the lorde, "Ne spare nought,
Bot hye that hyt were wroght."
'Oppon a day, stylle as stoon,
He sent eftyr masons anoon.
Thay schuld ordeyn and dyuysse
To make a waye with qweyntysse
Out of on tour into that othyr,
And a mason and hys brothyr
Vndirtoke anonryght
Hyt schulde be qwentlyche dyght
That he schulde with hir speke
That was in the toure steke.
That on masson was a clerke,
And made so qwentilich the werke
That to leuedy come the knyghte,
When he wolde daye and nyghte,
That no man myght the wyser be
Bote the leuedy hyrselfe and hee:
So qweyntlich hit was wroght,
The lorde persaued hit nowt.
'O daye to hire he cam,
And hys leue than he name
A rynge of hir fynger scho tooke,
As tellys the Romans booke,
And put hyt on hys,
And [sayed], "Lemman, were thou thys,
f. 62ra And late my lorde see hit aryght,
And brynge hyt me agayn er nyght."
He dyde on the renge anoon,
And took hys leue, and dyde hym to gon.
Ate the met as he sate,
The lorde the rynge vndir[y]at,
And hadde merueyle in hys thout
How the rynge was thydir broght.
After mete the way he nam,

2924 sayed] *om.* 2930 vndiryat] vndirrat

And to the leuedy sone he cam.
Tho the lorde hadde yswore,
Ȝyt cam he in byfore,
And kest the rynge in hyre barme
Forto saue hom bothe fra harme,
And tok hys leue, and dyd hym to gon,
And the lorde cam in anoon,
And sayed, "Dam, were hys thyn rynge
That was ate oure bygynnyng
The first gyfte that I gaf the?
That rynge late me see!"
"Sire," scho sayed, "thou myght wel,
And many anothir iuwel."
"Dame," he sayed, "lat ham bee!
I wyl no mo than that see."
To hyre forcer scho gan goon,
And broght the rynge anoon
That lay loken in hir tie—
Thus scho bleryd hyre lordys eie.
'Anoon as the lorde was agoone,
The styward come in anoon.
The leuedy tolde hym al that cas,
How hyr lord bygylyd was,
And sayed, "Sire, doute the nowt,
Al thy wylle schal be wroute,
And I wylle telle the anoon
Whilke manere and howe [to doon].
Saye thou hauest in thyn contree
Slane a man of grete bounte.
Therefore were thy londys lore,
And thou were outlawde therfore.
And saye thou hase a leue wyfe,
A lemman that hys nouȝt thy wyfe,
And scho hys comen in a message
To come hom to thyn erytage.
And he wylle besyche the
That he mot thy lemman see,
And thou schalt graunt hym anon—

2934 cam] c *written over 2nd minim of* n, *1st minim eras.* 2942 ate] hate (h *exp.*) 2960 to doon] *om.*

And I wyl be redy to goon,
In anothir tyre than thys—
To se me whan hys wyl hys.
And whan he hase sene me hys fylle,
Thanne mowe we hauen oure wylle
To gone wan we wyllen in fere;
Thanne wylle he no talys here,
Nowthyr of me no of the,
Bot wene that I thy lemman be."
'Quod the stywarde, "That may nouȝt fye!
And he se the with hys eye,
Anon as he haues a syght
He wyl knowe the anoonryghte."
"Sire," quod scho, "be myn hode,
f. 62vb My rynge schal make oure parti goode
That he on thy fynger see.
And sythyn he fande hyt here on heye,
Therfore dout the nought,
Thys schal been al hys thought:
As a rynge was lyche anothyr,
So may a womman be lyche anothir.
There schal the knote of gyle be knyt—
The rynge schal blynde hys wyt."
'The styward went and was glade
Forto make hys lorde made,
And tolde hym that hys pes was nome,
And how hys lemman was comen,
And hadde broght the messages
To come home to [hys] erytage,
And asked hym leue forto wende,
And hys louerd was ful hende,
And sayed, "Yf thy lemman hys comen,
Forsoth, scho hys welcome!
Late hyre take tonyght rest;
Tomorne scho sal be my geste."
'On the morne to the mete scho cam,
And by the hond the lorde hyre nam,
And faste by hym he hyr sete,

2986 schal] t *eras. at end of word* 3000 hys] my 3006 be] b *written over* v

And made hyre to saye hys mete,
And `he´ karf hys mete with hys knyf,
And sat and byhelde hys wyf,
And in gret thout he was
Where hyt were hys wyfe er hit nas.
Alse he sat in mornynge,
Anon he thout oppon the rynge,
And thout anoon in hys thought
That hys wyf was hyt nowt,
Bot as a rynge was lyche anothyr,
So was a womman liche anothyr,
And sate stille and made hym glade,
And thus hys wyf made hym made.
When the bordis were adoun,
Scho made semlant forto swone,
For scho wolde ben agon
Into the toure anoon,
And thyder scho was sone brought
That hire lorde wyste hyt nowt.
'The lorde he ne forgat hyt nowt;
Scho was algate in hys thought
For the merueyle that he syghe.
He went into the tour on hygh.
To the leuedy when he cam,
In hir armes scho hym nam.
He was blyth as bryde on bogh,
And wende al were god ynowe,
And dweld with hir al tha nyght
Til on the morne the day was bright.
'The styward let take al hys good,
And bere hit into se flood
Into a god schype and trewe
That was maked al newe.
When the wynd was good to goon,
The senescal tok hys leue anoon.
The lorde was bothe good and hynd,
And gaf hym leue forto wende,

3011 And he] And scho `he´ (he *interlin. above* scho, *and in left margin with mark for correction*) 3022 hym] y *written over two minims* 3037 nyght] y *written over two minims*

f.62rc And hymself broght him in way
Into the see a myle or tway
Wyth tru[m]ppys and oþer mynstralcie,
Wyth many maner of melodye.
The lord halpe with myrthe and playe,
Tollyd hys oune wyf away!
Thay token leue and wente otwo,
And cysten as loue schulde do.
The schyppe saylyd ouer the sonde,
The lorde went agayn to londe.
[. . . . .]
Into the tour the way he nam;
He lokyd both forth and bynne,
And fande no man therinne.
Than gaf hym hys hert anoon
That hys wyf was goon
With the senescal away.
Than sayed he walaway,
That euer was he man boren!
Than was al hys myrthe lorne;
He lepe out of the tour anoon,
And than brake hys neke boon.
'Thus was the goodman schent,
And with hys wyvys wylys blent.
Sire Emperour,' quod Marcius,
'Ryght on thys manere and thus
Schal thy wyf bygile the
And thou leue hir, so mot I the.
Hyreself with hyre wylys alone
Haues gylyd my felawes ilcon,
And me scho wille, yf scho may,
Er tomorwen that hyt be day,
Forto bryng thy sone to sorowe.
Certys he schal speke tomorowe:
Thou schalt wyet er aut longe
Whethir of thaym hase the wronge.'
Quod the Emperour to Marcius,
'That were me leuer, by swet Ihesus,

3049 trumppys] truppys 3050 maner] a *written over* e 3056 *see note*
3080 aut] a *written over* o

Than anythyng that men telle couth,
To here my sone speke with mouthe
Forto see the ryght way
Who were gylty of thaym tway.'
'Sire,' quod Marcius, 'be stille.
Tomorwen thou schalt haue thy wille.'
When the lady herde thys,
Scho was swyth sory, iwys.
Than wolde scho telle no more,
Bot al that nyght syghyd sore.
Oppon morwen ryght at prime
The Emperour thout tyme.
In the paleys withouten the halle,
Thare he lette asembyle alle—
Erlys, barouns, sympile knyghtys—
Forto here iugge the ryghtys
Bytwen hys sone and hys wyfe
Whethir schuld lese the lyfe,
For he hadden sworen hys hoth,
Were he lyf, were he loth,
He schuld dye withouten delay
Who were founde gylty that day.
When thay wystyn wat [was] to doone,
The pepyle was semyld sone,
And ilke man hyed bylyue f. 62va
Forto haue the childe on lyue.
The Emperour come out of hys halle,
And sete hym doun among thaym alle.
The Emperes was broght with pryde
And set adoun by hys syde.
The childe was anoon efter sent
To come byfore the parlement.
The childe was forthebroght;
Many a man was glade in thought.
Byfore hys fader he fel on knee,
And cryed, 'Mercy, for charyte!'
And sayed, 'Fadyr, I haue no gylte
Of thyng that hys oppon me pute;

3098 sympile] y *written over 2 minims* 3106 was] *om.*

Certys no more than hadde he
That hadde ben dronke on the see
Na hadde Goddys help ben neye
That broght hym to a roche on hye,
And thourow myght of Godys sonde
He was founden and broght to londe.'
'Certis, sone,' quod the Emperour,
'Hyt were vs lytil honour
Bot we myght on wylle dwelle,
And suffyre the thy tale telle.'
And thay sytyn stille ilke mane,
And the childe hys tale bygane.

A Tale [*Vaticinium*]

'There was a man that was bolde
[. . . . .]
And hadde a vertu that was hyghe:
Alle men louede hym that hym syghe.
Anothyr vertu Gode on hym layed:
He wyst wat alle fouls sayed.
Bysyde hys fadyr court a myle,
In the se was an ile,
And was no man in bot on,
A hermete in a roche of ston.
The fadyr and the sone o day
Went thyder forto play,
And thay rowed and were hot.
Ryght byfore oppon the bote
Thre rauenes lyghte adoun,
And made a gret gargoun.
The child was wys and of no bost,
And hadde wyt of the Holy Gost,
And wat thay sayden he vndirgat,
And hadde mykyl wondir of that,
And hys ore fast he drowe,

3134 *see note* 3137 Gode] o *written over another letter* 3147 Thre] h *written over* r lyghte] t *written over* e 3148 made] d *written over* t 3152 wondir] w *written over* v

And byhelde hys fadyr and loughe.
'Hys fadir asked, that by hym sate,
Why he loge and at wat.
"Fadir," quod he, "so mot I the,
I louke ate the rauens thre
That sayden in har gargoun,
Anon as thay seten adoun,
That I schulde hyreafter be
Man of so gret pouste
That thou schuldest by glad to fonde
To gyf water to my honde,
And myn moder glad to hye
To brynge a towayl myn handys to drye."
The faders hert was ful of pryde,
And thout hyt schulde nougt so bytide,
And tok hys sone by the hode, f. 62vb
And threw hym into the salt flod.
'When he was in the se kast,
To dye he was sore agast.
The wynde blew, the se was wod,
And bare the childe into the flod.
Thorow helpe of Gode þat syt on hye
He neghyd sone a roche nye;
Out of the water he went anon,
And clame vppon a roche of ston,
And there he was iuel dyght
Twa dayes and twa nyght,
Ther he sate on the roche on hye,
That no sokyr he ne see.
Ihesus gan sokur hym sende—
Thare come a fyscher that was hende.
When he come the roche nyghe,
He kest vp hys eyen and sygh
The child oppon a roche harde,
And drew hym fast thyderwarde.
To the roche when he cam
The childe into the bot he nam.
Thar come a strem that was wode,

3156 he] h *written over* l 3171 was] *foll. by* se caste *exp.* 3173 was] *altered from* wod, a *written over* o, s *written over partial* d

And bare ham into the salt flode
So fere fram there the child was bore
That alle hys knowlech was lore,
And he aryued fayr and welle
Vndir a nobil castille.
Out of the bot the childe he nam,
And into the castel sone he came
To the warden of the castel,
And solde hym the childe bone and fel.
Anoon aste the childe was knowen,
He was byloued with he and lowe,
Alle that in the castel were,
And many wynter he dwelde there.
 'In the londe thare he was
The kynge bytydde a woundir cas:
Thre rauens with a lothly crye
Sewyd the kynge euer ful nye
Were he rode or were he ȝede,
That al the londe thareof tok hede.
The kynge was schamyd therfore,
That hym were leuere ben vnbore.
Ouer alle hys lond hys bref was sente
To aselen a comuyn parlyment
To wyt conceyl of ham alle
Of that kas that was byfalle.
The warden of the castel
Let atyren hym ful wel,
And the child with hym nam,
And to the parlement he cam.
When the parlement was nome,
And the pepyle al come,
The kynge walde no lenger dwelle—
Wat hym greuyd he gan telle,
And to the pypyl he sayed this:
"Who can telle me why hyt hys
That the rauens on me crye,
And brynge me out of that vylanye
That the rauens crye no more,

3193 child] childis 3203 that in] *written twice* 3206 bytydde] *2nd* d *written over* e 3216 kas] *foll. by* thas 3225 to the] *over eras.*

Wherefore me schames sore? f. 62vc
I wyl gyf hym alf my londe,
And sykyr hym trewly on honde
That I may gyf, by my lyf,
And my dogter to ben hys wyf."
'The childe th[at] fram the castel cam
These wordys vndirnam,
And that wyt God hym gafe,
That on fouls lydyn he couthe.
The childe hys mayster in concel nam,
And sayed, "Mayster, that I am
That can of the sothe telle
Why thys rauens crye and ȝelle,
And delyuer the kynge
Of alle hare lodly crying."
"Sone," he sayed, "yf thou art bolde
To do that thou hauest tolde,
To the kynge wille I goon,
And put forth thy nyddis anoon."
"Mayster," he sayed hardylich,
"Put forth oure nedys boldelych."
Hys mayster tok the way anoon,
And byfore the kynge he gan goon,
And sayed, "Sire, hire hys a mane
That rydilich telle can
Why the rauens on the crye,
That dos the al that vylanye,
And make ham take away thayr flyght,
And thou wol holden that thow hase hyght."
The kynge byhelde the childe faste,
And gret loue to hym cast,
And sayed, "Certis, that haue het
I wylle holden, and ȝyt do bet."
Byfore alle the baronage
He sykyrd hym of that mariage.
'Byfore the kynge he knelyd adoun,
And bygan hys resoun,
And sayed, "Sire kynge, as ȝe moue see,

3235 that] the 3244 alle] a *written over another letter* 3245 yf] y *written over* ȝ

Ȝonder standys rauens thre,
Twa males and o femel
[. . . . .]
That o rauen was ful holde;
In a wedyr that was colde,
And for he was nouȝt of myght
To fynde hys make mete aryght,
For glotonye he brake hys fayth,
And bete hys make and droue hire awaye.
Hys make flee hest and weste,
And fond forto do hir best,
And met a rauen that was bolde,
A ȝonge rauen and nowt holde,
And soght a make and hadde noon,
And took hyr to hys make anoon,
And oueral about he drowe,
And fand hys make mete ynowe.
The colde wedirs was agoo,
Vngyr, colde, and al wo.
The holde rauen was hote of blode,
And sowt hys make has he were wode,
And fande ham both there thay were,
H[ym] and hys make yfere.
He chalanged hire for hys;
f. 63ra The tohyr sayede he chalanged amys.
Hyrefore thay cryen oppon the
That art kynge and hauest pouste,
And thay been in thy lond lent,
And thou schalt gyfe the iuggement.
Whan the iuggement hys gyuen,
Yf euermore, wyl ȝe leuene,
Hyre thaym annymore crye,
Hardylich put out my eye."
'Euer or he walde goon,
The kynge gaf iuggement anoon.
"For the holde rauen brak hys fayth,
Wyth wronge drof hys make away,
That iuggement I gyfue:

3269 *see note* 3270 o] to 3273 aryght] a *written over* o 3281 to hys] to *and* h *over eras.* 3289 Hym] Hire 3298 annymore] a *written over* o

The ȝonge that helpe hyr forto lyue,
He schal haue that he ches,
And the holde go makelees."
When the iuggement was gyuen
The ȝonge rauen schulde ben aboue,
The kynge no sawe ham neuermore.
Than leuede he the childys lore,
And loued the childe as hys lyf,
And gaf hym [hys] dogter to wyf,
And was sesed with alle hys thynge,
And byleued with the kyng,
And ferde swyth myry and wylle—
And hys fader in powerte fel.
In hys countreth, soth to telle,
He ne myght nout for schame dwel,
And wenten thyne, hys wyf and hee,
Fer into anothyr countre,
And lyued thare, he and hys wyf,
And lade swyth sympyl lyf.
'The childe let priuelyche inquere
In what stad hys fadyr were.
Thay fande hem that went to spye
In the toun of Plecie.
Than went he agayn anoon
As fast as he myght goon
With hys fet oppon the grounde,
And sayed, "Sire, I haue founde
That thou byden aspye
In the cite of Plecie."
The childe dyght hym rychliche,
And went thydir astiliche.
Into Plecie when he was comen,
Ner hys fadir hys in was nome.
To mete when he was redy to gon,
After hys fadir he sent anoon,
And hys modir, a good wyf,
Forto gladen hom of hare lyfe.

3311 Than] a *written over* e 3313 hys] *om.* 3334 dyght] d *written over minim*
3336 when] h *written over another letter*

'When thay comen into the halle,
Thay [were] fayer resa[yu]ed alle.
The childe askyd watyr anoon,
And hys fadir bygan to goon,
And the water wolde haue fete,
Bot he was sone let.
Hys modir wold the towel haue broute,
Bot othir wolde suffry hyt nouȝt.
And the child altogydir syghe,
f. 63rb And fadir and modir neghid nee,
And by the honde both he nam,
And sayed, "Forsothe, ȝoure sone I am.
Fadyr, nowe hyt hys byfalle
That I herde the rauens telle.
I tolde ȝow withouten lesyng
What thay sayeden in hyr gaulyng,
For I hire cryhyng vndirstode,
Therfore thou puttyst me in the flod;
Bot Ihesus held me by the hond,
And broght me soune to londe.
Fadir, hadde I than be dronken,
And in the salt flod sonkyn,
So God schild me fram curs,
Now thou myghtyst fare the wars!"
Than walde the sone speke no mare
[. . . . .]
And kyst hym and hys modir in fere,
And made thaym swyth fayer chere,
And gaf thaym londe and tresour,
And thay leuedyn in mykyl onour.'
Quod the Emperour sone to þe Emperour,
'Hyre fel the fadir lytil honour
That for a wille of hyghe blode
Put hys sone in the floode.
Fadyr, so hase thou talent
To sla me without iuggement,
And certys I haue no more gylte
Than he that was in the see pute;

3343 were] *om.* resayued] resauyed 3348 towel] tow *over eras.* 3366 *see note*

Bot the Emperes loues me nout,
Therefore hit was hir thout
With wichecraft and with nygrimancie
[To] ordayne that I schulde dee.
Myn maysters loked in the mone,
And tolde me wa[t] was to doone,
And sythen I was aftir sent,
Hadde I spokyn, I hadde ben schent,
And my seuen maysters also.
Thus was my welle tornyd into wo,
And alle was thorow thy wyvis rede
For scho wolde that I hadde ben dede.
Certys, sire, thus hyt hys—
Do now what thy wille hys.'
The Emperour was ful of godnesse,
And sayed anoon to the Emperes,
'Dame,' he sayed, 'wat sayes thou?
[. . . . .]
Avise the wille of thyn a[n]swere,
For the hede that I bere,
Bot thou may the fayrer skere
Of that myn sone haues tolde here,
For alle the men that beres breth,
Thou schalt dye on schentfol deth!'
The Emperes, sothe forto telle,
Was combird wit fynde of helle
That scho myght nout forsake
That let the treson make
With wychecraft and felonye
Forto make the childe to dye,
And sayed, 'My lord, Sire Emperour,
For Godys loue and thyn honour,
Ordeyn wat thy willys bee,
Wat thou thynkest do by me, f. 63[rc]
For certis I may forsake nowt
The fame that on me hys broght.
That thy sone haues sayed, iwys,

3382 To ordayne] Ordaynde 3384 wat] was 3395 *see note* 3396 answere] awswere 3404 scho] c *written over another letter* 3406 felonye] y *written over 2 minims*

Certeynlich soth hyt hys;
Hyt was altogydir my red,
For I wolde he hadde ben dede.'
  Thus the thef the Emperesse
Knowleched hyre wykkednese
Thorow the fyndys entysment,
And anoon scho was schent,
And bounden swyth fast,
And hadde hire iuggement at the last.
Thus the childe wan hys lyf,
And the Emperesse lees hire lyf.
[. . . . .
. . . .]
And maynted hys son aryght
Bothe by day and by nyght,
And hys clerkys t[wa] and fyue
Tha holpyn to saue hys sone on lyue
With seuene talys that thay tolde—
The seuen clerkys that were so bolde—
Agayns the wyle traytoresse,
Hys stepmoder the Emperesse.
  Therefore the Emperour
Dyde thaym swyth mykyl honour;
In alle thynges that he thout,
By hare concel alle he wroght,
And was wyduer al hys lyf—
He wolde neuer haue no wyf.
That was algat in hys thout,
For tresoun that scho hadde wrogt,
He ne durst dele with no mo
Lest thay wrogten more wo.
To lyue gode lyf he bygane,
And bycam a chast man,
And paynyd hym with al hys myght
To holde ilke man to ryȝt,
And lyuede in myrthe and solas,
And dyed wan Godys wylle was,
And went into heuen-riche

3425 *see note* 3428 twa] thre

Thare ioye and blysse hys euer ilyche.
To that ilke blysse brynge vs Gode,
That euer in erth ȝed schodde.

Amen, amen, for charite.

3453 euer] neuer

TEXTUAL AND EXPLANATORY NOTES

The notes provide detailed commentary on the relationship of D with the other Middle English manuscripts and French Version A*, as well as discussing emendations and any difficult or unusual words or phrases. Whilst the commentary makes reference to the wider context of Middle English literature, it does not provide a comprehensive discussion of sources or analogues, an area already covered in some detail by Campbell, *Seven Sages*, as well as Chauvin, *Biblographie*, and Runte, Wikeley, and Farrell, *Seven Sages*. Any source and analogue discussion in the notes is drawn from the information given in these works.

Quotations from A, Ar, B, E, and F are taken from Brunner's edition. The line numbers refer to Brunner's numbering of the text, except for quotations from after l. 2740, when the numbers given are those for the individual manuscripts.

Quotations from C and R are taken from Campbell's edition (C alone is quoted, unless any variant reading in R is of interest).

Quotations from A* are from the edition published by the CRAL, edited from Paris, Bibliothèque Nationale, 2137. There is as yet no single edition of A* with variant readings from the very many manuscripts, so it must be borne in mind that any details pertaining to A* in the following notes are based on this one manuscript alone. An on-line edition by Hans R. Runte is currently in preparation (http://myweb.dal.ca/hrunte/FrenchA.html, accessed 12 June 2005).

*

1 *Rome*: Constantinople at the beginning of K and D* (Campbell, *Seven Sages*, p. 149, note to l. 7); Sicily in the *Dolopathos*.

4 *Deocclicius*: the Emperor is called Diocletian in all the Middle English versions extant at this point, and in versions A*, L, and S; H has Pontianus; K, Vespasian; D*, Marcomeris, son of Priam; and the *Dolopathos*, Dolopathos (Campbell, *Seven Sages*, p. 149, note to l. 6).

6 *Helie*: unique to D. Four Y-group manuscripts name the first Empress: Mylycent (B), Dame Milisant (C, R), Ilacent (F). She is not named in the French source. Other versions naming the Empress are the Welsh (Eva), and the *Dolopathos* (Auguste) (Campbell, *Seven Sages*, p. 149, note to l. 12). In D* she is the daughter of the King of Carthage.

8 The Prince is not named in D or A*. The five Y-group manuscripts extant here call him Florentine (E, B, C, R, F). In As and H he is called Diocletian; in most versions of I, Stefano; and in the *Dolopathos*, Lucinius

(Campbell, *Seven Sages*, p. 150, note to l. 25). Campbell speculates about the possibility of influence from *Octavian*, in which one of the princes is called Florentine, or Florent, and notes the occurrence of the name in some Old French manuscripts of *Amis and Amiloun*, and in Gower's 'Tale of Florent'.

11–14 *The Emperour wax an old man . . .*: the theme of lineage and succession connects the *Seven Sages* not only with numerous Middle English romances such as *King Horn*, *Havelok*, *Bevis of Hampton*, or the Reinbrun section of *Guy of Warwick*, but also with its source *The Book of Sindbād* and other eastern works. Like *Bevis of Hampton*, works such as *Barlaam and Josaphat*, the *Tūtī-Nāma* (the Persian 'Parrot Book', which incorporates a version of the *Sindbād*), *The Book of Šimās*, as well as *The Book of Sindbād*, all begin with an old, childless king worrying about his lack of an heir. In such works, however, the problem of succession tends to be accompanied by the problem of the education of the prince, for to ensure that one's heir is successful, one must first ensure he is wise. This is preserved in the *Seven Sages* with the Prince's instruction in the seven liberal arts, but is rarely a feature of romances, in which education usually means acquiring prowess in arms. On the relationship between *The Book of Sindbād* and *The Book of Šimās*, see Belcher, 'Diffusion', pp. 44–47; on the *Seven Sages* and the *Tūtī-Nāma*, see Campbell, *Seven Sages*, pp. xiv, xcviii, n. 3.

16 *Tha the childe*: this is perhaps suggestive of an elided form (*thatte*) in an earlier state of the text (see also l. 1291), although *tha* without the definite article also occurs in D at ll. 763, 1698, 206, 2794, 3037, and 3429 (the form is attested by the *MED*).

28 *Bancillas*: the names of the Sages in D are basically the same as those in the other Middle English versions and A*, the most notable differences being Maladas for Malquidras (in various forms), and Marcius instead of Maxius/Maxencius (Martino in A*). On the names of the Sages in other versions, see Campbell, *Seven Sages*, p. 151, note to l. 53. D does not include the more detailed descriptions of the Sages to be found in A* and the Y-group; compare, for example, the introduction of Bancillas in C:

Maister Bancillas spak þan;
For of þam was he oldest man.
Lene he was *ond* also lang,
And moste gentil man þam omang;
Ful p*ar*fiteli he kouth his p*ar*tes,
And sadly of al þe seuyn artes. (ll. 53–58)

Wright transcribed Bancillas as Baucillas.

33 Unlike A* and the Y-group, D has no mention of the Sages competing for the Prince's education by offering ever-decreasing estimates of the number of years the instruction would take.

44 *reche*: in the context of teaching, one might expect *reche* to mean 'comprehend, understand', but the preposition *into* instead of *in* suggests the sense of 'take': 'I will teach him to take into his heart all the learning that we seven clerks know'.

64 *his*: the use of an unetymological initial *h* is ubiquitous throughout D (*his* or *hys* is the preferred form for 'is'). It is also found, for example, in forms such as *hee* for 'eye' (ll. 2094, 2830, 2877), or *her(e)* for 'ere' (ll. 507, 943).

74 *Mayster Caton*: the Y-group identifies Caton with Cato, supposed author of the *Disticha Catonis*. A* only mentions this later, in the introduction to Caton's tale *Avis*. Caton also appears in the composite romance *Generides* (dated to the late-fourteenth century) as the companion of Sereyne, daughter of the King of Syria. Of the two Middle English versions, Caton is mentioned by name in the introduction to the couplet version (*A Royal Historie of the Excellent Knight Generides*, ed. Frederick J. Furnivall, Roxburghe Club (Hertford, 1865) p. 1). Both this and the other, stanzaic version later refer to him simply as one of the Seven Sages. Sereyne explains how the Seven Sages were cast out of Rome into the sea, and how Caton came ashore on the coast of Syria and became chief counsellor to the king. Like the *Seven Sages*, *Generides* includes the 'Potiphar's Wife' motif: Generides is falsely accused of attempted rape by his stepmother who had tried to seduce him, and later is falsely accused of seducing the daugther of the Sultan of Persia, and is saved through the intervention of several of the sultan's counsellors. A French source for *Generides* is usually suggested, though none has been discovered. It is worth remarking that the French sequels to the *Seven Sages* bear many resemblances to the composite romance in their great length and involved, interwoven plot lines. At least some of these sequels were also known in England: Lewis Thorpe has demonstrated that Gower knew the *Roman de Marques* and used it for his story 'The Tale of the False Bachelor' in Book II of his *Confessio Amantis* ('A Source of the *Confessio Amantis*', *Modern Language Review*, 43 (1948), 175–81).

84 D follows A* in describing Jesse as beardless: *Il n'ot ne barbe ne grenon* (01.022); the Y-group omits this detail.

87 *attente*: the only example cited by the *MED*, meaning 'striving, effort'.

116 In A* and the Y-group the place to which the Prince is taken first of all is specified as the consistory, *þ*at *is a stede wiȝ inne Rome, / þer men makeȝ wise dome* (A l. 143–4).

128 *sette aprise*: cf. the earlier *sette to lore* (l. 16). D's contracted use of *aprise* for *à aprise* makes clear the word's Old French etymology, and the familiarity of its redactor with this form. The Old French prose version

A* uses *aprendre* to describe the Prince's education: *Li sage le conmencierent à aprendre* et *à enseignier* (02.019).

129 *stude*: cited under 'stede (n. (1))' by the *MED*, meaning 'a religious house, convent, monastery'. However, since there is no religious context, I have glossed it as a variant of *studie*, meaning 'a place of learning' (the form is attested by the *MED*).

133–4 *A studie thay fonden swyth faire, / And a stude of good eeir*: as for l. 129, the *MED* cites *stude* under 'stede (n. (1))', but with the meaning of 'building site', perhaps reading *fonden* as the past tense of *finden* ('found'). However, I have glossed *fonden* as the past tense of *fonden* ('built, constructed'), and *stude* as 'a place of learning' (in line with *stude* in ll. 129 and the variant *studie* in l. 134).

148 *The seuene sciens*: both A* and the Y-group name the seven liberal arts, with varying degrees of precision (see Brunner, p. 212, note to l. 171). The Prince's education not only connects the *Seven Sages* with eastern works in which succession and ensuring the wisdom of one's heir are important themes (see note to ll. 11–14 above), but also with the medieval tradition of the Mirror of Princes (of which Book VII of Gower's *Confessio Amantis* is a notable Middle English example in the tale collection genre). In the *Dolopathos* this emphasis on the Prince's education is even more pronounced. However, some versions of the *Seven Sages* also include courtesy as an important educational consideration, emphasizing its modification in the light of romance. In Version K, for example, the Emperor has a master accompany the Prince throughout his education by the Seven Sages, in order to teach him courtesy (Speer, *Sept Sages*, ll. 347–54). Later, the new Empress persuades the Emperor to summon his son home to Constantinople by saying he will learn chivalry and courtesy better there than in Rome:

> ~ Ja fust il miels en cest païs
> que a Romme, che m'est avis,
> et si veïst chevaleries
> et apreïst des cortoisies. (ll. 443–6)

161 In A* the child has learnt everything in the seven years; in the Y-group (excepting F and E, which also say seven years: see Brunner, p. 212, note to ll. 184–5), he disputes with his masters in the fourth year, argues over astronomy in the fifth, and is subsequently tested by his masters in the sixth year of education.

177 *wa*[*s*]: the form *wa* also occurs at ll. 703 and 1940, but is not recorded in *LALME* (nor in the *MED* or *OED*), and therefore has been treated as an error.

180 *Aste the*: the manuscript's *Aste* is clearly an earlier, elided form for 'As the', and was tolerated by the scribe, who nevertheless supplied the definite article. Cf. ll. 701 and 3201, and the note to l. 2153, on *Whent the*.

184 Unlike A* and the Y-group, D has the testing of the Prince take place whilst he is still in bed. D expands the exchanges between the Sages and the Prince to roughly three times the length of the other Middle English versions and A*, showing a marked preference for direct speech, noticeable throughout the poem.

206 *awale*: a variant attested by the *MED* for *avalen* (from the Old French *avaler*), 'to sink, drop down'.

218 The detail of the Sages making the bed as it was before is unique to D. The line contains an example of non-expression of the subject pronoun (the plural ending of *Maden* indicates that the Sages, not the Prince, make the bed); see also, for example, ll. 447, 1405, 1538, 1974, 2821, 3052, 3261, and 3405.

223 D alone places the death of the Prince's mother at this point; in the other versions she dies shortly after the birth of her son. By having her die in his absence and his father remarry *Sone aftir* (l. 225), the replacement of the Empress gains in import. Version H draws on similar feelings of unease about the switching of mother for stepmother by having the dying Empress tell her husband that she knows he will remarry and ask him to allow his new wife no power over the Prince, requesting that he be educated away from home (Campbell, *Seven Sages*, p. 150, note to l. 18).

235 *iolyf ob blode*: the *MED* cites *ob* as a variant for *of* when followed by a word beginning with *b*. The Emperour's lust as a motive for remarriage is unique to D. Earlier emphasis on the Emperor's advanced age (l. 11) establishes him as a *senex amans*, a type familiar from numerous comic stories such as Chaucer's *The Merchant's Tale*, or the *Seven Sages*'s own *Puteus*, a popular medieval story appearing elsewhere in Petrus Alfonsi's *Disciplina clericalis* or Boccaccio's *Decameron*, for example. Gower later used a *senex amans* as the central figure in the *Confessio Amantis*, another framed tale collection (although Amans's age is not revealed until the end of the poem). In both the *Seven Sages* and the *Confessio*, the instruction or advisement of the *senex amans* is the purpose of the tales. In the *Seven Sages*, the lover is also a ruler, and in Gower's work political allegory is never far from the surface (most notably in Book VII, which concerns the education of Alexander by Aristotle, but more generally in how the concept of self-governance of the individual as lover is related to good government of the state).

251–2 Such narratorial asides are not uncommon in D, cf. ll. 279–80, 293–5 etc.

261 This use of the seasonal *topos* common to romance is particular to D.

265 In A*, A, E, and B the Empress says she has been married for seven years at this point; in F the squire who tells the Empress of the Prince says she has been married for three years; in C and R, as in D, no reference is made to the length of the Empress's marriage. C and R have the Empress told of the Prince *Sone efter*, and *efter* respectively (l. 281); similarly, in D the *Emperasse was sone tolde* (l. 253). If the narratives of A*, A, E, B, Ar, and F are in strict chronological order, then it would suggest that the Prince must be older on his return to Rome than in D, C, and R. However, it seems we should understand that the Emperor's remarriage took place shortly after the Prince's departure, and not after his testing by the Sages, although it is recounted at this point in the narrative: later in the Y-group texts (but not A*) the Emperor says his son has been away for seven years. D, C, and R avoid this possible confusion.

287 *The lady sayed thare* [*scho laye*]: this emendation supplies the expected rhyme with *daye*, cf. *Al the nyght thare scho lay / Til a myl byfor the day* (ll. 1590–1).

288–90 Only D has the Empress insist on her husband sending for the Prince that same day, in response to the Emperor's vague, but unwittingly ominous *He schal com hom to thee* (l. 286). In A* the Emperor promises to send for him the following day; in the Y-group (except for F, which is silent) he tells her she will see his son the next day.

296–304 There is no mention of necromancy in the French source; only C and R have a similar interpolation, in which the Empress procures the counsel of a witch to contrive the Prince's death should he speak within seven days of his arrival at court. It is placed earlier in the text, however, after the Empress is told of the Prince. Necromancy was '*explicitly* demonic magic' (Richard Kieckhefer, *Magic in the Middle Ages* (Cambridge, 1989), p. 152), and this may make sense of the episode at the end of the poem when the Empress confesses her guilt because she is *combird wit fynde of helle* (l. 3403). The demons conjured by necromancers could prove difficult to control, and in medieval *exempla* 'the Fiend himself [was] shown as a lying and untrustworthy servant' (*ibid.*, p. 174; on the subject of necromancy, see also Richard Kieckhefer, *Forbidden Rites: A Necromancer's Manual of the Fifteenth Century* (Pennsylvania, 1998)). The alliterative romance *William of Palerne* also includes a stepmother well-versed in the arts of witchcraft and necromancy: *But lelliche þat ladi in ȝouþe hadde lerned miche schame, / for al þe werk of wicchecraft wel ynouȝ che couȝþe; / nede nadde ȝhe namore of nigramauncy to lere* (*William of Palerne: An Alliterative Romance*, ed. G. H. V. Bunt, Mediaevalia Groningana, 6 (Groningen, 1985), ll. 117–19). She transforms her stepson the Prince of Spain into a werewolf because she wishes her own child to be heir.

304 *For brynge*: a rare example of the plain infinitive in D (see also ll. 603 and 1308), most likely a remnant of an earlier state of the text.

338 A line is probably missing here (though there is no lacuna in the manuscript). Campbell, however, suggests that ll. 337–9 may comprise a triplet (Campbell, 'Study', p. 42, n. 4).

339 *todon*: meaning 'undone, ruined'. This is the only usage cited by the *MED*.

344–5 Only D mentions the stepmother's responsibility for the threat of death; F makes reference to the stepmother's culpability, but in general terms: *Yf he speke to morowe yn bowre or yn halle, / Hys stepmod*ur *schall do vs hange all* (ll. 299–300).

352 *asee*: the only occurrence of the uncommon verb *asen*.

357 *myght*: the manuscript's *syght* makes no sense, since it is the Prince's speech, not his sight, that is affected; therefore the more general *myght* (defined by the *OED* as 'an active power or faculty (of the heart, soul, brain etc.)') has been supplied as the probable rhyme-word of the original.

361 [*a*] *wondir cas*: the indefinite article has been supplied in conformity with all other occurrences of the phrase, at ll. 202, 330, 417, 669, 873, 1214, and 2790.

362–7 The themes of counsel and strategy and how they connect the *Seven Sages* with the genre of romance have been explored by Geraldine Barnes (*Counsel and Strategy*, especially pp. 116–20).

365 *al*[*l*]*er*: the manuscript's *aler* is not listed as a variant in either the *MED* or the *OED*, hence the emendation. An alternative would be *al*[*re*], since inflected forms for 'all' survived from Old English in the south-west Midlands dialect in which the original of D was written. This form could have been corrupted to *aler* by the northern scribe of D, or a previous one, unfamiliar with the inflected form.

366 *bettir*: most likely a contraction of 'but' and 'there', although the spelling *bet* is unusual and may be a corruption. The suffix *-tir* occurs elswhere in, for example, *nastir* (l. 162), and *wastir* (l. 164).

373 *deye*: the original must have read *spille*, to rhyme with *stille* (l. 372); clearly, the scribe of D was unfamiliar with this intransitive usage, meaning 'die', although it has been left untouched at l. 658, where it also occurs in rhyming position.

376–7 Similarly in F the Prince specifies that his masters should *Saue me wyth a tale a day* (l. 324).

396–7 In the other versions all the Sages accompany the Prince a certain distance then leave. In A* and F the Sages then repair *au bourc saint martin* (03.047) / *to boys seynt Martyn* (l. 348); the rest of the Y-group texts seem to betray a misunderstanding of the French in referring to St Martin's Wood as the place where the Prince has been educated. On the identity of this place, see Campbell, *Seven Sages*, p. 155, note to l. 482.

398–9 *And anon are the no*[*m*]*e / Ryght to the cite of Rome*: *the* for 'they' is perhaps a scribal error, but the form is recorded in *LALME* for areas including both the south-west Midlands and East Anglia, so may well have been in D's original or some intermediate state. Cf. the similar couplet at ll. 1918–19: *Oppon the morne the way the nome / Ryght to the cite of Rome*. In the other versions, the Prince is met before he reaches the palace (by the Emperor and his party in A*, A, E, and B; by the Emperor's men in F; and by the Empress and some knights in C and R).

400 ff. The scene between the Prince and his father is very close to the French source. In A, E, and B the Empress takes the Prince off on her own before the Emperor has realized that he will not speak; in F the Emperor asks his son what he has learned, but a message from the Empress summons him away before he should answer; in C and R the Empress takes the child away before he has even seen his father.

404–7 Yasmina Foehr-Janssens gives a psychoanalytical reading of the *Seven Sages* in which the Prince's silence symbolizes his incestuous desire (*Le temps des fables*, especially 'Le silence', pp. 152–8), aligning him with figures such as Oedipus: 'Ce silence est négation (meurtre?) du père' (p. 58). Foehr-Janssens sees the Prince as the focus of the story, the hero of his *roman de clergie*; seen from the Emperor's point of view, however, there is another possibility. Foehr-Janssens refers to Freud's essay on 'The Theme of the Three Caskets' (in which he argues that silence represents death), whilst discussing the motif of silence (p. 259, n. 39). If we recognize that it is the Emperor, not the Prince, who is at the centre of the dilemma for most of the work, the Prince's silence can be read in much the same way as Freud read Cordelia's silence in *King Lear*. The Emperor must choose his son, just as Lear must choose Cordelia over her sisters: both old men have to 'renounce love, choose death and make friends with the necessity of dying' (Sigmund Freud, 'The Theme of the Three Caskets', *The Standard Edition of the Complete Psychological Works of Sigmund Freud*, translated from the German under the general editorship of James Strachey, vol. XII (London, 1958), 289–301 (p. 301)). Reading the Prince's silence in this way connects it with the theme of succession and the anxieties this occasions in the older generation, a theme that lies behind the work as a whole, as highlighted by the final tale *Vaticinium*.

432–9 This exchange between the Emperor and Empress is unique to D.

447 *Yf euermore shal haue speche*: another example of non-expression of the subject pronoun (*Yf euermore* [*he*] *shal haue speche*). See the note to l. 218.

448–9 The Emperor similarly hands his son over to the Empress in A*, but the French text adds that the child would not go with her at first, then his father commanded him, and he did not wish to disobey.

452 *vowch . . . saue*: as the *OED* states, this sense—'to confer or bestow (something) *on* a person', with separable verb and adjective—is frequent in fourteenth-century romances, and it includes this example.

463 *men wenes*: D uses the singular verb form in conjunction with *men* elsewhere at ll. 646, 2653, 2710, and 3400.

469 In F the Empress says they should kill the Emperor and be king and queen of the land together. D* also has her promise to kill the Emperor (Campbell, *Seven Sages*, p. 155, note to l. 512).

483–7 The Empress's contrivance of the signs of attempted rape is the first of many occasions in both the frame and inset stories such as *Avis*, *Puteus*, or *Inclusa* in which women manufacture or manipulate how things seem. *The Book of Sindbād*, in tales such as *Gladius*, *Zuchara*, *Catula*, *Pallium*, and *Elephantinus*, is even more preoccupied with how women evade accusations of adultery by constructing alternative readings of the signs.

487 *vysages*: the plural form is unusual, but the *OED* cites one other instance of this, used to mean the 'face or surface of the earth'.

495–6 This accusation of potential strangling or rape is the same in A*; in A and B the accusation is of potential rape; in E, murder; in C and R the Empress says the Prince would have *done al his will* (l. 550), and murdered her; and in F she says he actually has raped her: *Thys thefe hath done me velonye, / In my chaunbur he hath leyn me bye* (ll. 398–9). Geraldine Barnes notes the similarity between the Prince and Floris in *Floris and Blanchfleur* (which follows the *Seven Sages* in the Auchinleck Manuscript): both are accused of breaking a sexual taboo (in the case of Floris, of sleeping with Blanchfleur, whom the Emir intends to marry; see Barnes, *Counsel and Strategy*, p. 116). Similarly, Bevis in *Bevis of Hampton* (which precedes the *Seven Sages* in Cambridge, University Library, MS Ff.2.38) is falsely accused of deflowering Josian, daughter of the King of Armenia, whilst Josian's attempted seduction of Bevis parallels the Empress's overtures to her stepson in the *Seven Sages*. There are further similarities between the two works: both concern themselves with problems of inheritance (in both, a wicked mother-figure—the Prince's stepmother in the *Seven Sages*, the hero's actual mother in *Bevis*—attempts to keep the hero from his heritage), and in both, the hero is saved by the intervention of his master(s) (the Seven Sages, and Saber in *Bevis*).

506–7 *I schal neuere hete brede / Here the thyfe traytour be dede!*: a variation on the common Middle English phrase *as ever I ete bred*, meaning 'as I live'. The Emperor uses it again at ll. 1632–3: *I nyll tomorwen ete no brede / Er the* *thef traytour be ded*. Cf. *Fro this forth shal I nevere eten bred / Til I myn owen herte blood may see* (Chaucer, *Troilus and Criseyde*, Book II, l. 444).

528 *Erlys and barrons*: in F it is the steward who saves the Prince's life.

583 *fyne appul-tre*: a pine tree in the other versions. In C and R the word used is *pine-appel* and *pyne appeltre* respectively (l. 612): if this was in D's source it might explain the change to *fyne appul-tre* as a scribal error or misunderstanding. There are apple trees (and pears) in the garden in A, E, and B as well as the pine tree.

582–5 The Empress in D reveals more of the story in her preamble than she does in the other versions. This strategy is repeated elsewhere in the poem, before the Sages' tales as well as the Empress's. F follows D in this respect at the beginning of both *Tentamina* and *Avis* (see note to ll. 2119–22).

586 *quod Emperour*: the absence of the definite article is suggestive of an elided form (*quoth'Emperour*) in an earlier state of the text, and of the scribe of D still being able to read the line in this way in spite of the spelling (although his usual practice is to include the definite article). See also ll. 712, 1496, 2389, and 2766. All occurrences were emended to *quod* [*the*] by Wright.

592–643 *Arbor* **('The Tree').**
The heading *Fyrst Talle*, and all subsequent headings, are those written in the left margin by the scribe.

594 *a knyȝt*: in A*, *.I. borjois* (06.001); in the Y-group, a burgess, except for C and R, in which he is a man of great renown. After this, in all the other versions except F, the burgess goes away on business, returning to find the *hympe* growing out of the old tree.

603 *tree see*: a rare example of the plain infinitive in D (see also ll. 304 and 1308).

609 *hym*: the neuter pronoun *hym* refers to the branch. It is used again in l. 611, and in l. 633, where it refers to the tree.

611 *lettyde*: D is unique in its considerable wordplay between *lettyde* ('obstructed') and *latte*, *lette* (ll. 615, 622) and *lette*, *lete* (ll. 618, 620), meaning 'allow(ed)', and 'caused something to be done' respectively.

623 *to dede*: 'To die'. A rare form: the *MED* cites only one other example.

636–41 The Empress in D applies the moral more obliquely, maintaining the symbolism. Compare, for example:

Gode sire, gent and fre,
þat olde tre bitokneȝ þe.
þe ȝonge bitokneȝ þi sone wode,
þat is isprонge out of þi blode.

He sschal be sone forht idrawe,
And maister, and þou his knaue. (A ll. 611–16)

The tree as genealogical image is found in eastern works such as *The Book of Šimās* in the King's dream: see Belcher, 'Diffusion', pp. 46, 53; Perry, 'Origin', pp. 29–30, or at the end of one of the Persian versions of *The Book of Sindbād* where the King chooses to abdicate in favour of his son, much as the man in *Arbor* chooses to cut down the old tree so that the young one may flourish: 'Thank God that thou hast a worthy successor in thy son . . . Thy day and night are over: it is now his day. The tree which time has dried up, I should marvel were it to bear fruit. When the branches of the willow are decayed, who looks to it for shade? What can be better for thee than that thy son should succeed thee, and preserve thy name upon the earth' (Clouston, *Sindibad*, p. 117).

662–3 This insight into the child's emotions is particular to D. A similar instance occurred at ll. 556–7: *Now his the childe t*[*o*] *prison brouȝt; / Mykile sorowe was in hys thout*.

663 *A kast on hym a ruful hye*: I have glossed *A* as the unstressed personal pronoun (here *he*), common in other South West/south-west Midlands writers, such as Langland and Trevisa (see also the note to l. 1929). Alternatively, it could be read as the weak form of *and* used elsewhere in D (see the note to l. 1205).

670 *pytte*: the rhyme-word *gylte* (l. 671) indicates that the original must have read *pylte* rather than *pytte*, and the scribe of D was unfamiliar with the form (which the *MED* cites as chiefly south-west Midlands and South West, the dialectal region of D's original). The scribe also replaces *pylte* (with *pute*) at ll. 3121 and 3378.

685 *sy*[*cur*]*lyche*: Wright transcribed this as *syrtnlyche*, but more likely is *syrculyche*, an error for *sycurlyche* (a word with which the scribe had trouble: see also the note to l. 734, and l. 2491, where the *k* of *sykyrlyche* has been written over *r*). I have emended it in the light of l. 846, *sycurlyche*.

686 *by Good*: this unusual employment of *Good* for 'God' also occurs at ll. 989, 1440, 2133, and 2231. The form is not recorded in the *MED*.

701 *Aste the*: see the note to l. 180. Wright mistranscribed this as *Afte*, and it was defined speculatively in the *MED* as 'after' (this was the only example cited).

726–893 ***Canis*** **('The Dog').**
A later hand has written the tale number (2^{d}) and the Sage's name (*Bancillas*) in the margin by the heading. This practice continues throughout the manuscript for the different tales (*nouercae* is written to indicate a tale of the Empress). The other versions begin with details of the tournament

before mentioning the knight. It should be noted that *Canis* is the eighth story in F, with *Puteus* in second place, and only the end of the tale survives.

732 *hagge*: presumably a variant of *age*, although not listed in the *MED*. The use of initial *h* is noticeable throughout D: see the note to l. 64.

734 *sycurliche*: although the manuscript's *syrcurliche* is listed in the *MED*, it is given as an erroneous form, hence the emendation (see also the note to l. 685).

744 *Knyght ordaynde a day*: Wright emdended this to [*The*] *knyght ordaynde a day*, but *Knyght* could simply be a plural form with zero-ending. The knight does arrange the tournament in E (see Brunner, p. 214, note to l. 703, who also interprets D in this way), but in the other Middle English versions and in A* the tournament is not arranged by the knight, who happens to live nearby. This would make better sense of ll. 748–9, which presumably should read, *The knyght of hit* [*herde*] *telle / In his felde thay wolde dwelle*. Wright also emended D in this way, but this seems inconsistent with his earlier emendation: if the knight arranged the tournament himself, he would not need to hear secondhand that it was to take place in his field.

745 *May*: Trinity Day in the other versions.

748 *The knyght of hit* [*herde*] *telle*: see above, note to l. 744, and cf. *Tho the Emperes herde telle* (l. 2261).

754 *norises two*: three nurses in the other versions; they are introduced earlier in the tale, and the duties of each are detailed. For example, A says of the child:

Hit hadde of þre norices keping:
þe ferste ȝaf hit soukeȝing,
þat oþer norice hi*m* scholde baþe,
Whan hit was time, late and raþe,
þe þridde norice hi*m* sscholde wassche,
þe child was keped tendre an nessche. (ll. 713–18)

In As there is only one nurse; in the Welsh version, the *Dolopathos*, and the *Sindbād* versions, there is no mention of nurses at all (Campbell, *Seven Sages*, p. 158, note to l. 789).

762 *In a toure thay clymbyd on hyghe*: this perhaps echoes the French: *les norrices . . . monterent aus creniaus du mur par les degrez* (09.011). Of the Y-group, only C and R describe the nurses' vantage-point, and then only indirectly as *a preue place bisyde* (l. 813).

763 *tha*: emended to *tha*[*t*] by Wright, and at ll. 1291, 1698, 2794, 3429 (though not at l. 16). The form is attested by the *MED*.

767 *An olde toure*: in the other versions the adder lives in the wall beside which the nurses have left the child.

772 D is the only version to mention music.

778 *hym*: there is some confusion as to the adder's grammatical gender (also in E and B; in A the adder is female, in C and R, male). *Scho* is used in ll. 775–7, and as well as the reflexive *hym* of this line, *he* appears in l. 780 (which, of course, could mean either 'he' or 'she'). The original most likely had *he* for 'he' at ll. 775–7, with D's scribe misreading this as 'she' and substituting his preferred form *scho*, then realizing his mistake when he came to *hym* in l. 778. Therefore he left the subsequent *he* of l. 780 unaltered, but did not bother to correct his previous mistake. Evidence that *he* was indeed used for 'she' elsewhere in the original (hence the scribe's misreading) is found at ll. 827, 1703, 1704, 1721, 1739, 1759, and 1782, where it was left unaltered by the scribe (*ho* for 'she' is also found in D: see the 'Glossary' for occurrences).

788 *here ȝe moun*: this common rhyme-tag and address to the audience occurs elsewhere at ll. 457, 1340, and 2645, and is used by the narrator of the poem as a whole and by the Sages in their tales, where the audience in question is the Emperor and by extension his court, although D makes no direct reference to this: the Sages sometimes begin their tales with an address to the Emperor alone (see ll. 1674 and 2467), but the Prince's story, *Vaticinium*, is the only one explicitly told to the whole court: *And thay sytyn stille ilke mane, / And the childe hys tale bygane* (ll. 3132–3).

792–3 The other versions say only that the child was not hurt.

793 *Bote* [*lay*] *alle stille and sleppe*: D employs the verb *lay* elsewhere when describing sleep, hence this emendation. Compare *And lay slepyng stille as stoon* (l. 980), *Thay felle on slepe and lay stille* (l. 2745). Another possibility suggested by the *MED* is that *stille* is an error for *stilde*, 'was silent'.

795 *That into the ȝerd the worme flyghe*: not in the other versions.

797 The fight is bloodier in the other versions: in A*, A, E, and B the greyhound bleeds over the cradle and in all of them we are told that the adder is ripped to pieces.

801 This detail of the dog's howling is also in A*, but not the other Middle English versions.

805 In the other versions the nurses find the cradle, rather than the greyhound, first.

808 *Thay two norise was were*: D sometimes employs a singular verb with a plural noun qualified by a number. See also, for example, l. 2366 and accompanying note.

812–19 Again, the redactor of D reveals his propensity for direct speech (A* has a little, but there is none in the other Middle English versions).

814 *eten*: the French has *mengié* (10.016), and B has *gnawe* (l. 779); the other Middle English versions merely say that the greyhound must have slain the child.

822–9 D is the only version in which the lady sees the nurses running away and sends a swain after them. In A*, A, E, and B she meets the nurses as they are fleeing; in C and R she is in the hall with the nurses when they discover the cradle.

838–9 The lady swoons in the other versions.

840 D is the only version in which the knight is alerted by the sound of his wife's cries; in the other versions he is coming home anyway.

849 In the other Middle English versions the lady says she will kill herself if her husband does not kill his greyhound.

855–6 Cf. A*, in which the greyhound *mist les deus piez devant en mi le piz* (11.007); in A, and similarly in E and B, the dog *him welcomed wiȝ fot and tail* (l. 799); in C and R the greyhound is running around and barking because of the venom from the adder, but then *He fawned his lord fast with his tail* (l. 883).

859 *And smot out the rygge-boon*: the same in A, C, and R; in the French source the knight cuts off the greyhound's head; E and B merely say that the knight slew the greyhound with his sword.

860–9 This device, the man *glad / To do that the knyght bade* (ll. 862–3), is particular to D; in the other versions the knight discovers pieces of the adder's body by the cradle and finds the child alive inside.

877 At this point in the other Middle English versions the knight makes a short antifeminist speech before calling in the other people to tell them what happened:

He said: 'Sorow cu*m* to þat man,
And sertanly right so it sale,
þat euer trowes any womans tale.
Allas,' he said, 'for so did I!' (C ll. 900–3)

When the others arrive (in A* as well as the other Middle English versions), the knight reiterates that the greyhound's death was brought about by trusting woman's counsel.

882–5 This is D's most original alteration of the tale and the only ending in which the knight dies. In A* the knight goes into self-imposed exile; in the Y-group he goes, variously, to the forest or desert, where we are told that he suffers greatly. In F, however (the text resumes at this point) he sells his land and travels across the sea as a pilgrim. In As and H the knight goes in exile to the Holy Land (Campbell, *Seven Sages*, p. 159, note to l. 920).

In A (similarly in E and B) the knight, on discovering his son alive, had said:

> Ne be þat man neuere iborewe,
> But in euel wat*er* adreint,
> þat euer leue wi*m*mannes pleint. (ll. 812–14)

It may be that these lines were in the source of D and suggested its novel ending, in which case D has comically transformed the knight's declamation into a self-fulfilling prophecy.

900 *No nouȝt he ne schal by boundon so sore*: the text appears corrupt at this point, though the sense is preserved. The original may have read something like *Ne schal he be ybounde sore*.

904–11 Only D tells us of the Empress's sorrow and plotting throughout the rest of the day (and again later, at ll. 1482–91); in the other versions the Emperor goes straight to his wife in his chamber. A* does have something similar at this point, however: when the Emperor goes to his wife, we are told that the Empress *fu moult iriee pour ce qu'ele ne pot acomplir son bon* (11.022).

928–89 ***Aper*** **('The Boar').**
D alone begins by telling us of the boar; A* and the Y-group (except for F) commence the tale with details of the forest and how the boar was feared. F begins by telling us of the swineherd who lost a boar one day. Reluctant to go home to his master for fear of a beating, he climbs a tree and, being hungry, eats of its acorns: then we are told of the fearsome boar.

930 A hawthorn in the other Middle English versions except for F, in which it is an oak. In A* the tree is a service-tree or sorb-apple tree (*alier*, 12.006). In the *Sindbād* versions it is a fig tree (Campbell, *Seven Sages*, p. lxxxiii).

945 *hoode*: C and R also have hood; in A* he fills *son giron* (12.007) and then begins to fill *l'autre giron* (12.008); A, E, and B follow the French, translating *giron* variously as 'barm', 'lap', 'sleeves' ('barm' most likely an error arising from the scribe having misunderstood 'lap' as signifying the part of the body, rather than the part of clothing (the *MED* defines 'barm' as the part of the body only)), and 'arm' (most likely an error for barm). See the 'Introduction', 'The Relationship of Dd.1.17 with the Other Manuscripts', for the textual implications of D's agreement with C and R against the Old French and the other Middle English versions.

948–9 *Tho the knaue hadde a syȝt / Of the bore he hadde a* [*fr*]*yȝt*: an alternative emendation is that of Wright, reading *Tho* as 'then' rather than 'when': *Tho the knaue hadde a* [*fr*]*yȝt, / Of the bore he hadde a syȝt*.

952 *hyhyde*: mistranscribed by Wright as *byhyde*, and thus cited by the *MED* as one of only two examples for *bihien* ('hasten').

953 The other versions (except F) add that the boar saw there was no fruit, or not as much fruit, on the ground as there usually was. In F the boar runs to the tree, finds plenty of acorns underneath, eats them, and lies down.

960 *the tree were rote-fast*: this is different from the other versions, in which the boar makes the tree shake: *þe tre wagged als it wald fall* (C l. 995). In F, of course, the boar does not attack the tree.

976 *The tohir*: this form is not listed in the *MED* or *LALME*, but *LALME* does list *y^e-toher* as a West Yorkshire form, so it seems probable that *the tohir* belongs to the repertoire of D's northern scribe, along with *The tohyr*, found at l. 3291. Similarly, the form *whehir* occurs at l. 1225.

977 *And claude the bore vndir the syde*: D is closest to the French here, in which the herdsman scratches the boar *desouz le ventre* (12.017); in the Y-group he scratches the boar on the back, and then (except in F) on the stomach too.

978 F is similar in expressing the boar's pleasure:

> He clawed þe boor on the bakk
> And full well lykud he that.
> He thoght þat he clawed so swete,
> That at the laste he felle a slepe. (ll. 667–70)

982 *And rent hys wombe with the knyf*: in A* and the Y-group (except for E, C, and R, none of which specifies) the herdsman wounds the boar in the heart.

986 *an*: emended to *an*[*d*] by Wright. The form is attested by the *MED*.

995 *Eemperour*: this variant spelling, attested by the *OED*, appears only once in D.

997 Ar is extant from this point. Ar, E, B, C, and R contain a longer version of the preamble to the fourth tale: the Emperour sends for his torturers and commands them to flog (not in B) then hang the Prince, much to the disapproval of the barons. The Prince is flogged then led away to the gallows with cries of pity from the onlookers; he meets his master on the way. In Brunner's opinion, A and D are independent abridgements of this longer version, which must have been introduced into the story with the English parent version, or a French text immediately preceding it, since it is not in the extant manuscripts of A* (215, note to ll. 937–52). Both A* and A, but not D, also specify that the Prince's death will be by hanging.

1001 In Ar, E, B, C, and R the onlookers urge Ancilles to use his learning to plead for the Prince's life (see Brunner, p. 215, note to ll. 957–8 for the textual implications of this).

1007 *Ancillas*: A* calls the master Augustes; Ar, Maxilles.

1026 *That ȝe bytyde swilk a cas*: the subject pronoun *ȝe* is mistakenly used both here and at l. 1501 in place of the object pronoun. Similarly, l. 2081 has *I* in place of *me* (*I ne schal nouȝt bytyde that cas*), suggesting the scribe or redactor of D did not properly understand this construction (although it is used correctly elsewhere).

1027 *Ypocras*: on Hippocrates here and in other Middle English literature see Campbell, *Seven Sages*, p. 160, note to l. 1086.

1028 *cosyn*: in the general sense of a blood-relative, or kinsman. The person in question is Ypocras's nephew (cf. l. 1054, *Hys emys bokis he vnselde*). The other versions refer to him as such, except for E, which uses 'cousin' throughout. In H the nephew is Galen (Campbell, *Seven Sages*, p. 160, note to l. 1087).

1034–7 These lines are virtually identical to those spoken by Bancillas before his tale (ll. 714–17), typical of the redactor's recourse to stock phrases in the linking sections.

1046–1163 ***Medicus*** **('The Physician').**
In F *Medicus* is the twelfth tale, the final one of the fragment; the fourth tale is *Tentamina*.

1046 *fysysian*: none of the other Middle English versions uses this noun, preferring to say, for example, *Of leche craft was non his pere* (A l. 1004).

1049 D differs from the other versions in its portrayal of the nephew as a feckless youth who undergoes a change of heart, teaching himself medicine from his uncle's books. In the others, Ypocras does not wish to teach his nephew (in the Y-group he taught him for a while, but stopped when he saw that his pupil was overtaking him in wisdom), so the child teaches himself. As Campbell observes, the child's apparent dullness in D is 'in accord with a convention of ancient and mediaeval story', Perceval being another example of this (*Seven Sages*, p. 161, note to l. 1107).

1057 At this point in the other texts Ypocras sees that his nephew has taught himself, and is envious or angry. D is unique in having Ypocras grow envious later in the tale.

1062–3 D alone says Ypocras did not go to Hungary himself because he was old; A* has nothing on this point; the Y-group texts simply say he could not go, except C and R which say he was loath to go.

1063 *And hys blode wax ale colde*: in standard Galenic medicine the blood was thought to cool with age. See Nancy G. Siraisi, *Medieval & Early Renaissance Medicine: An Introduction to Knowledge and Practice* (Chicago and London, 1990), p. 103.

1064 *He let atyre wile a fyne*: D alone follows the French in giving details of the boy's dress (*Il conmanda son neveu à atorner* (14.007)), but makes no reference to his horse, which is mentioned in both A* and the Y-group. Wright emended *a* to *a*[*nd*], but *a* here is from the French *à fin*, meaning 'at or to the end' (see the *OED*, *afine* and *well-a-fine*, 'right well, well indeed').

1072 *fysenamye*: diagnosis by physiognomy is unique to D; in the others the nephew examines the urine of either the child only, or of the child and both his parents. A* is similar to D in that the nephew looks at the child then the king and queen before asking for the urine—obviously his visual examination of the family suggests something amiss.

1076–9 This anticlerical interpolation is peculiar to D.

1082 There are no maidens in the other versions.

1084–93 D compresses into this one diplomatic speech a sequence of exchanges in the other versions in which the not-so-diplomatic nephew has to work hard to persuade the queen to tell him the identity of the child's father.

1087 *schryue*: the choice of confessional diction is particular to D.

1092 *swat*: the *MED* includes this example under its definitions for *swot* ('sweat'), but suggests it may be an error for *bote*, which is found in the other Middle English versions:

> I ne mai do þi sone no bot,
> But ȝif i wite þe sothe rot,
> Of what man hit was biȝete. (A ll. 1061–3)

Certainly, this is similar to D:

> And bot thow telle how hit hys
> I may nought hel thy sone, iwys.
> Of hys hele he ase ne swat
> Bot thow telle wo hym bygate. (ll. 1090–3)

Nevertheless, *swat* is unlikely to have been a simple mechanical error, and it may have an unfamiliar, colloquial meaning here (some of the meanings given in the *MED* have a medical context). Even if the original rhyme-word of l. 1093 was *bygot* rather than *bygate*, this could still have been rhymed with *swot* (as a weak rhyme), rather than *bot*. Furthermore, *I ne mai do þi sone no bot / But ȝif i wite þe sothe rot* seems to be paralleled by D's *And bot thow telle how hit hys / I may nought hel thy sone, iwys* rather than by l. 1092. In view of this uncertainty, I have allowed *swat* to stand.

1098 In the Y-group the queen says the events took place one April (C and R specify twelve years ago). In A* the queen's lover is *li quens de namur* (15.001); in the Y-group he is the Earl (King in Ar) of Navern. On the frequent occurrence of Navern in Middle English romances, see Campbell, *Seven Sages*, p. 161, note to l. 1169.

1102 *And so he* [*was*] *getyn, iwys*: an alternative is Wright's *And so* [*was*] *he getyn, i-wys*. I have preferred *he* [*was*] as *was he* is rare in D; also cf. B: *And soo he was on me biȝete* (l. 1079).

1108 *he helyd the childe ol and sound*: the other versions are more detailed here, telling how the nephew prescribes a particular diet, varying slightly in each. In A, for example, he tells the queen

> But for he was biȝeten amis,
> Hit mot boþe drink and ete
> Contrarius drink, contrarius mete:
> Beues flesch *and* drinke þe broþt. (ll. 1082–5)

1110–11 Only D tells how the queen gave the nephew gifts to encourage him to keep her secret.

1113 D has compressed a longer exchange in which Ypocras questions his nephew about the prince's illness and cure.

1122–39 In the other versions the nephew first brings one plant, and is then told by his uncle that there is a better one; he is killed whilst fetching the second plant. Although D has only one plant, the scene includes more dialogue, which creates a tension and a build-up to the murder, increased through the narratorial aside *Quod Ypocras, euer uorthym wo* (l. 1130), and through the way in which Ypocras entices his cousin to pluck the herb by promising to teach him of its powers (unique to D).

1133 *dyggy*[*t*]: the scribe has mistakenly written the preterite or past participle form *dyggyd* instead of the contracted form for the infinitive and pronoun, *dyggyt*; he uses the contraction correctly at l. 631.

1137 *fauchon*: A* says *son coustel* (15.016); all the other Middle English texts say it was a knife (except for C and R which do not specify the weapon).

1139 At this point the Y-group texts, but not A* or D, mention that Ypocras buried his nephew secretly.

1141 *And bernyd hys bokys ilkon*: C and R omit this detail. Campbell (*Seven Sages*, p. 161, note to l. 1224) refers to the fable in which Hippocrates, as librarian, burned the books at Cos in order to conceal his plagiarism.

1143 *For no man schuld lerne of ham good*: only D spells out Ypocras's motive for burning his books. At this point the Y-group texts say God saw Ypocras's actions and repaid him with illness.

1146 *a maladye*: dysentery in A* and the Y-group (*menesoun* (A l. 1122)).

1148–9 D is unique in pointing out the consequences of Ypocras having burned his books (the other versions, except for C and R, come close to this at the end of the tale when Ancilles asks the Emperor if Ypocras profited by killing his nephew and burning his books). D has drawn attention to the books throughout the tale, telling us how the child *Hys emys bokis* . . .

vnselde (l. 1054) and how he healed the prince *As taught hym Ypocras booke* (l. 1107)—both details are absent in the other versions.

1151 At this point A* and the Y-group relate how Ypocras filled a barrel full of water then pierced it full of holes, each of which he stopped with a plug, and anointed around the holes; when he removed the plugs, the water stayed in the barrel, to the amazement of his neighbours. Making a grotesque analogy between the barrel of water and his own dysenteric body, Ypocras then remarked that although he could stop the water from flowing out of the barrel, he could not stop his dysentery. In the Y-group he tells his neighbours that the illness is a just punishment for having murdered his nephew, the only person who could have saved his life (cf. D ll. 1150–1). D's omission of this episode highlights its tendency to cut any extraneous material: the irony of Ypocras's death is clear enough without this sequence.

1156–63 D's emphasis on the Prince as his father's protector in his old age is similar to the French:

vous n'avez que .I. filz *et* celui volez vous destruire pour le dit de vostre fame. ∗ vous estes viel home *et* savez bien que jamés n'en aurez plus enfant. ∗ Et se vos ainsint le volez destruire, si vous en aviegne il ausint conme il fist ∗ ypocras de son neveu. (16.004–6)

The other Middle English versions do not mention this.

1168–71 This mention of the courtiers' relief and the Empress's sorrow is particular to D.

1172 *Scho* [*ofte*] *syghyd* [*sore*] *amonge* (MS *Scho syghyd and swore amonge*): whilst the original does make sense, the metre is somewhat defective. The text has not been emended on these grounds alone, but also in the light of l. 571: *And ofte syked sore amange*. Both ll. 1172 and 571 describe the Empress before she begins one of her tales, and the redactor often reuses stock phrases at similar moments in the story. The lead up to the following tale (*Gaza*) and most of the tale itself is wanting in F due to a missing folio. It is placed fifth in the collection, as in the other versions.

1176–87 The Empress's speech is much shorter than the exchange between her and the Emperor in the other versions.

1190–1279 ***Gaza* ('The Treasure').**

1192 *Emperour of Rome*: Octavian in the other versions.

1194–5 See Campbell, *Seven Sages*, p. 162, note to l. 1318, for details of the proverbial wealth of Octavian in Middle English literature.

1194 *a toure*: all versions except D, C, and R say that the tower is called Cressent (Oroysaunt in E (l. 1225)).

1196 *seuen clerkys*: two in C and R.

1203 One or more lines are missing here (though the manuscript has no lacuna), hence the sudden shift to *the othir* of the two remaining clerks. Presumably they contained a description of the other clerk; in the other versions he is portrayed as a miserly individual and is given the guardianship of the Emperor's tower.

1205 *And haddyn both childryn a wyf*: Wright emended *a* to *a*[*nd*] here and at ll. 1928 (an error for the following line, where *a* actually occurs: see note to l. 1929), 2168, 2188, 2376 (ll. 1930, 2170, 2190, and 2378 respectively in Wright: line numbers for some sections of the text are inaccurate). The form is attested by the *MED* as a weak form of 'and'.

1210–15 This insight into the clerk's motivation for the robbery is unique to D.

1216–19 The description of the robbery is much longer and more detailed in the other versions.

1218 *Thay wente and breken that tour*: towers dominate the architectural landscape of the *Seven Sages*, as Yasmina Foehr-Janssens has observed (*Le temps des fables*, pp. 268–78). As well as *Gaza*, there is the tower in *Roma* which Geneuer ascends to frighten the Saracens into retreat, and the tower in which the husband locks his wife in *Inclusa*, penetrated by her lover. One might also add the pillar in some versions of *Virgilius* (including this version), which supports the magic mirror and is undermined by the clerks: *A piler that stode fol heyghe, / Heyer wel than ony tour . . .* (ll. 1881–2). Towers or other buildings as symbols of power are common throughout so-called 'Matter of Rome' romances in which the destruction of the city parallels the destruction of the ruler/father, and *The Seven Sages of Rome* is certainly affiliated with such works in this respect. In *The Seege or Batayle of Troye*, for example, we are told how Priam walls the city and builds himself a tower in which to live; the text ends with the Greeks breaking into Troy, penetrating the tower, and killing all inside. In many versions of the Alexander story, the hero throws his father Nectanabus down from a high tower (Gower, for example, uses this version in the *Confessio Amantis*, VI, ll. 1789–2366); and in Lydgate's *Troy Book* Ulysses constructs a fortress after dreaming he will be killed by one of his kindred.

1229 The other versions detail the thieves' means of entry (in A*, A, Ar, E, and B they use picks to break through the tower wall; in C and R they make a hole under the earth and block it with a stone after leaving).

1231 *a deppe caudron of bras*: D best preserves the French (*une chaudiere à tainturier* (17.024)); in the other Middle English versions the clerk makes a ditch and fills it with lime and pitch (tar and pitch in C and R).

1234 *And helyd thare the cawdron stode*: again, D echoes the French in having the clerk cover the trap; A*, however, is more elaborate: *puis prist* *branchetes* et *petites vergetes, si mist desus la chaudiere* et *la couvri de terre par desus* (17.025). The Y-group omits any reference to this.

1255 *smyt of my hede*: the reason for this is spelled out in A*: *car puis que je aurai la teste coupee, ne serai je pas conneuz, ne mes lignages n'i aura ja reprouche* (18.013); the other Middle English versions each reflect this in part. F's *Gaza* is extant from this point, the start of the tale wanting due to the loss of f. 141.

1257 *Byrye hit in Cristyne graue*: only C, R, and B have something similar here: And *hide it in som preue pit, / So þat na man mai knaw it* (C ll. 1385–6); *And loke thow bury it pryuyly* (B between ll. 1289–90). In A*, however, the Empress later asks her husband, et *la teste son pere, pour coi ne la mist il en .I. bel cimetiere?* (19.017), and this is echoed by the Y-group (except F).

1266 *a forme*: this usage is not glossed in the *MED*, whose definition of 'a burrow or retreat', usually of a hare, seems unlikely here. It may simply mean 'a pit': in the Y-group the son throws the head in a privy (*gong*), subsequently referred to as a 'pit' in A, C, and R (F has *gong pytte* (l. 1017)). Similarly in A*, *il la jeta en une des fosses son pere* (18.015).

1273 As with *Medicus*, D omits the end of the tale as superfluous to the overall message of the story (*Than he had that hys fadir gate, / Hys fadir deth he al forgat* (ll. 1272–3)). In the other versions, the clerk goes home and tells his family what has happened. When the other clerk discovers the headless corpse and is unable to recognize it, he orders it to be dragged through the city: whoever shows signs of emotion on seeing the body must be related to the dead man. When the clerk's relatives see the corpse they do indeed reveal their sorrow, but in order to escape suspicion the son wounds himself and this is given as the reason for their distress.

1284 *lyste*: transcribed by Wright as *lyfte*, and glossed by the *MED* with one other example as 'an evil person' (under the entry for the adjective *lift*, as a noun). The correct reading must be *lyste*, however (see the following note), defined by the *MED* as '?a cunning or crafty person; ?evildoer' (only one occurrence is cited, from John Mirk's *Festial*).

1285 *nyght*: the original must have read *nyste*, (or some variant form) to rhyme with *lyste* (l. 1284). The *MED* cites *nist* as belonging to the south-west Midlands: obviously the scribe of D was unfamiliar with this rare form, part of the dialect of the original.

1286 *Vppe o[n]*: the manuscript's reading *Vppe of* is not supported by any examples in either the *MED* or the *OED*, and has therefore been emended.

1294 *stud[e]*: neither the *MED* nor the *OED* lists the manuscript's *studye* as a possible form for this sense of 'place', hence the emendation. The form *stude* would have belonged to the south-west Midlands dialect of the original, and the scribe's unfamiliarity with this most likely led to the error, compounded by the fact that in ll. 129–34 *stude* and *studye* are used interchangeably to mean 'a place of learning' (both forms are listed in the *OED* for this sense). However, *stude* for 'place' is preserved elsewhere at l. 1738, rhyming with *dude*, but most probably has also been substituted at ll. 2561 and 2607, leading to the corrupted rhyme of *stede* with *dyde*.

1297 *Hys o maystir*: the *MED* glosses this usage of *o* as 'own', but I have preferred 'one' (i.e. the child met 'one of his [seven] masters').

1308 *my sone teche*: a rare example of the plain infinitive in D (see also ll. 304 and 603).

1312 A line is missing after this (though the manuscript has no lacuna). The other Middle English versions provide no clues. The usual rhyme-word for *Lentulus* is *Ihesus*, and so it is possible that l. 1313, which ends with an oath, has been corrupted in its rhyme, from *Ihesus* to *lyf* (the scribe's eye skipping to the rhyme of the next line, transposing it to the end of l. 1313, and then omitting the next line altogether, which would have ended in *lyf* to rhyme with *wyf* in l. 1314).

1318 All the other versions mention the wife here, so it is possible that l. 1318 should have ended with a rhyme on 'wife' (perhaps *of hys wyf*). The French reads: *il ausi avenir* con*me il fist au riche home de sa fame* (20.012).

1333–1473 ***Puteus* ('The Well').**

1333 *a man*: a Roman in the other versions. In A* he had neither wife nor heir and was persuaded to marry by his friends. In the other Middle English texts (except F) the man rejects his neighbours' daughters and takes a wife from further afield: we are told she was full of vices. In F the man has already been married twice, but in spite of this *He wedded hym a wyfe sauage / Thorow couetyse of herytage* (ll. 535–6). Campbell suggests that this feature of F has been taken from the beginning of *Tentamina* ('Study', pp. 65–66).

1335–8 D best reflects the French here, the Y-group texts omitting the contrast of young wife and old husband. In F the wife's lover is a squire, newly arrived in town; in the other Middle English versions, the woman's former lover follows her from her home town. All the other versions mention the Roman curfew law at this point (D reserves reference until ll. 1413–17), and is similar to F in not mentioning a curfew as such (Campbell, 'Study', p. 73), and in having death as the punishment for offenders. The punishment for breaking this law is public whipping in A*; in the Y-group (except F) the offender is driven through the town.

1339 In the other Middle English versions (except F) we are told the husband was aware of his wife's nightly departures. One night he pretends to be drunk and feigns sleep. Taken in by this (this final detail is also in F), the wife rises to meet her lover.

1355 In A*, A, Ar, E, and B the husband goes to the window and confronts his wife before she realizes she has been locked out.

1365–6 The husband's desire to see his wife shamed in public is unique to D (see also ll. 1375–6).

1390 *adrynge*: the original must have read *adrenche* to rhyme with *wenche* (l. 1389), the scribe replacing this verb with the one with which he was familiar.

1398 In all the other Middle English versions but F the husband hears the door shutting and asks who is there. In A* he goes to the well and asks if she is there; his wife replies from the house.

1399–1400 *The godman was ful vuele my*[*t*]*t*[*e*]*; / He sowt hys wyf in the pytte*: the manuscript's *ful vuele myght* is clearly a corruption. A possible emendation is my *ful vuele my*[*t*]*t*[*e*], meaning 'with great evil' (that is, the husband was in a great deal of trouble).

1405 *And loue hir so myche*: another example of non-expression of the subject pronoun (*And* [*he*] *loue hir so myche*). See the note to l. 218.

1417 At least one line is missing here (though there is no lacuna in the manuscript). The other versions suggest D still has the sense of the passage and may only be lacking a single line to rhyme with l. 1417 (the following lines, as mentioned above, occur at the beginning of the tale):

In þat toun was ane vsage
þat halden was with maist*er* *and* page:
þat whoso war tane in þe toun
Efter curfu bel vp or down,
Seriantes sold þam tak ful sone
And hastily in preson done;
And on þe morn for ani thing
Bifor*e* domes-men þai sold hi*m* bring;
þan thorgh þe toun men sal þam driue. (C ll. 1527–35)

1430 *tho*: emended to *tho*[*u*] by Wright (and at l. 1571). The form is attested by the *MED*.

1432 *to*: the *MED* includes this form for the preterite singular of 'take' as a south-west Midlands variant, the dialect of D's original.

1445 In the Y-group (except for F) the watchmen give the wife a chance to take her husband back inside, which she rejects.

1446–55 The husband's excuse of looking for his spaniel is unique to D.

1466 In C and R the wife's lover joins her in the house.

1469 Only in D and F is the husband is killed.

1486 *scho fonded hyre flyght*: *flyght* probably has some loose, colloquial meaning here: the phrase may mean, 'she set about her aim, purpose'.

1492 *of sythes*: emended to *of[t] sythes* by Wright (l. 1493 in his edition). Forms without the *t* are attested by the *MED*.

1501 *that ȝe sal bytyde*: see the note to l. 1026.

1509 *That gret gyng hys wyf*: this line is cited in the *MED* under *gangen* for the phrase *gangen gret* ('be with child, be pregnant'), but this makes no sense since the wife does not become pregnant in the story. *Gret* may mean 'of high rank': in A* the king marries the steward's wife at the end of the story (in the Y-group he eventually gives her to one of his noblemen who, in C and R at least, marries her), so although we are not told of her fate in D, the information may have been in the original. On the other hand, the line may be simply corrupt (it has an unusually small syllable count). A possible alternative for *gret* might be *gert*, meaning 'compelled': the steward does indeed compel his wife to sleep with the king (if this were the case, the verb *gyng* would have the sense of 'to act', or 'to do').

1516–1629 ***Senescalcus*** **('The Seneschal').**
John Gower adapted *Senescalcus* for Book V of his *Confessio Amantis* (see pt. 1 of my M.Phil. dissertation, Denham, '*Seven Sages*', which also traces the close relationship between the tale in the *Confessio* and D). In F, *Senescalcus* is replace by a unique story, *Parricida*. Due to the loss of f. 144, only the beginning remains and may be summarized as follows. A knight had one son, a prodigal child who, having spent all his money, planned to kill his father. One day he feigned sickness and told his father that only the flesh of a wild boar that lived in the nearby forest could cure him. The father rode out to the forest where his son, along with twelve other men, attacked him and cut him to pieces. The story breaks off with news of the knight's death spreading through the city.

1516 *Pule*: D follows the French here; in the other Middle English versions the king governs both Puile and Calabre. As Campbell remarks, 'Apulia and Calabria, being nearly associated geographically, were often referred to together in mediaeval story' (*Seven Sages*, p. 165, note to l. 1691). Puile is also the location for *Inclusa*.

1517 *That hatyd wymmen of alle thyng*: only A and B follow the French in mentioning the king's preference for sodomy, and even so the scribe of A has either misunderstood the word or attempted to disguise it by writing *sodomiȝte* as *so do miȝte* (*Wimmen he louede swiþe lite, / And usede sinne sodomiȝte* (l. 1554, MS so do miȝte)). Ar and E mistakenly say the king loved women or took great delight in women respectively (Campbell, *Seven Sages*, p. 165, note to l. 1693).

1526 *Salner*: this reference to Salerno is unique to D.

1538 *When herde thys thythyng*: another example of non-expression of the subject pronoun: see the note to l. 218. Wright supplied the pronoun: *When* [*he*] *herde thys thythyng*.

1539 *comfordede*: an unusual form: the *MED* has no examples of *comforten* as an intransitive verb, but the *OED* does include the rare definition 'to take comfort' for the intransitive form. The only example cited, however, is much later in date, from Shakespeare's *As You Like It*, II, vi, 5: *Live a little, comfort a little, cheere thy selfe a little*.

1541 *hys medicyne*: in A* the doctor gives him barley bread and spring water; this is the same in A, Ar, and E, although spring water is not specified (A says barley water). B, C, and R do not mention these medicines. In all the Y-group texts the doctor also administers a plaster to the king's swollen body.

1554–7 Only in D does the king specify the kind of woman he would like.

1563 In B the steward himself suggests the bribe.

1570–5 The scene between the steward and his wife is longer in the other versions. The wife initially protests, but finally assents in obedience to her husband's will.

1579–89 D follows the French most closely here in the exchange between the steward and the king in which the former requests that the bedchamber be dark; the other Middle English versions compress the scene and omit the dialogue. One detail of A* that D (also C and R) omits is the steward clearing the room of the king's men.

1590–3 Only in D is the wife said to be sorrowful; in the other versions we are simply told that *li rois jut avec la dame* (23.022). These lines may be an adaptation of ones originally describing the steward's distress, which is emphasized in the other versions. Compare *Al nyght scho sykkyd and sorow made* (D l. 1592) and *He sighed* and *sorowd al þat night* (C l. 1764). In any case, the lines bear a strong resemblance to ones used to describe the Empress elsewhere in the poem, thus illustrating the redactor's formulaic style:

> Myghte no man the lady glade;
> Scho syghyd and sory semlant made . . . (ll. 904–5)
> Scho syghyd and sory chere made;
> Myght hyr that day no man glade. (ll. 1854–5)

1597 *Thow most that lady ryse*: the line can be read as *Thow most* [*make*] *that lady ryse*, where the infinitive *make* is understood from the context. However, the *MED* notes that *risen* is sometimes used with the sense of *reisen*, to rouse somebody from sleep, so an alternative reading would be simply, 'You must rouse that lady [from sleep]'.

1598–9 D follows A* in having the king insist on keeping the wife longer; at this point in the other Middle English versions, the steward tells the king that the woman is his wife. In D, the king recognizes her himself.

1607 Perhaps some lines are missing from D here. In all the other versions the steward answers the king, saying he did it for the money.

1611 *Thow schalt be angyd and todrawe!*: B offers the most original alternative to the king's threat: the steward is led out of the town, bound naked to a post, and killed by having molten silver and lead poured into his mouth (reminiscent of the death of Crassus in *Virgilius*).

1622–4 D echoes the French here: *vous estes si couvoiteus de oir les paroles à ces sages* (24.005).

1647 *Withouten* [*any*] *proses of lawe*: this phrase occurs elsewhere at ll. 533, 1871, 2075, and 2118, and *any* has been supplied here in conformity with the other examples.

1676–1847 ***Tentamina* ('The Trials').**
The fourth tale in F, told by Ancyllas.

1676–7 F is closest to D in simply telling us the old man had a young wife. In A* the old man's friends advise him to take a wife, and he gets himself a beautiful young blonde. In the other Y-group texts the man has been married twice before in his youth, but in his old age his servants advise him to take a young woman as his wife.

1681 *Sche bygan to loue a clerke*: the other texts do not include this here, although we are later told that the wife had her sights set on the town priest (in F she tells her mother at the start of the tale that the priest has been wooing her), adding she will not have a knight for a lover, because knights cannot keep an affair secret.

1685 *merryghe*: literally, 'marrow', but used figuratively to denote 'vital energy'. The meaning here seems to have been extended to sexual energy, virility.

1696 D is unique in having the daughter devise the trials herself; in the other versions her mother invents the schemes. At least one line is missing after this (though the manuscript has no lacuna); because D differs from the other versions, they provide no clue. It seems probable that only one line is wanting: when the daughter takes leave of her mother on the two subsequent occasions, a four-line linking passage is used to cover her journey home. For example:

> And at hir moder leue he nam;
> Toward hyr oune house ho cam,
> And by the way as scho ȝede
> Scho thout oppon a schreud dede. (ll. 1782–5)

The line in question, 1696, would form the third line of such a passage:

> The douter took hire leue anoon,
> And dyde hyre hastylych to gon,
> And thout hyr lorde forto proue . . . (ll. 1694–6)

1701 *nobil pers*: D follows A* here; the other Middle English versions do not specify a pear tree.

1703 *On of hyr men with hyr he nam*: not in F: the wife cuts down the tree herself, as she does in A*, because the servant refuses. In the other Y-group texts the gardener is reluctant but, in spite of this, the tree is felled (we are not told whether he does it, or whether the wife has to do it herself).

1707–8 Only D has the lady leave the remains of the tree in the hall for her husband to see when he comes home. In A* the servant is carrying the tree in when the husband arrives; in the Y-group (except F) the husband goes to his orchard and sees what has happened; in F the wife puts the tree on a fire.

1714 In the other Middle English texts the wife adds that she felled the tree to make a fire to warm his bones.

1719 *He ne sayed nouȝt al that he thout*: either a line is missing after this (there is no lacuna in the manuscript), or two lines have been compressed into this one, hence the internal rhyme on *nouȝt/thout*, reminiscent of ll. 1732–3:

> Thow he were stille and spake nouȝt,
> Thow wost neuer what [was] hys thout.

1722–7 Only in D does the daughter report what has happened to her mother in this way; A* is similar to some extent, but has the information presented in a series of short question-and-answer exchanges between mother and daughter.

1729 *as I mot go*: cf. *so mot I go*, l. 1779. Neither the *MED* nor *OED* cites these variants of common phrases such as *so mot I the*, meaning 'as I may live', 'so may I live', or 'upon my life'.

1734 [*he*]: Wright supplied *scho* here, but I have preferred *he* to the Northern scribe's own form of *scho*. The scribe left *he* unchanged at ll. 1721 and 1739, either side of the line in question, though he did use *scho* elsewhere in this tale.

1740 *kenet*: defined by the *MED* as 'A small hunting dog, small hound; also, a dog, cur'. In A* it is a *lissete* (25.044); in A, C, and R the animal is a *gre biche* (C l. 1972); in the other Middle English texts, a greyhound. The other versions have much more detail than D for this episode, mentioning the kind of clothes the wife was wearing, for example.

1750–2 This reasoning on the part of the husband is only in D.

1756–7 *Scho thout tho, "[He] that wil sp[e]re, / To haue a lemman for hys f[e]re."*: the text has been corrupted here (MS *Thay that wil spare / To haue a lemman for hys fare*; not emended by Wright). The following suggestions are offered: the manuscript's reading of *thay* in l. 1756 conflicts with *hys* in the following line, and *fare* must surely have been *fere* in the original (it occurs elsewhere in the poem as a rhyme-word at ll. 463 and 1425). This would have rhymed with *spere*, a south-west Midlands form for *spare*: this dialect form may have been unfamiliar to subsequent scribes and could account for the corruption. Similarly, *thay* may have been substituted for *he* at some point by a scribe thinking it to be the third person plural pronoun, and accustomed to translating this form. In their emended form, the lines may be understood as 'He will excuse that, [namely] to have a lover for his spouse', *hys fere* being the wife's way of referring to herself.

1760–7 Again, only D has the daughter give such a report.

1785 F includes an additional episode here in which the wife kills her husband's hawk, telling him it had scratched her.

1789 *maungerye*: cf. F: *Sey þou wylt haue a mangerye* (l. 832). The other Middle English versions use 'feast' instead. In F the dinner guests are to be both their families.

1796 This reference to the guests' *riche grene* robes, and, subsequently, the wiping of the clothes are details particular to D.

1801 *solace*: the *MED* cites this example from D, giving it the speculative definition of 'cleaned'. It is the only usage listed for this meaning, but an example is given in which *solace* means to clean shoes.

The text of F ends at this point due to the loss of f. 141.

1802 In the other versions the husband confronts his wife the following morning, not after the departure of the guests.

1813 In the other Middle English versions (except E) the husband is helped by a barber-surgeon, not his brother. In A* he is alone. The scene is much more detailed and grisly in the other versions; in the Y-group texts the husband takes three dishes of blood, one for each misdeed. On bloodletting in medieval medicine, see Siraisi, *Medieval & Early Renaissance Medicine*, pp. 137–41.

1819 In the other versions the wife sends for her mother and tells her what has happened. She resolves never to take a lover.

1820–31 These concluding details are unique to D.

1824–5 There is nothing similar in A* to the husband's threat of the same punishment if she misbehaves again, but in the Y-group the husband promises to double the number of dishes of blood in such an event.

1826 *I ask ȝore*: the *MED* glosses D's usage under *yare* as 'eagerly, earnestly'. In the context of the preceding *Sire . . . mercy*, however, I have glossed the phrase as 'I beg for mercy or pardon'.

1866–7 D follows A* in having the Empress portray her husband as covetous of his Sages' stories. This particular slant is lost in the other Middle English versions, which simply say, *Þou leuest tales of losengrie / Of falsenesse and of trecherie* (A ll. 1945–6). The motif of covetousness is an appropriate introduction to the story of Crassus, the Emperor who lost Rome through his love of gold, and John Gower adapted *Virgilius* for the Covetousness section of the *Confessio Amantis* in Book V.

1869 *Crassus*: C and R call the Emperor Cressent (the name of the treasure tower in *Gaza* in A* and all the Y-group texts except C and R (Oroysaunt in E)). In Ar he is named Carfyus or Carfus.

1876–2079 *Virgilius* **('Virgil').**
F substitutes *Armiger*, another original tale, which may be summarized as follows. The nephew of a renowned squire is imprisoned for stealing and awaits death by hanging. The squire offers to take his place in prison and the nephew (who is freed, but supposed to make amends for his crime, and return to rescue the uncle) goes on the rampage, killing and stealing. By the day of execution, the nephew has not returned and the squire is killed. The nephew continues stealing until he, too, is hanged.

D cuts the introductory material of *Virgilius* in which we are told of Virgil's other devices (a perpetual fire guarded by an image with a bow and arrow and ultimately extinguished by a Lombard, and two other images of men on opposite gates of the city, which are said to throw a ball from one to the other). D's omission is in keeping with its tendency to prune material inessential to the plot or moral of the story. Gower made the same decision when retelling the tale in the *Confessio*.

1878 *Merlyn*: Virgil in all other versions, hence the tale's title. Merlin also has a magic mirror or globe in Spenser's *Faerie Queene*, III, ii, 21, and whilst critics have cited *Virgilius* as an analogue, the fact that Virgil's part is taken by Merlin in this text has not been noted. See Johnson, 'Walter W. Skeat's *Canterbury Tale*' for a discussion of *Virgilius* as one of several possible sources for Skeat's portrayal of Virgil as a necromancer in his imitative Middle English composition *The Deyers Tale*.

1880–9 D follows A* in having the mirror placed on a tower; in the other Middle English versions the mirror is held in the hand of another of Virgil's images. D is unique in specifying that the mirror works by casting light over the city, not by reflecting distant objects: [*It*] *schon ouer al the toun by nyght / As hyt were daylyght* (ll. 1884–5); *the myrrour was so clere / That kest lyght fer and nere* (ll. 1894–5). The redactor of D may have been thinking of the famous lighthouse at Alexandria that protected the city in this way and may well have been the prototype for Virgil's mirror. The other versions do not say exactly how the mirror works. In Chaucer's *Squire's Tale* the knight tells Cambyuskan that the mirror given to Canacee:

> Hath swich a myght that men may in it see
> Whan ther shal fallen any adversitee
> Unto youre regne or to youreself also,
> And openly who is youre freend or foo. (ll. 133–6)

Chaucer may or may not have been influenced by the *Seven Sages* (the story of Virgil's mirror was common): the mirror is taken *up into the maister-tour* (l. 226), and the gathered masses *seyde that in Rome was swich oon* (l. 231).

1896–9 In the other versions the king summons all the wise men in the land and then the two clerks volunteer. The clerks are not said to be brothers in Ar, E, B, C, and R.

1900 *bathe*: here, and at l. 1925, the scribe has substituted some form of the very rare rhyme-word *beie* for the more familiar northern *bathe* (rhyming with *twae* and *twaye* respectively). This suggests the dialect of the original was south-west Midlands (see the section on the 'Dialect of D' in the 'Introduction' for a full discussion).

1916 [*thaym*]: the manuscript's *E* (used elsewhere as a brevigraph for *Emperour*) is clearly an error. Wright's emendation of *em* is not attested elsewhere by D, and I have emended to *thaym*, D's preferred form for this object pronoun.

1918 *the nome*: see the note to l. 398.

1920–8 In the other versions the clerks hide the chests on the night of their arrival rather than waiting until the next day, and only in D are they buried in a field: in A* the chests are hidden one at each city gate, and the other Middle English texts specify that one is hidden by the east gate, under the image that held the ball, and the other by the west gate. Presumably D has the clerks leave *redy markys* (l. 1926) to show where the treasure is concealed because the chests are buried in a field and not under a specific landmark.

1928 *stille a ston*: an example of elision, the final *s* of *as* being supplied by the initial *s* of *ston*. Cf. *schul todryue* at l. 2692.

1929 *A comen to the Emperour anon*: in the other versions the clerks go to the Emperor the following morning. I have glossed *A* as the unstressed personal pronoun (here 'they'); see also the note to l. 663. Alternatively, it could be read as the weak form of *and* used elsewhere in D (see the note to l. 1205).

1933 The clerks make the Emperor promise them half the treasure in the other texts.

1934 *For a sweuen vs come tonyght*: the future tense is intended here. C and R omit all reference to the clerks' claim to locate the treasure through dreams.

1937 *And I wole do we[r]for of myn*: not emended by Wright, although the scribal word-division of *we for* is not preserved. The *MED* defines the verb *don wherfore* as 'to pay a fee for a privilege or service', therefore the Emperor is telling the clerks that he will pay them *of myn* (out of his own money) if they recover the hidden treasure. See also l. 2859 and accompanying note for another example of the possessive pronoun standing alone in rhyming position. The *OED* lists no forms for 'wherefore' without a medial *r*, hence the emendation. D also contains one instance of 'therefore' without a medial *r* (at l. 2859, in a similar context, as mentioned above, and similarly divided by the scribe as *the for*: both examples suggest the scribe was unfamiliar with the construction). The *MED* lists *þefor* as a form occurring in error.

1940–57 The other Middle English versions compress the following scene in which the first treasure-chest is 'discovered'.

1944 In the other versions the Emperor and his men accompany the clerks, not just the one man.

1957 *smyte*: the *OED* suggests this might be related to the noun *smit* (a blow or stroke) and to the verb *smite* (to strike), and originally denoted a small piece struck off. It is comparatively rare, the *MED* citing examples from only two texts in addition to the *Seven Sages*.

In A*, C, and R the second clerk promises a second treasure at this point.

1958–75 This scene is not in the other versions, which cut straight to the finding of the second treasure.

1974 *Ham tolywryd a man anon*: from *toliveren*, 'to deliver'. Another example of non-expression of the subject pronoun ([*He*] *ham tolywryd a man anon*). See the note to l. 218.

1989 The clerks promise the Emperor an even greater treasure at this point in the other versions (in A* they add that it is under the mirror) before going home for the night.

1995 *the day bryght*: an unusual verb, meaning 'grew light', 'dawned'. This is the only occurrence cited in the *MED*.

1996–7 *On the morwen tho the day sprong / Thaym thought in hare bed ful longe*: the impersonal construction *Thaym thought . . . ful longe* ('it seemed a very long time to them') does make sense here, but cf. the earlier *Amorwen when the day spronge, / In thayr bede thay thought longe* (ll. 1964–5, *thought* here meaning 'made a plan, plotted, schemed'). However, since both lines do make sense, and it is impossible to determine which, if either, contains the error, I have left the text as it stands.

2002 *goldehord*: D's usage of this Old English word is the latest cited by the *OED*. However, it is used by Gower in his retelling of *Virgilius* in Book V of the *Confessio Amantis*, ll. 2118, 2128; it is possible that Gower took the word from the *Seven Sages*, since this is the only time he ever uses it (see Denham, '*Seven Sages*', pt. 1, p. 17).

2008 In the other Middle English versions the clerks tempt the Emperor by telling him the treasure under the mirror belonged to Virgil.

2016 *The clerkys toke mynours anoon*: in A* the Emperor had taken miners with him to help recover the first treasure: *Il amena mineeurs, si commencierent à miner là où li devinierres dist* (29.014). At this point in A* (and in A, Ar, E, and B), however, the clerks go to the mirror alone. In C and R we are told: *þan take þai men* and *mani toles* (C l. 2296).

2019–21 The other versions do not emphasize the problem of having to destroy the pillar's foundations. These three lines make sense of the subsequent episode in which the clerks use fire to bring down the mirror: *The fyere was hote and bernyd faste, / And malt the soudyng at the last* (ll. 2040–1).

2024–41 D differs considerably here. In the Y-group the clerks tell the Emperor (who is there with them) he will have the treasure tomorrow, then go to their inn and devise *anoþer ginne* (A l. 2110), namely, to take fire to the mirror and burn the foundations. Having done this, they leave the city. In A* the episode is much shorter. It seems the text in D is either corrupted or simply nonsensical. It is unlikely that the clerks would set fire to the foundations of the pillar then go back to see the Emperor before returning to their inn. It seems the redactor of D, having introduced the fire at this earlier point, nevertheless goes on to copy the sequence of events in the other versions even though they now defy narrative logic.

2042–3 D follows A* in having the mirror fall down when the clerks have only just left town: *Il n'orent mie grantment alé quant le mireoir chai,* ⁎ et *que les pilers de marbre pecoierent par mi* (29.029). In the other Middle English versions the clerks watch the mirror fall then leave the city.

2064–9 In the Y-group Crassus is bound (to a table in A). D is unique in specifying ground gold: in the other versions molten gold (and silver in C and R) is used. In the different versions a variety of facial orifices are filled.

2081 *I ne schal nouȝt bytyde that cas*: see the note to l. 1026.

2091 A line, or lines, is missing here (though the manuscript has no lacuna): most probably the extant line formed part of a formulaic couplet similar to those found throughout the poem when the child is led to his death, which share similar rhymes. For example:

> The tormentours wer ful rade
> To do tha the Emperour bade (ll. 1290–1)

As the childe was forth ladde,
Ryght als God Almyghty bade (ll. 2441–2)
Toward the deth he was lade;
Than was the Emperes glade. (ll. 2748–9)

2097–8 *let hys* [*eyen*] *glyede* / *Oppon* . . .: Wright also supplied *eyen*. This use of *glyede* is the only example cited by the *MED* under the definition '?of the eyes: to fall upon (sb.), glance at'.

2119–22 D (also F) reveals more of the tale than do the other versions. F is quite close to D:

For yf þou do so, mote hyt fare by þe,
As hyt dud be a burges of þys contre
That wroght ouyr hastelye,
For hys wyuys tale he slewe hys pye. (F ll. 1476–9)

2141–256 ***Avis*** **('The Bird').**
Numerous versions of the story of the tell-tale bird are found in medieval literature (see, for example, Clouston, 'The Tell-Tale Bird'). In Middle English, analogues include Gower's tale of 'Phebus and Cornide' in Book III of the *Confessio Amantis*, and Chaucer's *The Manciple's Tale*. Gower follows the Ovidian version of the story quite closely (*Metamorphoses*, Book 2, ll. 531–632), but it is probable that Chaucer also knew the version in the *Seven Sages* (see pt. 2 of my M.Phil. dissertation, Denham, '*Seven Sages*', which also traces the close relationship between Chaucer and the Midland Version).

2143 *a popyniay*: a magpie in the other versions. The bird is also a parrot in *The Book of Sindbād*, but this can only be a happy coincidence. The other versions (except for E and F) tell us the pie spoke in the French, or Romance, language.

2146 In F the wife seeks another lover because her husband *yn bedd lay full stylle,* / [*Sch*]*e þoȝt he dud not all hur wylle* (ll. 1506–7). A priest called Peter woos her, but she is initially afraid to begin an affair because she knows the bird will see and tell her husband.

2153 *Whent the*: the manuscript's *Whent* may be the remnant of an earlier elided form *whente*, and was tolerated by the scribe, who nevertheless also supplied the definite article. Cf. *aste* at ll. 180, 701, and 3201, where the scribe has also included the definite article.

2153–4 *Whent the goodman was went,* / *Than was the lemman after sent*: see pt. 2 of my M.Phil. dissertation (Denham, '*Seven Sages*') for comparison with Chaucer's *And so bifel, whan Phebus was absent,* / *His wyf anon hath for hir lemman sent* (*The Manciple's Tale*, ll. 203–4). Chaucer's use of *lemman* has occasioned much commentary, not least by the Manciple himself (see ll. 205–37, and also Norman Blake, *The English Language in Medieval*

Literature (London, 1977), and J. D. Burnley, 'Picked Terms', *English Studies*, 3 (1984), 195–204 (pp. 202–4)).

2154 In the other versions (except F) the lover is afraid to enter because of the pie.

2157 [*sc*]*h*[*o*]: I have followed Wright in emending *the* to *scho* here, though an alternative emendation would be *tho*, for 'then'.

2161 *a knaue*: a *chamberiere* in A* (32.016); a maid in A, Ar, E, and B; in C, R, and F the lovers set up the trickery themselves.

2163–82 The devices employed to fool the bird vary from one version to another. A* is very similar to D, having the water and the torch, but *.I. maillet de fust* (32.016) instead of *Grete blowen bladdyrs* (2179). In the other Middle English versions the character beats a basin to produce the sound of thunder and (in all but C and R, in which a torch is also used) a candle produces the effect of lightning. D is perhaps most detailed in its description of the trickery, including information on how the knave lit the torch from a coal, for example.

2183–96 This comic scene is unique to D.

2213–28 Rendered superfluous in the other versions (except F) because the wife hears the bird accuse her directly.

2234 Only D and F have the wife suggest her husband ask the neighbours about the weather: in the other versions the husband thinks of this himself. In C and R the burgess asks his servants, not the neighbours.

2241 *lyȝt*: this form for 'lightning' is not listed in either the *MED* or *OED*, and was clearly dictated by rhyme. Cf. the more common *lyghtyn* at l. 2189.

2250 In A*, A, Ar, E, B, and F the husband breaks the bird's neck (her back in C and R).

2252 In the other versions the burgess discovers the trickery, finding some of the devices left on show. He chases his wife out of the house, except in F, in which the wife and her lover eventually kill him.

2257 *Quod the* [*Emperour*], *'Maystyr Caton* (MS *Quod the maystyr caton*): since it is the Emperor who is speaking, Wright emended the text using the common rhyme word *anon*: *Quod the emperour anon*. Wright obviously assumed the scribe had mistakenly substituted one name for the other. However, I prefer *Quod the* [*Emperour*], *'Maystyr Caton . . .'* This means the scribe merely omitted one word, *Emperour* (something which he often does), rather than made an uncharacteristic substitution. If we look at the other Middle English versions, we see that in most the Emperor addresses Caton in a similar fashion, using either *Caton*, or *Master* (the line numbers for Ar, E, and B are those of the individual manuscripts):

Anon þemp*er*our saide þan,
"Catoun, bi hi*m* þat made man . . ." (A ll. 2303–4)
P*ar*fay, mast*er*, it schall not soo. (Ar l. 1331)
Mayster, quothe the Emp*er*oure tho . . . (E l. 2357)
Nay, mast*er*, by my hede . . . (B l. 2386)

This suggests such a form of address may have been present in the Middle English parent version. Finally, whilst Wright's emendation is simpler and smoother in terms of metre, my *Quod the Emperour, 'Maystyr Caton . . .'* is similar to the other lines in the poem in which the Emperor responds to the Sages at the ends of their tales: for example, *Quod the Emperour to Mayster Iesse* . . . (l. 2617). See also ll. 896, 1164, 1474, 1848, 3082.

2279–82 Unusually, D discloses less information about the tale than the other versions (except F). In A*, for example, the Empress says, *il ausint avenir conme il fist au roy herode, ⁎ qui tant tint en despit le dit de sa fame pour le conseil des .VII. sages* q*ue il em perdi la veue* (32.056).

2279 *That thou wilt* [*lese*] *thyn honour*: Wright also supplied *lese*. This phrase is commonplace in D: cf., for example:

Thou schalt lese thyn honour
As dyde Crassus the Emp[er]our . . . (ll. 1868–9)

2280 *Herode the Emperour*: Herod is not named in F.

2289–430 ***Sapientes* ('The Wise Men').**

2291 A line is missing in D after this (though the manuscript has no lacuna). Comparison with A suggests what the missing line might have been:

And hadde seuen clerkys wyse . . . (D l. 2291)
He hadde wiȝ hi*m* seuen wise,
Als ȝe han, of grete prise. (A ll. 2333–4)

2292 *a vsage*: in F this custom is said to have been part of Roman law at that time.

2295 Another line is missing after this (though there is no lacuna in the manuscript). Again, the other versions provide some clues:

. . . whaso dremyd any nyght,
And come vnto þe clerkes ful right
And broght a besant til ofring . . . (C ll. 2589–91)

The missing line most probably told us the dreamer would come to the clerks; the line perhaps ended with *cam*, to rhyme with *nam*.

2299 *And wannyn riches*: in F we are told the clerks amassed almost all the gold in the land and made a treasure house *ryght aboue Rome yate* (l. 1616).

2303 *A*[*n*]*t*: possibly just an error for *and*, but *ant* is found four other times in D, all around this point, at ll. 1939, 1945, 1992, and 2102.

2305–10 D follows the French very closely in its description of the Emperor's malady: *Li enperieres avoit tel maladie que, quant il voloit chevauchier hors de rome, il avugloit ne n'en pooit issir* (33.004). The Y-group differs, saying the Emperor was struck blind one day as he left Rome, not that he would become blind only when trying to leave the city. F adds that the blindness came on when the Emperor passed by the clerks' treasure tower.

2316 In the other versions the clerks ask for a respite of a fortnight.

2321–6 The redactor of D has compressed what is a much longer episode in the other versions in which the clerks search for Merlin. They have been told to look for a fatherless child and finally come across a boy being taunted for having no father (on the similarity of this episode to one in *Arthour and Merlin*, see Campbell, *Seven Sages*, p. 175, note to l. 2635 ff.). In all versions except F the scene is interrupted by the arrival of a man on his way to the clerks to have his dream interpreted. Merlin is able to tell the man both what his dream was and what it means (a revelation of gold buried beneath his dunghill). The clerks ask Merlin to come to Rome to explain the Emperor's illness. As usual, D's omission of this episode is in keeping with the redactor's policy of cutting extraneous narrative material.

2329 *schortys wordys*: an unusual occurrence of adjectival inflection, or perhaps just an error on the scribe's part since the phrase occurs without inflexion at ll. 247, 2473, 2489, 2500, and 2863.

2344–6 In the other versions Merlin also mentions the seven *walmes* here. This is perhaps an oversight on the part of D's redactor, because when Merlin does mention the *walmes* at l. 2363, he does so in a way that suggests we ought already to have been aware of them.

In F the cauldron is full of boiling lead.

2346 In F Merlin also blames the clerks' treasure tower for the Emperor's blindness: *And ye schal neue*r *wyth eyen see, / Tyll the golde ydeled bee* (ll. 1694–5).

2366 *wyssys*: the singular form of the second person present tense is used here with the noun *seuen clerkys*, as is sometimes the case in D when a plural noun is qualified by a number. See also, for example, l. 808 and accompanying note.

2386 A adds, *His heued was in to þe caundroun cast* (l. 2503).

2389–400 D is closest to the French in having Merlin respond to the Emperor's request for advice by telling him to kill the remaining six clerks: the other Middle English texts cut straight to their death.

2404 The other Middle English versions end here, saying the Emperor could see again (in C and R Merlin washes the Emperor's eyes). F tells us the gold in the clerks' treasure house was shared out among the poor, the Emperor regained his sight, and Merlin stayed with him as his counsellor. As the malady was different in A* and D, we have the following coda in which the Emperor rides out of Rome and discovers he can now see when outside the city walls.

2444 *Maystir Iesse*: Lentylyon in F (l. 1061), where *Vidua* is the sixth tale.

2467–616 ***Vidua*** **('The Widow').**

2469 In A* the sheriff lives *en loherainne* (36.002).

2470 *That was lot hys wyf to greue*: the other versions tell us how much the husband loved his wife, and (except in F) how much she loved him. F elaborates still further:

He wolde neuyr let hur goo
Halfe a myle hym fro
To churche nod*ur* to chepyng
On hur was all hys moost lykyng. (ll. 1080–3)

2472 In the other versions (except F) the knight has recently been given this knife.

2475 *croume knyfe*: a curved knife. Although the adjective *croume* or *croumb* is quite common in Middle English, the *MED* cites only D for this particular usage.

2476 *The schyref woundyt hys wyf*: in the thumb in A*, E, and B; in C and R, the finger; in A and Ar, the stomach (*wombe*, l. 2563). In A* the husband is making an arrow when the accident happens. F has a longer scene in which the wife wounds herself whilst peeling a pear.

2477–8 In A*, A, Ar, and B the husband died because he had a feeble heart.

2479–82 Only D has the husband refused burial in a churchyard because he committed suicide. D is close to A* in which the husband is also buried outside the town, but at a new cemetery. The other Middle English versions do not specify his place of burial.

2487–8 The other versions (except F, which is even shorter than D here) detail her friends' attempts to persuade her to go home and start a new life.

2495 *Lete hyr dwel al hyer stille*: Wright mistranscribed *stille* as *scille* (the cross-stroke on the *t* is clearly visible), and the *MED* subsequently glossed this under *skil* as the phrase *al her skil* ('as long as she wishes'). Probably only one line is missing here (there is no lacuna in the manuscript); this speech is unique to D, so the other versions provide no clues.

2499 In the other versions her friends make her a lodge by the grave; in F she makes it herself.

2506 A line is missing after this (though there is no lacuna in the manuscript), probably the second half of a formulaic couplet such as the one at ll. 570–1, which begins with a line identical to 2506:

> Scho wippe and hir hondis wronge,
> And ofte syked sore amange.

2510 *thre thefys*: only one thief in F.

2521–4 In the other versions the knight asks permission to enter her lodge. She refuses, he asks again, then she agrees to let him in. In C and R he is first refused three times.

2531–2 The knight's admiration of the widow in D is close to the French: *Li chevaliers regarda la dame, * Ele fu bele* et *coloree conme rose* (37.020–21); but A*, unlike D, does not tell us he was unmarried.

2533–42 The knight's wooing in D is very different from the other versions in which he talks to the lady, telling her mourning cannot bring back her husband and she could start a new life and love some other knight. The lady says she will never love another. In F, however, there is no mention of conversation: when the knight has warmed himself at the fire, he goes back to check the gallows.

2555 In the other versions the lady offers to help if he will marry her (in E and B she asks him to be her lover, and he then makes the offer of marriage).

2560 *the cors*: D is the only version in which the corpse is never referred to as being that of the lady's husband. In all the other texts except F, the woman refers to the body as *my lord*, for example. In F, at the end of the tale, the knight asks the lady if the corpse was her husband. The widow in D merely calls the corpse *hym* or *he*.

2562 D omits reference to the actual digging up of the body. In F the knight refuses to disinter the corpse, so the lady does it herself, then carries it on her back to the gallows and hangs it up. In the other versions the knight does not object to digging up the body but refuses to hang it on the gallows (usually saying he would be considered a coward if he did so), so the lady does it instead.

2581 Some lines are missing after this (though there is no lacuna in the manuscript), presumably in which the lady offers to wound the corpse and prepares to do so. In D the lady draws a knife; in the other versions she takes the knight's sword.

2582 *schete*: the *OED* glosses this as 'sheath'. However, since this is the only example it cites for this form (unusual in this sense in not having the *-th(e)* ending), and since the line reads *hire schete*, I have glossed this as 'cloak, robe' (the form is attested by the *MED*).

2586 At this point in the Y-group texts (except F) we are told the knight now realizes the lady's true nature: *þanne þe kniȝt wel vnderstod, / þat fals and fikel was hire blod* (A ll. 2697–8).

2589–90 The other versions make no reference to the thief having lost his teeth in a *countek*.

2600 F has a further incident: the knight says the other corpse was missing two fingers, so the lady takes a sword and cuts off three.

2601 *this char hys heued!*: the *MED* glosses this use of *char* as 'ironically: ?change (someone's mind)', but I have preferred '?let this alter his head', since the lady is literally altering the corpse's head by knocking out two of its teeth.

2601–8 This ending is unique to D. In the other versions the knight repudiates the lady because of her behaviour towards her husband's body.

2625 In A*, C, and R the story is told the following morning.

2635–8 This preamble to *Roma* differs from the other versions in which the Empress asks her husband if he knows why people celebrate the Feast of Fools. Although this idea is probably connected with later references to how Geneuer gave his name to January (see next note), the Feast of Fools is not mentioned again (see Brunner, p. 222, note to l. 2738, and Campbell, *Seven Sages*, p. 179, notes to ll. 3057, 3058).

2636 *Geneuer*: the other texts name Geneuer (Gyneuer (l. 2730)) later in the tale: Genus (A*, F, C, R), Gemes (A), Junius/Junyus (B, E), Julius (Ar). The form of name in D reflects the popular belief that Geneuer gave his name to the first month of the year, a detail mentioned by all versions except D. In Ar, because the clerk is called Julius, he is said to have given his name to July. Although E and B called the clerk Junius, they still claim that his name was given to January.

2638 *Schend the kynge`s´ and h[are] hoste*: there are three kings in *Roma*, hence the interlineation correcting *kynge* to *kynges*. The possessive pronoun *hys* was left uncorrected, however, hence my emendation to *hare*, cf. *Thre kyngys and hare hoste* (l. 2733). Not emended by Wright, and without interlineation.

2645–739 ***Roma* ('Rome').**

2647 *Thre haythyn kyngys*: D is unique in having three kings instead of seven.

2650 *agyed*: the specific definition of 'ruled, governed (a city)' is only cited by the *MED* for the related verb *gien*, not *agien*.

2659–60 D follows A* here; in the other Middle English versions the old man who speaks is not one of the sages. D consolidates further in making this sage Geneuer (in A* this is not specified).

2666–7 Geneuer's request to be the last sage to save Rome is particular to D. D is also unique in having the sages each save Rome for one day, mirroring the frame-tale in which the Seven Sages each save the Prince's life for a day. In A* the sages are also supposed to save Rome each day in turn, but this is said to go on for a period of seven months until the city is running short of provisions.

2673–6 The other versions tell us of his device at this point; D saves the description for the following day.

2679–80 D follows A*, F, C, and R in having Geneuer order the Romans specifically to arm themselves; in Ar, E, and B he tells the Saracens to prepare for battle.

2680 *a[s] wel as* (MS *al wel as*): the usual form for the 'as . . . as' construction in D is *as* . . . *as*, hence this emendation. The form *als* for 'as' is found at l. 2442, and *alse* occurs at l. 3015, but since neither *als* nor *alse* are found in D in the 'as . . . as' construction, I have preferred *a[s]*.

2684 *the heyghest tour on hyghe*: in A* the tower is called Cressant; in E, Crassus; in B, Cressus; in Ar, Carfus; and in F, Gressus. C and R, like D, give it no name. These various names appeared earlier in the poem as the name of the treasure tower in *Gaza*, or as the name of the Emperor in *Virgilius*.

2685 *a wondir tyre*: the other versions detail his costume: a garment covered in squirrel tails, and either one or two masks. C and R give the most detail:

A garment to him gert he mak,
Side *and* wide *and* wonder blak.
He gert it dub, fra top til to,
With swerel tailes ful blak also.
þan gert he ordain a vesere
With twa faces *and* fowl of cher*e*,
With lang noses *and* mowthes wide,
And vgly eres on aiþer syde;
With eghen þat war ful bright *and* cler*e*,
And brade ilkone als a sawser*e*;
With brade tonges *and* bright glowand,
Als it war a fire-brand. (C ll. 3101–12)

A finishes here, the rest of the text being lost due to missing leaves.

2688 In the other versions Geneuer also uses a mirror as part of his trickery.

2692 *As al the worlde schul todryue*: another example of elision, the final *t* of *schult* being supplied by the initial *t* of *todryue*. Cf. *stille a ston* at l. 1928. At least one line is missing here (though the manuscript has no lacuna). The text in A* runs as follows: *Lors conmenca à ferir des .II. espees* * et *à fere une escremie* et *une si fiere bataille que li feus* et *les estancelles voloient des espees* (40.011).

2712–13 D follows A* in having the Saracens believe God has come to fight them on behalf of the Christians; in B and F Geneuer is mistaken for Jesus; in Ar, for a devil; and in C and R some think he is an angel sent by God, some the devil.

2717–18 *He wylle sle Syre Mahoune / And oure othyr goddys ilkon*: Islam in D is portrayed with the ignorance typical of popular writers of the time: *Syre Mahoune* is called a god, the Saracens are represented as polytheists, and, as l. 2712 shows, the author fails to recognize the Christian and Muslim god as one and the same. This is in keeping with many of the other items contained in Cambridge, University Library, MS Dd.1.17: the *Seven Sages* is found alongside a variety of anti-Islamic texts, as well as geographical writings on the Orient (see the full list of contents given in the 'Introduction'). Bearing in mind the origin of the *Seven Sages* in *The Book of Sindbād*, the presence of the *Seven Sages* amongst the more confrontational material about the Orient in Dd.1.17 (or, indeed, the presence of the anti-Saracen tale *Roma* in the *Seven Sages* itself) points to the complex, ambiguous relationship of West to East during the Middle Ages. Although *Roma* is not in *The Book of Sindbād,* there is an eastern analogue in the *Pañcatantra* (see Campbell, *Seven Sages*, pp. cviii–cix).

2733 All the other versions except A* and E tell us Geneuer subsequently became Emperor of Rome.

2787–3081 ***Inclusa* ('The Imprisoned Wife').**

2802 D follows A* in having the knight search for the lady for three weeks; in the other Middle English versions he travels for three months (in B only one month).

2805 *Puyle*: in A* the knight comes to Hungary, having set off from Monbergier; C and R also say Hungary, in spite of having named Hungary as the knight's homeland. In Ar the knight arrives in Pletys, probably a scribal error for Plecis (see Brunner, p. 223, note to l. 2918). *Plecie* occurs in D in *Vaticinium* as the place where the child's parents are found (l. 3327). All the other texts also name Puile.

2811 *Hadde* [*a swythe*] *fayere iuwel*: the scribe also seems to have recognized the need for emendation here, since there is a mark ('+') in the left margin beside this line that is used elsewhere to prompt correction (l. 3011). Another such prompt has been overlooked at l. 2851.

2817 The wife's companion is unique to D.

2818–19 This detail of the lord keeping the key to the door on his person is also in A* and F; C and R mention it later (l. 3348). After this the other versions tell us the lord is engaged in a war. D handles this information differently: the knight learns of it from an innkeeper and so when he presents himself to the lord he offers to fight against his enemies (ll. 2838–

60). In the other texts the knight offers his services to the lord and the lord welcomes him, saying he is in need of help because he is in the middle of a war. Consequently, the knight in D seems more resourceful.

2821 *Bot when wolde comen hyr to*: another example of non-expression of the subject pronoun: see the note to l. 218. Wright supplied the pronoun: *Bot when* [*he*] *would comen hyr to*.

2832–3 *And by the syght he wyst hir thoght / That was the lady þat he hadde sowt*: this line is most likely corrupt, since it makes little sense that the knight knew the lady's thoughts by looking at her: rather, he simply recognized her as the lady he had been seeking. Ar has the following:

> And þo wyste þe knyȝt, sauns doute,
> þat it was þe lady bryȝt (Ar ll. 1974–5)

The original of D may also have used some form of *sauns doute* as a rhyme at the end of l. 2832, instead of *hir thoght*.

2833 In the other versions the knight sings to the lady and we are told that she wants to speak with him but does not dare. In C and R the narrator adds that her lord *sat biside vnder a tre, / At þe ches, a knyght* and *he* (C ll. 3293–4).

2838–52 This scene at the inn is unique to D. At this point in the other versions the knight introduces himself to the lord (earl in the other Middle English versions). The knight stays with the lord in the Y-group (as he does later in D), but in the French version *Li sires le fist herbergier en la vile chiez .I. bourjois riche home* (43.001), a detail which echoes D here.

2839 A line is missing here (though there is no lacuna in the manuscript), which probably used the rhyme word *cam*.

2849 F also says the war had lasted two years.

2851 *man*[*nes*]: the *MED* cites this example in its unemended form for the verb 'to behave like a man, act bravely'. The manuscript reads *mande*, but the shift to the past tense after the present tenses of ll. 2847–50 seems strange. However, there is a mark ('+') in the left margin against this line that is used elsewhere to indicate the need for correction (l. 3011), so it seems likely that *mande* should have been *mannes* but the correction was left unexecuted (see also l. 2811 for another example).

2859 *Forto helpe the*[*r*]*for of thyne*: the possessive pronoun can stand alone and D uses it elsewhere in rhyming position at l. 1937: *And I wole do we*[*r*]*for of myn*. The *MED* lists possible meanings for such pronouns: one is wealth, and in this earlier example (from *Virgilius*) *of myn* refers to the Emperor's money: he is telling the clerks that he will pay them *of myn* (out of his own money) if they recover the hidden treasure (see note to l. 1937). The example in l. 2859 is vaguer, but probably means 'yours' in the sense of 'your war', referring back to the previous line. Not emended by Wright, with the scribal word-division of *the for* preserved (cf. the scribal *we for* in l. 1937 cited above, both examples suggesting the scribe was unfamiliar with this construction). The *MED* lists *þefor* as a form occurring in error.

2860 In the other versions the knight explains his presence by telling the lord he killed a knight in his own country and so dare not return home. Again, D introduces this information in a very different way (see below, note to ll. 2953–94).

2880–90 The lady employs a similar device in all the other versions except E, F, C, and R, in which she throws down a love letter. See the 'Introduction', 'The Interrelationship of the Manuscripts', for the textual implications of this detail.

2885 *karole*: the word usually means a ring of some sort, but the context here clearly precludes such a sense. A possible meaning is 'a chain or braid' (made from the rushes), derived from the changing of partners in some ring dances (*karoles*). The *MED* includes this tentative definition for D's usage.

2891–8 In A* the knight waits eight days before approaching the lord about building next to the tower and requests a house *où je me deduiroie plus priveement* et *mon harnois y metroie* (43.011); in the other Middle English texts the knight says he would like the house to live in.

2895 *Lenand to*: this is the only example cited by the *MED* for the speculative definition '?to adjoin (sth.), ?be very near to (sth.)'.

2906–10 The other versions include a much longer scene in which the knight confides in one mason (in all except E he is said to have come from another country), asking him to make a secret entrance from his house to the lady's tower. When the mason has completed the task, however, the knight kills him *For fered þat he sold oght say* (C ll. 3401–4).

2913–23 These lines are unique to D, telling us that the knight visited the lady when he desired for a period of time and that she gave him the ring one day after he had been visiting for a while. The other versions tell of the knight's first visit to the lady in some detail and it is then that the lady gives him the ring.

2924–6 Again, unique to D. See the section on 'The Midland Version' in the 'Introduction' for a full discussion of the many changes the redactor has made to this story and the originality of his treatment.

2930 *vndiryat*: the manuscript reads *vndirrat*, and the *MED* lists this as an error, suggesting *undiryat* as the correct reading. Perhaps at some stage of copying the *y* in *undiryat* was mistaken for a long *r*.

2935–6 The text appears corrupt at this point: *yswore* in particular makes little sense. The *he* of l. 2936 (and ll. 2933–4) is clearly the knight: although the lord left first, the knight came to the tower before him (because of the secret entrance). Cf. C:

> þe erl hies to þe lady fre;
> Bot þe knyght come lang or he. (ll. 3455–6)

2938 In A*, Ar, F, C, and R the lady puts the ring in her purse; later D tells us she placed it in her *forcer* (l. 2949).

2941–4 In the other versions a brief conversation precedes the husband's asking after the ring, in which the lady expresses her unhappiness at being locked in the tower and her husband tells her he keeps her there because he loves her so much.

2942–3 Only D says the ring was the husband's first gift to his wife; in B, the ring was his New Year's gift to her.

2953–94 In the other versions the husband concludes that one ring may easily resemble another and spends the night with his wife. From ll. 2991–2 we see this conclusion is exactly what the wife anticipated and desired in D. The other texts now differ considerably from D: the next day the lord goes to hear mass then asks the knight to accompany him on a hunt. He declines, saying he has just heard that he can return safely to his own land, and that his beloved has brought the news. He invites the lord to dine with them and when the lord leaves for his hunt the knight goes to the lady, leads her out of the tower to his house, and disguises her in clothes and jewels as if she were a lady of his country.

2960 *Whilke manere and howe* [*to doon*]: not emended by Wright. *To doon* is a common rhyme-tag throughout the poem. For example:

> Myn maysters loked in the mone,
> And tolde me [wat] was to doone . . . (ll. 3383–4)

2985 *be myn hode*: a common oath in Middle English.

3023–8 The lady's feigned swoon is unique to D, once again indicating her control. In the other versions the lord takes leave of the knight when the meal is over and then the knight quickly dresses the lady in her own clothes and takes her back to the tower before her husband arrives to see if she is really still there.

3039 In the other versions the lord goes to church the following morning; meanwhile the knight brings the lady from the tower and dresses her in the clothes of the previous day. He asks the lord permission to marry her and the lord, with great irony, gives his own wife away.

3047–52 Only in D does the lord escort the lovers at the beginning of their journey in this way. C and R also mention minstrelsy, but in a slightly different context:

þe prest þam weddes swith sone.
And als tite als þe mes was done
þan was þar*e* made grete menestrelsy . . . (C ll. 3687–9)

3052 *Tollyd hys oune wyf away!*: another example of non-expression of the subject pronoun ([*He*] *tollyd hys oune wyf away!*). See the note to l. 218.

3056 Probably just one line is missing here (there is no lacuna in the manuscript), which used the rhyme-word *cam*: the other Middle English texts say that the earl went to the tower to see, or to speak with, his wife.

3066–7 In the other versions the husband is distressed when he learns he has been tricked, but he does not kill himself.

3079 *Certys he schal speke tomorowe*: the theme of speech and silence is common to wisdom literature. Although the Prince is suspected when silent, it is this very silence that endows his subsequent speech with power. The conclusion of *The Book of Sindbād* places special emphasis on wisdom, and the earliest of the Persian versions includes several maxims, the last of which is pertinent here: *Beware of speaking, except on occasions when thy speaking may be useful. So speak, that when thou speakest again, thy words may be the same—nay, better* (Clouston, *Sindibad*, pp. 114–15).

3096–7 In the other versions the Emperor goes to church before calling the assembly.

3106 *When thay wystyn wat* [*was*] *to doone*: not emended by Wright. The emendation makes better sense of the passage: the people assemble when they hear that judgement is to be passed rather than when they know what to do (presumably they already know the procedure for attending an assembly). Cf. l. 3384: *And tolde me* [*wat*] *was to doone*.

3120–1 The misrhyming of *gylte* and *pute* (repeated at ll. 3377–8: *And certys I haue no more gylte / Than he that was in the see pute*) shows the scribe of D to have been unfamiliar with what must have been the original reading, the less common *pylte* (which the *MED* cites as chiefly south-west Midlands and South West, the dialectal region of D's original). Cf. the note to l. 670. At this point in the other versions the child tells his father he knew through looking at the stars that he would die if he spoke a word before this time; in D the Prince tells of this after his story.

3134–378 ***Vaticinium*** **('The Prophecy').**
Vaticinium is brief in comparison with similar stories in which heroes are taken away from home such as *King Horn*, *Havelok*, *Bevis*, the Reinbrun section of *Guy of Warwick*, and the several Constance romances. In Version H of the *Seven Sages*, however, *Vaticinium* is fused with an early version of the romance *Amis and Amiloun* (known as *Amici* in the *Seven Sages* tradition), prolonging the story with various adventures (*Vaticinium* frames the other tale), whilst again emphazing its affiliation with the

romance genre. Version H is represented in Middle English by the prose version printed by Richard Pynson, Wynkyn de Worde, and William Copland in 1493, 1506?, and *ca.* 1555 respectively. Apparently, *Vaticinium* and *Amici* also circulated independently of the *Seven Sages* in the Gaelic oral tradition: see J. G. McKay, 'Cànain nan Eun/Language of Birds', *Scottish Gaelic Studies*, 3 (1931), 160–87.

3134 There is at least one line missing after this (though there is no lacuna in the manuscript). In the other versions we are told the man had a son and the child was a certain age (about twelve years old in A*; seven in F; fifteen in the other Middle English texts), so it is likely the rhyme-word for *bolde* was *olde*.

3135–38 These lines detailing the child's gifts are particular to D.

3138 *He wyst wat alle fouls sayed*: as several critics have observed, the child in *Vaticinium* is reminiscent of the biblical Joseph, both sharing prophetic powers, both being spurned by their families as a result and subsequently gaining advancement in a foreign country through their interpretative ability. This may have been purposeful on the part of the *Seven Sages*'s author: the Empress's false accusation of the Prince in the frame-tale is analogous to the incident of Joseph and Potiphar's wife and could have suggested a tale for the Prince that reflected the rest of Joseph's story.

3142 *A hermete in a roche of ston*: D best preserves the French in which we are told that father and son set sail *por aler à .I. reclus qui estoit seur .I. rochier* (48.002). The Y-group texts say they were going to an island, except for B, which does not specify the purpose of their journey, and F, which says they *thoght to wynde bothe yn fere / Into a straunge londe to dwelle there* (ll. 3453–4).

3147 *Thre rauenes*: D is the only text with three birds, paralleling the three ravens that follow the king later in the tale. A* has *.II. corneilles* (48.002); E, C, and R two ravens; Ar and B two crows; and F two rooks.

3149–56 These lines are unique to D: in the other versions the father wonders what the birds are saying and the child tells him he can understand them. The child's laughter at his father in D is a fine stroke of characterization coupled with his innocent, but insensitive speech in which he tells his father how he will one day surpass him.

3159–66 The prophecy motif also occurs in the story told by the Prince's master Syntipas at the end of the Greek *Sindbād*. Stephen Belcher cited this tale as a version of *Vaticinium*, but in fact only the motif of prophecy is analogous (Belcher, 'Diffusion', p. 50, n. 74). The story concerns a sage's son who, according to an astrologer at the child's birth, is destined to become a thief at fifteen. His father attempts to avert this by giving his son an excellent education, but inevitably the astrologer's prediction comes true (this outline is taken from the summary given by Chauvin, *Biblographie*, p. 70, where the tale is entitled 'Le voleur predestiné'; there is no translation of the Greek text). It may be the case that this story influenced the choice of *Vaticinium* by the original redactor of the *Seven Sages* (if, indeed, it was in whatever version was known to the redactor, something that remains unknown), in which destiny is equally important. Other extant versions of the *Sindbād* still emphasize the role of destiny in the common tale *Lac venenatum* told by the Prince (this story occurs in the Syriac, Greek, and Old Spanish versions, as well as the *Seven Vizirs* and the *Sindbād-Nāma*).

3163 The extant text of Ar ends here.

3167–8 This insight into the father's pride is unique to D. In the other versions the father tells his son he will prove him false, before casting him into the sea.

3170 *And threw hym into the salt flod*: *Vaticinium* is also similar to the numerous episodes in longer romances in which a prophecy proclaims how a son will kill his father: Alexander in several accounts; Edippus in the Thebes romances such as Lydgate's *Siege of Thebes*; Paris in those versions of the Troy story derived from the *Excidium Troiae* (*The Seege or Batayle of Troye* in Middle English); Telegonus in several accounts including Lydgate's *Troy Book* and the *Destruction of Troy*, and even Judas in *Titus and Vespasian*. Like the child in *Vaticinium*, most of these sons are exposed to death or sent from home in the hope of averting the prophecy. In *Vaticinium*, however, the dark crime of parricide is replaced, or read symbolically, by the less threatening reality of the child becoming greater than his parent. Such an alternative is certainly appropriate in a tale told by a prince seeking to persuade his father not to put him to death.

3171–4 These lines detailing the child's fear and the inclement weather are particular to D.

3182 *That no sokyr he ne see*: the other versions tell us the birds kept him company and told him he would soon be helped.

3184–90 The child's rescue is more detailed in C and R: he cries to the fisherman for help, who takes pity on him and takes him on board. The child tells him what has happened and the fisherman says he will take him to a castle where he is well known.

3191–4 The details of their long journey are unique to D, although l. 3193 is echoed in some of the other texts, which tell us how far away the castle was: thirty leagues in A*; thirty miles in E and B; and simply a long way away in F.

3201–3 These lines remind us of the child's gift: *Alle men louede hym that hym syghe* (l. 3136). Only A* and B mention the warden had a wife, who also loved the child.

3201 *aste the*: see the note to l. 180.

3211–12 Only D tells us of the king's distress at his plight.

3219 In the other versions the child himself asks to be taken.

3245 In A*, C, and R the warden warns the child what might happen if he is wrong about the ravens. For example:

> Þe steward said: 'Lat swilk wordes be,
> For, son, þou may sone shend me;
> If þou tald a wrang resown,
> In euyl tyme come we to toun.' (C ll. 4009–12)

3261 *And sayed, "Certis, that haue het*: another example of non-expression of the subject pronoun (*And sayed, "Certis, that* [*I*] *haue het*). See the note to l. 218.

3269 Some lines are missing here (though the manuscript has no lacuna). In the other versions the child explains how the older of the two male birds had the female as his mate, and this is most likely the sense of the missing lines in D. D's *Twa males and o femel* parallels the French *C'est une corbe* et *.II. corbiaus* (A* 50.004). The other English versions have a lengthier explanation in which the child says the bird sitting alone crying is the female and the other two are the males.

3270 *That* [*o*]: not emended by Wright. The *OED* cites the manuscript's reading of *That to* as an error for either *That o* or *The to*. I have preferred *That o*, since *o* for 'one' is found elsewhere in, for example, the preceding line, whilst *the to* is not found in D.

In the other versions (except B) the child says the old raven had been with the female for thirty years (thirty-two in F).

3275 In the other texts the old raven deserts his mate.

3308–9 The misrhyme *gyuen* and *aboue* shows the scribe's unfamiliarity with the original form for the past participle of *give*, which must have been a form with *o* as the medial vowel, such as *ȝoue*.

In the other versions we are told that when the judgement was given the old raven cried out in sorrow and flew away, and the other two went off happily together.

3311–16 Of all the heroes of romances with the prophecy motif, the child is most like Edippus in achieving greatness through his powers of interpretation: Edippus becomes famous after solving the riddle of the Sphinx just as the child promotes himself at court by explaining the ravens' cries. These shared interpretative powers seem the most important similarity between the Prince and Edippus (see above, note to ll. 404–7).

3316 In A*, E, and F we are specifically told that the child becomes king after the death of his father-in-law; it is clear that he also becomes king in the other versions, because later in the story when the messengers tell his parents he will dine with them the next day, he is referred to as such.

3320–1 In the other versions the child's parents go unwittingly to their son's country.

3324–5 The child learns his parents are living in his land in the other versions (except C and R, in which this is revealed to him in a dream) and sends a servant, or servants, to tell them the king will dine with them. In A* the father's name is given as *Girart le filz thierri* (51.011); in all the Y-group texts but E it is some form of *Gerard Nories son* (C l. 4145); in E, *Barnarde norysshe sone* (E l. 3449).

3327 *Plecie*: D alone preserves the French here: *va, dit li rois, au plesseiz* et *demanderas .I. home qui novelement y est venuz* (51.011).

3345–9 In A*, C, and R, as predicted, the father holds his son's sleeves whilst he washes. F also says *Hys Fadur helde hys oon sleue* (F l. 2791) in spite of the fact that the child predicted his father would hold the basin whilst he washed his hands. Only in C, R, and F does the child permit his father to serve him; in the other versions he stops his father from carrying out the task. In none of them does the child allow his mother to hold the towel.

3353–65 The child's words to his father at the end of *Vaticinium* are similar to those of Chaucer's Custance to her father in *The Man of Law's Tale*:

> 'I am youre doghter Custance,' quod she,
> 'That whilom ye han sent unto Surrye.
> It am I, fader, that in the salte see
> Was put allone and dampned for to dye. (ll. 1107–11)

3357 *gaulyng*: this is the only example cited by the *MED* for *gouling(e*.

3366 One or more lines are missing here (though the manuscript has no lacuna): the other Middle English versions tell us the father was afraid his son would kill him. For example:

> When þe fader herd þis tale,
> In his hert he had grete bale.
> Al þa wordes ful wele he knew;
> He was so ferd him changed hew.
> He wend his son þan sold him sla,
> For þat he had hym serued swa.
> Bot þe kyng kissed þam both in fere,
> And said: 'Bese meri, and mase gude chere . . .' (C ll. 4225–32)

The last two lines of these from C match ll. 3367–8 of D quite closely in rhyme and content.

3395 Probably only one line is missing here (there is no lacuna in the manuscript). The Emperor's words of warning to his wife are not paralleled in the other English versions in which he merely asks if what his son has said is true. In this, D is closer to the French: *Fu ce voirs, dame? dit li emperieres à l'empereriz. gardez que vous ne me mentez mie* (A* 52.009).

3402–7 This reference to possession by the devil is unique to D: perhaps the redactor felt that the Empress, having lied throughout the poem, would not confess her guilt simply because the Prince had spoken. See also the note to ll. 296–304 for a possible connection with the Empress's necromancy.

3405 *That let the treson make*: another example of non-expression of the subject pronoun (*That [scho] let the treson make*). See the note to l. 218.

3416–17 The Empress offers various excuses in the other versions: she was afraid the Prince would have killed her and/or the Emperor and taken over the Empire; she wanted her own children to be heirs.

3421–3 The other versions tell of the Empress's death, by burning, in much greater detail.

3424–54 The end of the poem differs slightly from one version to another, but in general concludes in a formulaic manner. D is unique in telling of the Emperor's subsequent life as a chaste man, and E is also noteworthy: the Prince builds an abbey after his father's death and employs *vij schore monkys* (l. 3555) to read and sing for his father's soul.

3425 Some lines seem to be missing after this (though the manuscript has no lacuna), hence the sudden shift to the Emperor as the subject understood in l. 3426.

3453 *euer*: the manuscript reads *That neuer in erth ȝed schodde*, but *neuer* must be a scribal error for *euer*, the line meaning 'who ever trod the earth' (i.e. all mankind).

GLOSSARY

The glossary includes only those words or forms of words that are either not found in modern English or are very rare, or those whose form or change in meaning may render them unfamiliar to the modern reader. Therefore the glossary is not a comprehensive list of all definitions or forms for every word. For forms occurring more than five times, the first three usages are given, followed by *etc*. Parentheses are used to indicate alternative forms such as final *-e* and *-n*, unless one variant is noticeably dominant, in which case both forms are listed separately. Such parentheses are ignored in the alphabetical sequence. For words with several variant forms, the most frequent form is given as the headword; other forms are listed in order of frequency, and forms with the same number of usages are listed in order of occurrence in the text. The headword is not repeated at the beginning of any subsequent definitions within an entry. Verbs are listed under their infinitive form, if it is found in the text.

Words beginning with *þ* are filed with those beginning with *th*.

Words beginning with *ȝ* are filed after *g*.

Medial *y* is treated as *i*; *u* and *v* are distinguished according to pronunciation, although orthographically identical.

A question mark before an entry indicates a speculative definition.

An asterisk before a line number indicates an emended form; an 'n' after a line number indicates a discussion of the word in the notes.

Abbreviations

1 first person
2 second person
3 third person
adj. adjective
adj. phr. adjectival phrase
adv. adverb
adv. phr. adverbial phrase
aux. auxiliary
combs. combinations
comp. comparative
conj. conjunction
contr. contraction
correl. correlative
demons. demonstrative
fem. feminine
fig. figurative
freq. frequent
gen. genitive
imp. imperative
impers. impersonal
inf. infinitive
intens. intensifier
interj. interjection
interr. interrogative
intr. intransitive
lit. literally
masc. masculine
MED Middle English Dictionary
n. noun
neut. neuter
obj. object
pa. past
periphr. periphrastic
pers. pron. personal pronoun
phr. phrase
pl. plural
poss. possessive
pp. past participle
pr. p. present participle
pr. present
prep. preposition
pron. pronoun
prov. proverbial
refl. reflexive
rel. relative
sb. somebody
sg. singular
sth. something
sub. subject
subj. subjunctive
tr. transitive
v. verb

A

a *pron.* (in unstressed position) he 663n; they 1929n

a *adj.* one 381, 2664; ~ *day(e)* on an unspecified day, one day 1223, 2149, 2471

a *conj.*[1] and 1205n, 2168, 2188

a *conj.*[2] *stille* ~ *ston* see **stille** *adv.*

a *prep.* in 1455; at 2625

a *interj.* an exclamation (before a noun of address) 689, 1018, 1250 etc.

abate *v.* diminish (sth.), make less 2374. **abatynge** *pr. p.* diminishing, growing less 2381

abede *adj.* in bed 2171

abyde *v.* delay, hesitate 938, 1462, 2413; remain, stay (in a place) 1500; experience, endure (sth.) 2722. **abode** *pa. 3 sg.* waited 2825

abought *pa. 3 sg. sore* ~ bought dearly, paid a high price for 1209

about *adj.* in attendance 157; *was, arte* ~ was, are actively engaged or busy (in doing sth.) 1194; **abowte** 1180

aboue *adj. ben* ~ be successful, victorious 3309n

abrayder *pa. 3 sg. with pron.* ~ *of* upbraided her, reproached her (for sth.) 2214

acent *n.* see **asent, acent**

acente *v.* to assent or consent (to a proposal, plan, etc.) 241

acolde *adj.* cold, numbed with cold; *sore* ~ 2516

adoun(e) *adv.* down 424, 963, 973 etc.; **adown(e)** 614, 641, 969, 2006; **adon(e)** 483, 2381; *set, seten* ~ sat down 3113, 3160; *bordis were* ~ dining tables had been removed 3023

adrede *adj.* afraid 811, 943, 1435 etc.; **adrad(e)** 188, 192, 194, 1422

adrynge *v.* drown 1390n

aferd(e) *adj.* afraid (to do sth., of suffering sth.) 662, 1561

afryght *pp. were* ~ were frightened or terrified 2702

after *prep.* in order to get **aftyr** 1139; according to **aftyr** 2650; *senden* ~ send for (sth.), summon (sb.) 17, 273, 2154 etc.; **aftir, aftyr** 1042, 1060, 1527 etc.; **eftyr** 2135, 2902; **efter** 3114; *goon* ~ go to get (sb.) 2464, 2783; **afftir** 549, 719; **aftyr** 1328, 2138; *fare* ~ go to get (sb.) 306; **aftir** 290

agayens *prep.* before, by the time of 908, 1487; in opposition to (sb.) 2711; contrary to (sth.) **agayen** 2114; **agayn** 2281; to contradict (sb.) **agayns** 3432

agayn(e) *adv.* back to a place, back again 561, 829, 907 etc.; **agayen** 1324

agyed *pp.* ruled, governed (a city) 2650n

agoo(n) *pp.* gone 724, 2388, 2404, 2552, 2568; **agoone** 2953; **agon** 3025; of time, a period of time: passed, elapsed, come to an end 33; **ago** 563; of living things: passed away, dead 879

agreef *adv. take nowt* ~ do not take amiss 53

agremed *pp.* troubled 2311

ahey *adv.* upwards 350

ayer(e) *n.* heir 7, 268, 730; **eir** 255; **heyre** 1216

ayther, hayther *pron.* ~ . . . *othyr* each . . . the other 787, 2837

al *adv. al* . . . *so* in the same way as . . . so 2868

ala *interj.* an exclamation expressing grief, pity, concern; ~ *alas* 1173

albyssi *adv.* with difficulty, hardly (lit. 'with all effort') 1559

ale *adj.* all, the whole of 554, 1148; ~ *both* both of them **alle** 1998. **aller** *gen. pl.* *365n

ale *adv. with adjs.* entirely, utterly, very 1062, 1063; *with verbs* completely **al** 2220; *with advs.* entirely, quite 1910

alf *n.* see **half**

algat(e) *adv.* in all ways, entirely 1835; always 3030, 3440

alle *n.* all things 2133, 2231

alle, aller *adj.* see **ale**

alon(e) *adj.* only, alone 1376; **aloon** 397; *hymself* ~ 34, 57; *hyreself* ~ 3074

alse *adv.* also 1622, 1651

also *adv. and conj.* in the same manner 582, 890, 918 etc.; as 1439; **als(e)** 2442, 3015; *(as correl.)* ~ . . . **as** as . . . as 36, 70, 270 etc

altogydir *adj.* everything 3350

altogydyr, altogydir *adv.* in every way, completely, entirely 1177, 3416; **altogyder** 2632

amay *imp. sg. refl.* be frightened, alarmed 1536

amende *v.* mend one's ways 1459

amyd(e) *adv.* in the centre, in the middle 151, 597
amys *adv.* erroneously, wrongly 3291; *ferde, fares* ~ fared, fares badly 1152, 2338; *fare* ~ behave wrongly 2757; *doo* ~ do wrong 1777
among(e) *adv.* all the time, all the while, continually 2226; *ofte* ~ again and again, repeatedly 1172; **amange** 571
amorwen *adv.* on the morrow, next day 1467, 1964
and *conj.* if 343, 355, 2450 etc.; and **ant** 1939, 1945, 1992, 2102, *2303n; **an** 986n
angyd *pp.* ~ *and todrawe* see **hyng**
anhangede *pp.* put to death by hanging 2510
anyght *adv.* at night 1546, 1555
anny *adj.* see **ony**
anon *adv.* at once, instantly, immediately 242, 301, 406 etc.; **anoon** 651, 658, 672 etc.; **anone** 426, 548, 552, 1228; **anoone** 657, 1352, 1821, 2560; **on(n)oon** 1262, 2175, 2436; **onon** 2327; shortly, soon 398, 1929; **anoon** 1720, 1738, 2940; **anone** 228; **onnoon** 2533; ~ *(h)as* as soon as 1066, 2086, 2983; **anoon** 724, 1264, 1534, 1601, 2953; ~ *aste* as soon as the **annon** 3201n; *ryght* ~ at once, instantly, immediately **anoon** 2237
anonryght, anoonryght(e) *adv.* at once, instantly, immediately 508, 860, 2984 etc
anothyr *pron.* an additional thing 1909
answerde *pa. 3 sg. nowt* ~ answered nothing 405
ant *conj.* see **and**
appul-tre *n.* apple tree 583n, 598
aprise *n.* lore, learning, instruction *sette* ~ set (sb.) to learning, educated 128n
aqwere *v.* acquire (knowledge) 1081
ard *adv.* hard, firmly, securely 1731
ar(e) *adv.* before, until 1249, 1286, 1375 etc.; **or** 128, 161, 691, 2781, 3300; **her(e)** 507, 943; **er** 1633, 1904; **arre** 901
areryd *pp.*~ *cry* cried out 497
aryght *adv.* in the right way, properly, truly, well 1547, 2658, 2925, 3273, 3426
aryse *v.* move upwards 204
aryued *pa. 3 sg.* arrived 3195
arly *adv.* see **harlyche**
arme *n.* see **harme, arme**
armees *n. pl.* arms 472
arre *adv.* see **ar(e)**
artou *pr. 2 sg. with pron.* are you 192, 2368
asayed *pa. 3 sg.* tested the character or qualities of (a person) 2892
aschamed *pp.* embarrassed 2312
aschent *v.* treat (sb.) shamefully 916
as(e) *conj.* see **has**
ase *pr. 3 sg.* see **hase**
asee *pr. 2 sg.* see 352n
aselen *v.* ?convoke (a parliament) under seal (?*MED*) 3214
asembyle *v.* gather or assemble (a group) 3097. **asembild** *pp.* assembled 751
asent, acent *n. at on* ~ in complete agreement 1504, 2070
askyd *pa. 3 sg.* asked for, requested (sth.) 1533
asolyd *pp.* absolved 1573
aspye *v.* look for, seek to discover, search out (a person or thing) 1552, 3332. *imp. pl.* 238. **aspyed** *pp.* discovered (a person or thing that is concealed) 1943
as(s)tow *adv. with obj. pron.* see **has**
aste *conj. contr.* see **has**; *anon* ~ see **anon**
astiliche *adv.* see **hastilich, hastylich**
at *rel. pron.* that 2143
at *conj.* that 1556, 1907; so that 485
atyre *n.* clothing, attire 2529
atyre(n) *v.* attire (sb.) 1064, 3218
atte *prep.* at **ate** 2182, 2304, 2329 etc.; (come) to (a place) 1296; in the presence of (sb.) **ate** 2851; *toke leue* ~ take leave of (sb.) 1938
attente *n.* striving, effort 87n
atwyne *adv.* in two; *parte* ~ part 2486
aut *adv. er* ~ *longe* soon 3080
avise *v. refl.* reflect, take thought 3396
auisemend *n.* consultation 366
awale *v.* sink, drop down 206n
awantage, avantage *n.* benefit 715, 1035

B

badde *adj.* decayed, rotten 634; ill-behaved **bad** 1741
badde *pa. 1 sg.* asked, begged, or pleaded (for sth.) 276. **bede** *pa. 2 sg.* advised 1761
bael *n.* torment, misery 258; **bale** *brew, brewest, brewyst, browe* ~ see **brew(e)**
bandyn *pa. 3 pl.* see **byndys**
bare *pa. 3 sg.* carried 864, 2168, 3174,

3192; had 72; produced, yielded 1701; wore 2819. *pa. 3 pl.* ~ *away* carried away, stole 1219

barme *n.* lap 2937

baronage *n.* barons or nobles collectively 3263

bath *adv.* both 32

bathe *adj.* both 1900n, 1925

be *v.* ~ *for* be on the side of (sb.) 383. **ham** *pr. 1 sg.* am 613, 1248, 1424. **arte** *pr. 2 sg.* ~ *abowte* see **about**. **his, hys** *pr. 3 sg.* is 64n, 76, 198 etc. **ben** *pr. 2 pl.* are 1650. **been** *pr. 3 pl.* are 205, 695, 1366, 2367, 3294; **ben** 1504, 2365. **by** *pr. 3 sg. subj.* be 532, 535, 536 etc. **whas** *pa. 3 sg.* was 26, 40, 434 etc.; came to pass, happened **was** 713; *wat him, hym, hyre* ~ what was wrong with him/her **was** 190, 1061, 1175. **war(e)** *pa. 3 pl.* were 308, 756, 811. **were** *pa. 3 sg. subj.* were 1080; **where** 1289. **by** *pp.* been 1071

bed(e) *n. in* ~ *brought* put (sb.) to bed 564, 912; *to* ~ *brogt, broght* 1491, 1856

bede *v.* wait for 1972

bede *pa. 2 sg.* see **badde**

behoues *pr. 3 sg. the* ~ it is necessary that you 1545

belle *n. by Goddis, Goddys* ~ by God's (the church) bell 2283, 2457

benedicite *interj.* (as an exclamation) bless us, bless my soul, goodness 2185

berd *n.* beard 84

berde, bryde *n.* bird 2126, 3035. **bryddys** *gen. sg.* 2156

beres *pr. 3 sg.* holds up, supports (sth.) **berys** 2001; *with pl. n. as subj.* ~ *breth(e)* are alive 646, 3400

beryd *pp.* see **byrye**

beriel *n.* grave 2559

bernyd *pa. 3 sg.* burned 1141, 2040. **brent** *pp.* 1144

besyche *v.* beseech 2969. *pr. 1 sg.* 271; **bysyke** 1024, 1511

best *n.* beast, animal 936, 939. **bestis** *pl.* 741

bet *adv.* better 3262; *go* ~ go quickly **bete** 1005

betauȝt *pa. 3 sg.* entrusted (sth. to sb.) 324

bete *pa. 3 sg.* beat 3275

betyd *v.* see **bytyde**

bettir *adj. thow were* ~ you would be better off 578

bettir *conj., ?contr.* ?unless there 366n

by *adv.* nearby 942

by *prep.* with reference or respect to, as regards, concerning 2144; by means of 2234

by *pr. 3 sg. subj., pp.* see **be**

bybled(de) *pp.* covered, stained with blood 807, 810

bycam *pa. 3 sg. were he* ~ what happened to him 1617

byde *v.* invite 1787. *pr. 1 sg.* request, beg, or beseech (sb.) 924, 1188, 1319; **bydde** 588; command 511. **byddis** *pr. 3 sg.* commands 321; **bydeth** 1203. **bidde** *imp. pl.* command 311. **badde** *pa. 1 sg.* requested 276; commanded **bade** 1649. **bade** *pa. 2 sg.* advised 1723; **bede** 1761; commanded **byden** 3332. **bad(d)e** *pa. 3 sg.* 656, 829, 863 etc.; requested 1359. **baden** *pa. 3 pl.* urged 2488

bydeth *pr. 3 pl.* remain, stay *1202. **bode** *pa. 3 sg.* lingered 1003

byfalle *v.* come to pass, come about, happen, occur 706, 2298; fall to (one's) lot, happen (to sb.) 890; **befalle** 2119. **byfel(le)** *pa. 3 sg.* 1742, 2210; fell to (one's) lot, happened (to sb.) 222. **byfalle** *pp.* 3216, 3354; *how the cas was* ~ how it came about, happened 875

byfoulyd *pp.* soiled (sth.), befouled 1749

bygyn(n)e *v.* undertake (sth.) 67, 78, 164. **bygane** *pa. 3 sg.* came into existence, was created 84; brought (sth.) into existence, created **bygan** 1879. **bygune** *pp.* 2002

byhede *v.* behead 1295

byhelde *pa. 3 sg.* ~ *on* looked at 1055. **byhelden** *pr. 3 pl.* ~ *towarde* looked (in a certain direction) 333

byhoue *n.* benefit, advantage 2299

byleue *v.* remain, stay 48, 2037. **byleued** *pa. 3 sg.* 3315

bylyue *adv.* quickly 1429, 2691, 2750, 3108

byloued *pp.*~ *with* loved, cherished by (sb.) 3202

byndys *pr. 3 sg.* grips, holds (sth.) fast 1158. **bandyn** *pa. 3 pl.* bound, tied up, as with a cord 520. **bondon, boundon, bounden** *pp.* bound, tied up, restrained 500, 900, 3422; *harde* ~ strictly imposed 1413

bynym(e) *v.* take away, remove 1472, 1654, 2256. *pr. 2 sg. subj.* 2615. *imp. sg.*

705. **bynam(e)** *pa. 3 sg.* 708, 983, 2121, 2252. **bynom** *pp.* 2310
bynne *adv. forth and* ~ outside and inside 3058
byre *n.* ~ *he fette* he struck blows 957
byrye *imp. sg.* bury 1257. **byrid** *pa. 3 pl.* 1925. **beryd** *pp.* 2481
bysyde *prep.* (a certain distance) from (a place) 3139
bysyke *pr. 1 sg.* see **besyche**
byspake *pa. 3 sg.* spoke out 337
bytake, bitake *v.* entrust, put in (sb.'s) charge 31, 42, 79. **bytake** *pr. 1 sg.* 106. **bytoke** *pa. 1 sg.* 412; assigned **bytook** 1308. *pa. 3 sg.* ~ *vndyr hys hond* put in his charge 2869
bythoght *prep.* ~ *fening* see **fening**
bythout *pa. 3 sg. refl.* thought, considered 2669; devised, planned 1736; resolved, decided **bythought** 1051. **bythout(e), bythought** *pp.* intent (upon sth.) 173, 1380, 2880; intent, resolved 1490
bytyde *v.* happen (to sb.), befall, afflict 897, 918, 1185 etc.; **bytide** 582; **bytydde** 991; **betyd** 2618; happen, come to pass 336; **bytide** 3168. **bytyde** *pr. 3 sg. subj.* happen (to sb.), befall, afflict 1026n. **bytyd(d)e** *pa. 3 sg.* happened (to sb.), befell, afflicted 1033; happened, came to pass 589, 596, 925 etc.; **bitidde** 1214. **bytyd(d)e** *pp.* happened (to sb.), befallen, afflicted 1838, 2204; come to pass 2125
bytyme *adv.* quickly 1287; soon 2780
bitwene, bytwen *prep.* (of procreation) between 7, 730
bladdyrs *n. pl.* bladders 2179
blake *adj.* (of complexion) swarthy, dark 60
bled *v.* bleed 487
blent *pp.* blinded, deceived 3069
blere *v.* ~ *eye* hoodwink, delude (sb.) 1967. **bleryd** *pa. 3 sg.* ~ *ee, eie* 1404, 2952. **bleryd** *pp.* ~ *hy[s] eye* 2259
blys *n. heuene* ~ heavenly bliss 476
blode *n.* an offspring, son 498; a living being, a creature, a person 681; blood *hote of* ~ high-spirited 1269; lustful 3286; *iolyf ob* ~ amorous 235; (in oaths) *be my* ~ 812; *famed of* ~ foamed with blood 959; *hys* ~ *wax ale colde* his blood became entirely cold, his blood cooled 1063n; *hys* ~ *bygan to colde* his (sexual) desire began to lose fervour, slacken 1678; the supposed seat of emotion or passion *of hyghe* ~ 3373
blowen *adj.* inflated 2179
bode *pa. 3 sg.* see **bydeth**
bodun *pp.* ~ *wronge* harmed 632
bogh(e), bou *n.* branch, bough 610, 973, 3035. *pl.* **bowys** 638
bokys, bokis *n. pl.* books 1054, 1141, 1144, 1148
bolde *adj.* excellent, noble 2322, 2333, 3134; sturdy, strong 2515, 3278; forward, brazen 1335; brazen, shameless 2229; confident, assured, certain 2660; ~ *and feres* stern and proud 308
bolde *v.* grow bold, impudent 640, 1679
boldelych *adv.* without fear or apprehension 3250
bondon *pp.* see **byndys**
bon(e) *adj.* good ~ *sire* 1013; ~ *cosyn* 1124
bon(e) *n.*[1] ~ *and fel* bone and skin, the whole body 2481, 3200
bone *n.*[2] request, prayer 275, 546
borde-clothe *n.* tablecloth 1793
bordis *n. pl.* ~ *were adoun* dining tables had been removed 3023
bore *n.* boar 919, 925, 928 etc.
bore(n) *pp.* born 73, 815, 3193
borowe *v.* save (sb.) 2742; ~ *lyf* save (sb.'s) life 1038
bost(e) *n.* noise 2637, 2732; *of no* ~ without pride, modest 3149
bot(e) *n.*[1] boat 3146, 3190, 3197
bote *n.*[2] cure (of a disease) 625, 1127, 1537; *ther nyl bee no noþer* ~ there will be no alternative **botte** 630
bot(e) *conj.* but 65, 69, 79 etc.; unless 497, 500, 1090, etc.; except, other than 631. *adv.* only, no more than, only 14, 251, 1156, 1159, 2042; except, other than 1817, 2051
bothume *n.* bottom 809
bou, bowys *n., n. pl.* see **bogh(e), bou**
bounte *n.* goodness, virtue 2662, 2962
brayd *n.* sudden or quick movement, snatch 483; rash or hasty act **brayed** 2248
brayd *pa. 3 sg.* ~ *adon* pulled, cast, flung down 483
bras *n.* brass 1231, 2020
brede *n. fig. hete* ~ eat bread 506n; *ete no* ~ 1632
brede *pp.* grown up 768

bref *n.* a written mandate or summons 3213

breke *v.* shatter (a weapon) 747. **brak(e)** *pa. 3 sg.* 3067; pierced, burst 2179; ~ *hys fayth* broke his word or promise 3274, 3302. **breken** *pa. 3 pl.* break into, force entry 1218

bretful *adv.* full to the brim 945

brew *v.* ~ *bale* contrive harm or injury (of or for sb.) 2288, 2644; **browe** 643; ~ *deth* contrive or cause (sb.'s) death **brewe** 1489. **brewest, brewyst** *pr. 2 sg.* ~ *bale* 580, 1315. **brewed** *pa. 3 sg.* ~ *deth* 1285

bryddys, bryde *n. gen. sg., n.* see **berde, bryde**

bryght *adj.* having a fresh or rosy complexion; fair 1554, 2823

bryght *pa. 3 sg.* grew light, dawned 1995n

bryng(e) *v.* ~ *to nowt, nouȝt, nought* destroy, ruin 304n, 459, 1117, 2739; ~ *agayn(e)* return, bring back (sth., sb.) 2130, 2926; ~ *to honde* to bring (sb.) to (sb.) 341; ~ *adown* destroy (sb.) 641; ~ *in wille* bring (sb.) to the will or intention (to do sth.) 910. **broght** *pa. 3 sg.* ~ *in way* got (sb.) launched on a journey, sent off 3047. **brogten, broghten** *pa. 3 pl.* brought (sb. into a state or condition) 2300; ~ *vp* introduced 2292. **brought, broght, brogt** *pp. in bed(e)* ~, *to bede* ~ put (sb.) to bed 564, 912, 1491, 1856; ~ *agayn(e)* brought back 561, 907; ~ *in wille* brought (sb.) to the will or intention (to do sth.) 568; *in erth* ~ buried 2483; ~ *adon* destroyed, done away with (sth.) 2652

bryther *n. pl.* brothers 1897

brood *adv.* broad 1725

browe *v.* see **brew(e)**

buylys *pr. 3 sg.* boils 2345

burges, burgees, burgeis *n.* freeman of a town, a citizen with full rights and privileges 2120, 2126, 2141, 2246, 2251

C

can(e) *pr. 1 sg., pr. 3 pl.* see **conne**

cas *n.* state of affairs, situation, predicament 875, 897, 1104 etc.; **kas** 3216; *harde* ~ **caes** 222; event, occurrence 887, 1026, 1032 etc.; **kas** 1214, 1512, 1837; *wondir* ~, *kas* wondrous, marvellous event, incident, occurrence 202, 330, 361 etc.

castille *n.* castle 3196

castyn *v.* spread (a cloth) 1799. **kest** *pa. 3 sg.* cast, threw 969, 972, 1895 etc.; **keste** 2693; ~ *hys syght* turned his eyes, looked (up, down, at, etc.) **keste** 1224; ~ *hys hee* 2830, 2877. **kast** *pp.* ~ *vpperyght* laid (a woman) on her back 2540

catel *n.* money 1210

caudron *n.* cauldron 1231n, 1245, 2344 etc.; **cawdron** 1234; **caudrone** 2382

cautel *n.* ~ *he toke* he sought advice 2313

certenlych, certynlyche, certeynlich *adv.* certainly, surely 367, 2714, 3415

certys, certis *adv.* as an emphatic: indeed, surely 201, 282, 443 etc.; **certes** 119, 2776; **sertis** 1842; certainly 653, 993, 1283 etc.; **certes** 2614; *for* ~ 2716, 3412

chalanged *pa. 3 sg.* laid claim to (sth.) 3290, 3291

char *pr. 3 sg. subj. this* ~ *hys heued* ?let this alter his head 2601n

charite *n. for, per* ~ as an act of kindness, for the sake of charity; often simply as an intensive, common in entreaties and requests 678, 2359, 3454; **charyte** 3119

chast *adj.* chaste 3445

chasted *pp.* brought under control 1809

chastement *n.* punishment 1659

chasty *v.* rule or dominate (sb.) 1665

chatyse *v.* punish, chastise 1839

chere *n. made* ~ assumed or displayed a (certain) mien or expression 1854, 2268; *made thaym swyth fayer* ~ treated them very kindly 3368

ches *pa. 3 sg.* chose 3306

cheson *n.* reason or grounds (for a given opinion, decision, or act) 680

chest *n.* contention 1638

childys, childis *n. gen. sg.* child's 665, 1037, 1285, 1315, 3311; **chylde** 1323

cysten *pa. 3 pl.* kissed 3054

clam(e) *pa. 3 sg.* climbed 951, 955, 973, 3178

claude *pa. 3 sg.* scratched lightly 977. **clauyd, clouyd** *pp.* 920, 984

clavyng *n.* scratching 978

clepyn *v.* summon 1452. **clepid, clepyd** *pa. 3 sg.* 649, 828, 2238, 2401

clere *adj.* giving light, shining 1894

clergy(e) *n.* knowledge, learning 45, 82, 378, 2315; study 1078

clergyse *n.* skill in magic 1880
clerk(e) *n.* one who is educated; a learned person, scholar, master 1010, 1681, 1878 etc. **clerkis, clerkys** *pl.* 319, 988, 1076 etc.; **clerkes** 19, 46; **clercus** 180; **clerk** 1900
closyd *pa. 3 pl.* enclosed 2027
cnyt *pp.* see **knyt**
coffyn *n.* chest, box 1977. **coffyns, coffynys** *pl.* 1911, 1913, 1925, 1927
colde *v.* grow cold 824; *hys blode wax ale ~, hys blode bygan to ~* see **blode**
cole *n.* live coal 2168
colour *n.* complexion 1554
combird *pp.* possessed by (an evil spirit) 3403
come *pa. 3 sg.* came 7, 189, 424 etc.; **kam(e)** 280, 400, 608, 853, 1595. **come** *pa. 3 pl.* 228, 1296, 1443 etc.; **comen** 318, 1929, 2267, 3342; **com** 1233, 2701. **comen** *pp.* 1066, 2435, 2502 etc.
comfordede *pa. 3 sg.* took comfort 1539n
com(m)ande *pa. 3 sg.* commanded 718, 1478, 1634, 2137; **com(m)aunde** 996, 1327
company(e) *n.* group 104; a group of visitors or guests 1788
comuyn *adj. ~ parlyment* see **parlyment**
concel *n.* counsel, advice 2274, 2275, 2281 etc.; **conceyl** 3215; agreement, assent **consel** 240; a secret, private matter **counsel** 1111; *in ~ nam* took (sb.) into a consulation 3239; **councel** 1683, 2840; *nome in ~* taken into a consultation 2240; *hys ~ was nome* his advice was taken 2678; *take ~* deliberate, consider **counsel** 362
concels *pr. 2 sg.* advise 2392
conne *v.* possess knowledge or understanding 34; know 57. **can** *pr. 1 sg.* know 70, 82, 1252. **can** *pr. 3 sg.* knows 172. **cunne** *pr. 1 pl.* know 46; *with inf.* be able to, know how to **conne** 2009. **cune** *pr. 3 pl.* know 68; **cane** 77. **couthe** *pa. 1 sg. ~ of lare* possessed learning, was learned 94. **couthe** *pa. 3 sg.* knew 50, 163, 169 etc.; **couth** 2050; *with inf.* was able to, knew how to 2317, 2699; knew or had mastery of (a field of learning) 1149, 1151; *~ so mykyl good* had so much knowledge or understanding 1115; knew or understood (a language) *~ on* 3238. **couthe** *pa. 3 pl. with inf.* were able to, knew how to 2680. **couth** *pa. 3 sg. subj.* knew 122; *with inf.* would be able to, would know how to 2795. **couth** *pa. 3 pl. subj. with inf.* were able to, knew how to 3084
contak *v.* quarrel 1718
contek, countek *n.* discord, conflict 1890; a quarrel or conflict 2589
copinyere *n.* illicit lover, paramour, adulterer 2172
coppys *n. pl.* cups 1795
cordis *n. pl.* ropes, cords 513, 521
cors *n.* corpse 2560, 2605
cosyn *n.* nephew 1028n, 1117, 1119 etc.; **cosyne** 1065, 1150; **cosin** 1115; *~ of hys blode* a blood relative 1048
countreth *n.* country 3318
couth(e) *pa. 3 sg., pa. 3 pl.* see **conne**
couere *v.* regain 357
couetes *pr. 2 sg.* covet 1866
couetyse *n.* covetousness 1576, 1620, 1623 etc.; **couatyse** 1864
crake *n.* a bursting or splitting sound 2180
credyl *n.* cradle 780, 789, 790, 809, 864; **credile** 778
crepe *pa. 3 sg.* crept 1244
creuas *n.* crevice 768
crye *v. on me ~* cry at me 3227
crokyn *pr. p.* taking a crooked form or direction, bending 609
croume *adj. ~ knyfe* curved knife 2475n

D

day *n. oppon a ~* on an unspecified day, one day 608, 1118, 2871, 2901; *a ~* 1223, 2149; **daye** 2471; *on a ~* 12, 167; *o ~* 1682
daynte, dayenteth *n.* delight, pleasure 602, 606
dame *n.* used in addressing a woman of rank or postition; also in address to other women 282, 292, 437 etc.; **dam** 439, 834, 842, 2941; (as a form of address) mother 1770, 1778. *gen. sg.* mistress of a household's 2206
dawe *v.* dawn 2604
dede *n.* behaviour, conduct 740; deed 1692; **dyde** 1607; course of action 1785
dede *v.* die 623n
dee *v.* die 103, 653, 662 etc.; **dey(e)** 295, 373n; **dede** 623; **deyen** 915. **deye** *pr. 1*

sg. subj. 379. **deyd(e), deyed** *pa. 3 sg.* 223, 1153, 2455, 2478

delay *n. withouten (ony)* ~ without hesitation, assuredly, certainly 385, 1612

dele *v.* ~ *with* deal with (sb.) 3442

delyuer(e) *v.* set free 559; ~ *of* free (sb.) from (sth.) 3243

delue *n.* see **deuel**

delue *v.* bury (sb.) 2480; dig 1978. **doluen** *pa. 3 pl.* dug 1950

demed *pa. 3 sg.* ordained 345

depardus *interj.* by God, indeed 1715

depe *adv.* deeply versed (in sth.) 176

deppe *adj.* deep 1382

dere *adj.* dear, beloved 313, 323, 462

desauyde *pp.* deceived 1243

despyte *n.* an act designed to humiliate, insult, or harm someone 1661. **despites** *pl.* 1807

deth *n. the* ~ death as an event 2748

deuel *n.* a devil 499; the Devil, Satan **delue** 1359. **deuels** *pl.* 2364

dyde *n.* see **dede**

dyggyt *v. with pron.* dig it 631. *imp sg.* *1133n

dyght *v.* prepare (sb.) 289. *pa. 3 sg.* dressed 3334. **dyght, dyȝt** *pp.* prepared, arranged, put in order 1800, 1914, 1916, 2173; put, placed 1935; disposed 197; dressed, prepared **diȝt** 393; cultivated 595; built 2908; *iuel* ~ afflicted with suffering 3179

dyrworth *adj.* excellent, honoured, noble 1025

dyschys *n. pl.* dishes 1795

disputide *pa. 3 sg.* ~ *with* debated with 168

dyuyse *v.* explain (sth.) 2699

do *v.* do **doon(e)** 591, 1888, 2352, 2773; **don** 363, 2376; take, convey (sb. to a place) 1479; *was to* ~ was to be done, was going to happen **doone** 3106n, 3384; was necessary **done** 2208; ~ *to deth(e)* put (sb.) to death **do(e)** 657, 2448; ~ *by* act with regard to (sb.), do to 2429, 3411; ~ *to tormentrie* put (sb.) to torture 652; ~ *wyl by* have sexual intercourse with 1546; ~ *we[r]for* provide compensation or payment in return for something 1937n; ~ *in* put in 2896. **dustou** *pr. 2 sg. with pron.* do you act, behave 1746; do you **dostou** 2282. **doe** *imp. pl.* ~ *to deth* put (sb.) to death 2091. **dyde** *pa. 3 sg.* put 1232; acted, behaved (in a certain manner) 1705; *refl.* got ready (to go, ride), prepared, began 1263, 1695, 1794 etc.; ~ *oppon, on* put on (one's clothing, a garment, armor etc.) 2685, 2927; ~ *to bed* put (sb.) to bed 1588; did **dude** 1739. **dyde** *pa. 3 pl. refl.* got ready (to go), prepared, began 761, 821; **dydden** 1949; ~ *hym to wite* caused him to know, made known to him **dyden** 1956. **don(e)** *pp.* done **doun** 1761; ~ *with* had sexual intercourse with (sb.) 465; ~ *thayre wyle* done their will, had sexual intercourse 1353; *wyl* ~ rightly done; appropriate, fitting **doo** 1747; *haue* ~ finish (speaking), be quiet **doo** 2111; *medicyne ben* ~ cure be performed 2348; ~ *to dede* put to death 2758

doghter, dogter *n.* see **dougter**

dole *n.* see **dule, dole**

doluen *pa. 3 pl.* see **delue**

dome *adj.* (of persons) lacking the ability to speak; mute 2115

dorst *pa. 3 sg.* see **durst**

dostou *pr. 2 sg. with pron.* see **do**

dougter *n.* daughter 1688, 1691, 1720, 1772; **dogter** 1728, 3234, 3313; **douter** 1694; **doghter** 1778

doun *pp.* see **do**

doun *adv.* to a lower place, down, downward 976, 1795; **dowen** 328; **don** 2168; *sete hir, hym* ~ sat down 2504, 3111; *ly* ~ lie down 2190

dout *n. for hys fadir* ~ out of respect for his father 158

dout(e) *v.* fear, respect 1159. *imp. sg.* ~ *the nowt, nought* never fear 2957, 2989

douter *n.* see **dougter**

dowen *adv.* see **doun**

drede *v.* fear 1162. **drade** *pa. 3 sg.* 1614

dronken *adj.* drunk 209

dronke(n) *pp.* drowned 3123, 3362

drow(e) *pa. 3 sg.* drew (a weapon) 858, 981, 1137; pulled 1795, 3153; went 3282; *refl.* drew himself, went 778, 851; **drew** 3188

dude *pa. 3 sg.* see **do**

dule, dole *n.* sorrow 710, 884, 2455; *mykyl* ~ *he made* he lamented greatly 937; *make* ~ lament 2557

durst *pa. 3 sg.* dared 1615, 2722, 2879,

3442; **durste** 518; **dorst** 655. **durst** *pa. 3 pl.* 755, 804
dustou *pr. 2 sg. with pron.* see **do**
dwel(le) *v.* remain (somewhere or with sb.), stay 2058, 2501, 3319; tarry, linger 804; stay (in expectation of hearing sth.) 3130; delay (to do sth.) 3223; remain (in a certain condition), continue to be (as specified) ~ *on lyue* stay alive, live 541, 2083; ~ *on lyf(e)* 1040, 2131, 2262. *pr. 3 sg. subj.* remain (somewhere or with sb.), stay 118. **dweld** *pa. 3 sg.* remained (somewhere or with sb.), stayed 3037

E

ee *n.* see **hee**
eeir *n.* wholesome or fresh air 134
Eemperour *n.* Emperor 995n. **Emperour** *gen. sg.* 255, 722, 1200, 1639, 3371
eft *adv. neuer* ~ nevermore, never again 302
efter, eftyr *prep.* see **after**
eir *n.* see **ayer(e)**
elcon *pron.* see **ilkon**
ellys *adv.* otherwise, else 2429
emys *n. gen. sg.* uncle's 1054
Emperour *n. gen. sg.* see **Eemperour**
enchesone *n.* reason or grounds (for a given opinion, decision, or act) 673
endyng *n.* the ending or end of life, death 515
enmys *n. pl.* enemies 2866
entysment *n.* allurement 3420
er *adv.* see **ar(e)**
er *conj.* or 3014
erber *n.* see **herber**
erytage *n.* inheritance 2968, 3000
erlys *n. pl.* earls 528, 3098
erst *adv.* first 2578
ese *n. made ham at* ~ made themselves comfortable 1994
euelle, euyly *adv.* see **vuele**
euen *n.* evening 1939, 1958, 2625; **heuene** 1990
euen *adj.* exactly 140
euene *n.* heaven 375
euene *adv.* directly 1984; fully, completely 1985
euer *adv.* every time, on every occasion 1824; added for emphasis to the *adv.* **ere** ~ *or* 3300

F

fadir *n.* father 226, 342, 402 etc; **fadyr** 1271, 3120, 3143 etc.; **fader** 3118, 3317. *gen. sg.* 158, 1261, 1268, 1273; **faderes** 463; **faders** 3167; **fadyr** 3139
fayr(e) *adv.* beautifully, attractively 595, 603, 607; courteously, graciously, properly, duly 428; **fayer** 3343; (of speech) courteously, kindly, affably 1432; *as* ~ *as* exactly as **fayer** 2562; ~ *and welle* happily, safely 3195. **fayrer** *comp.* adequately 3398
fayth *n. brak(e) hys* ~ broke his word or promise 3274, 3302
falle *v.* befall (sb.) 1657. *pr. 3 sg. subj. ful* ~ may it turn out unluckily for 1406. **fel** *pa. 3 sg.* befell (sb.) 707, 3372; befell 1675; came (into one's mind, heart, thought etc.) **felle** 1212, 2834. **felle** *pa. 3 pl.* ~ *in* became engaged in (an activity) 2474; ~ *on slepe* fell asleep 2745. **falle** *pp.* slain, dead 798; fallen (into a state or condition) 2076
falnesse *n.* falseness 2763
fame *n.* ill repute 3413
famed *pa 3 sg.* ~ *of blode* foamed with blood 959
fande *pa. 3 sg.* found, discovered 1355, 1419, 2807 etc.; **fand** 1229, 3283; **fandir** *with pron.* found her 1407. **fande** *pa. 3 pl.* 246, 805, 2807, 3326; found out **fanden** 874. **fonden** *pp.* found, discovered 1414; used to state the existence, occurrence, or location of someone or something without reference to a specific act or time of finding **funde** 2565
fare *n.* commotion, fuss 698, 842, 2488, 2494
fare *v.* conduct oneself, behave, act (in a certain manner) 1207; ~ *amys* behave wrongly 2757; ~ *aftir, after* to go to get (sb.) 290, 306. **fares** *pr. 3 sg.* ~ *amys* fares badly 2338. **ferde** *pa. 3 sg.* conducted oneself, behaved, acted (in a certain manner) 484, 573, 1495 etc.; **ferd** 806; got along, fared 404, 1450, 3316; *how hit, hou hyt* ~ how it went, happened, turned out 771, 895, 2192; *how hyt* ~ how things were 2199; *how that* ~ how that happened, came about

2642; ~ *amys* fared badly 1152; ~ *ryght* was as it should be 1225

faste *adj.* (of love etc.) firm, strong, steadfast, unyielding 2792

fast(e) *adv.* tightly 1792, 3422; intently 2696, 3259; hard, much 2211; ~ *by* nearby 3009

fauchon *n.* sword 1137n

faut *n.* *for* ~ *of* for want of 1152

fede *v.* feed 942

fel *n.* *bon(e) and* ~ see **bon(e)** *n.*[1]

fel *adj.* fierce, cruel 1771; (of an animal) ferocious, savage, cruel 1762

felaw *n.* companion, associate 812, 817. **felaw(e)s** *pl.* 66, 68, 77, 1650, 3075; **felaus** 338

felde *n.* a field for jousting 749, 822; field 1922

fele *adj.* *many* ~ many many 1110

felonye *n.* act of treachery or craft 3406

femel *n.* female 3269

fening *n.* *bythoght* ~ without reservation, whole-heartedly 85

ferd(e) *pa. 3 sg.* see **fare**

fere *n.*[1] mate, lover 463; spouse *1757n; **feere** 244; *trewe* ~ faithful husband 1425

fere *n.*[2] a group of companions, associates, or followers *in* ~ together 1339, 3367; **feere** 263; *gone in* ~ go together 2977

fere *n.*[3] *for* ~ *to* for fear of (sth.) 1834

fer(e) *adv.* far 3193, 3321; ~ *no ner* farther nor nearer 1714; ~ *and nere* everywhere 1895

feres *adj.* *bolde and* ~ see **bolde**

fest *n.* *make* ~ hold a feast 1211

fet(e) *v.* find 2800; ~ *agayne* fetch, bring (sb.) back to a place, back again 829. **feche** *imp. sg.* fetch, bring 613. **fete** *pa. 3 sg.* fetched 2165; *byre he* ~ he struck blows **fette** 957. **fete** *pp.* fetched, brought 1970, 2438, 3346; *agayen* ~ fetched, brought (sb.) back to a place, back again 1324

fye *v.* work out successfully 2981

fyfte *adj.* fifth 71

fykyl *adj.* ~ *and false* false, treacherous, crafty 985

fylde *pa. 3 sg.* filled 1917. **fylden** *pa. 3 pl.* 2067, 2069

fynde *n.* *wit* ~ *of helle* with the Devil of hell, Satan 3403. **fyndys** *gen.* Devil's 3420

fine *v.* stop, put an end to 2860

fyne *adv.* see **wile a fyne, wylle a fyne**

fyrde *adj.* fourth 59

fische *n.* ~ *pole* see **pole**

fyscher *n.* fisherman 3184

fysenamye *n.* physiognomy 1072

fysysian, fesisian, fysisian *n.* physician 1046n, 1056, 1527, 1544

flee, flyghe *pa. 3 sg.* fled, retreated 481, 795. **flowen** *pa. 3 pl.* 822

flesche *n.* *by hyr* ~ *lygge* see **lygge** *v.*[1]

flyght *n.* *turnyd to* ~ fled 2723, 2725; ?aim, purpose *fonded hyre* ~ set about her aim, purpose 1486n

flod *n.* sea 3174, 3359; **floode** 3374; *salt* ~ 3170, 3363; **flode** 3192

floure *n. pl.* flowers 1121

fol, folle *intensive particle with adj. or adv.* see **ful**

foly *n.* a foolish course of action 78

fond(e) *v.* try, strive 747, 2668; **fondon** 637; **foundyn** 2236; concern or busy oneself (about sth.) 3163. **fonde** *imp. sg.* try, strive 2663. **fondys** *imp. pl.* try, strive 376. **fond** *pa. 3 sg.* tried, strived 3277; ~ *hyre flyght* **fonded** see **flyght**

fonden *v.* devise, invent 1488. *pa. 3 pl.* built, constructed 133

fonden *pp.* see **fande**

for *conj.* because of, on account of 584; in order that 1111, 2297; for the reason that, because 2060, 2818, 3302

for *prep.* because of, on account of 1162, 2061

forbere *v.* forgo 355; endure, forebear 370

forcer *n.* chest, casket 2949

fordide *pa. 3 sg.* destroyed 252

forgat *pa. 3 sg.* forgot 1273. **forgate** *pa. 3 pl.* 759

forlore *pp.* *was* ~ was doomed or lost; perished 711, 881; *hys worthy* ~ deserves to be lost 2347

forme *n.* ?pit 1266n

forme *adj.* first 373, 2514

forsake *v.* contradict, reject 65; deny (an accusation) 3404

forsoth(e) *n.* in truth, truly 65, 269, 292 etc.

fort *with v. forming inf.* see **forto**

forth *adv.* ~ *and bynne* see **bynne**

forthebroght *pp.* brought out (sb.), taken or led out 3116

forthgoo *v.* go forth or out 761

forthladde *pp.* led (sb.) out or away 2441
forthoght *pa. 3 sg.* was loath 15; regretted **forthout** 2246. **forthought** *pa. 3 pl.* regretted 2701
forto *with v. forming inf.* to 174, 230, 487 etc.; **fort** 44
forvngrid *pp.* extremely hungry 964
forwarde *n.* agreement, promise 2013
forwhy *conj.* ~ *that* on condition that, provided that 1829
fot *n.* foot, base 2026
foule *adj.* see **fule**
foule *adv.* in an unbecoming or unseemly manner 484; dishonestly 2259
fouls *n. pl.* birds 3138. *gen.* 3238
foundyn *v.* see **fond(e)**
four-cornarde *adj.* having four corners, rectangular 140
fra *prep.* from 973, 2085, 2938; away from **fram** 1082
freche *adj.* sober, not drunk 1226
ful *adv.*[1] completely 2578
ful *adv.*[2] ~ *falle* see **falle**
ful *intensive particle with adj. or adv.* very, quite 316, 457, 458 etc.; **fol** 1858, 1881, 2207; ~ *wille, wyle* very well, well enough 431, 954. **folle** *adv.* fully, completely 2067
fule *adj.* guilty, sinful, wicked 681; **foule** 2216; shameful **ful** 1661
fulfylde *pa. 3 sg.* carried out, executed 2385
funde *pp.* see **fande**

G

ga *imp. sg.* see **goon**
gadderd *pa. 3 sg.* gathered 945
gadlyng *n.* rascal, scoundrel 1589
gaf(e) *pa. 1 sg., pa. 3 sg.* see **gyf(e)**
game *n.* joy, happiness 358, 1298; tournament, jousting **gam** 765; business, proceedings **gamen** 147; amourous play **gamen** 2474; *how his this ~ goone* how has it happened 410; *oppon hyre ~* in jest 1454; *take ~* see to it (that sth. is done) 2656
gan *pa. 3 sg. aux. with inf.* forming phrases denoting actions or events as occurring (rather than as beginning to occur): did 402, 428, 489 etc.; **gane** 1348. *pa. 3 pl.* 1121, 1241; **gone** 1975, 2606; **gune** 1966; **goon** 1998; **gonne** 2340
gargoun *n.* chattering of birds 3148, 3159
gat *pa. 3 sg.* begat 1089. **getyn** *pp.* begat 1102
gate *pa. 3 sg.* got 1272
gaulyng *n.* croaking of ravens 3357n
gawe *imp. pl. with pron.* see **goon**
geme *v.* see **ȝeme**
gestis, gestys *n. pl.* guests 1797, 1802
getyn *pp.* see **gat**
gye *v.* rule, govern 5
gyf *conj.* if 48, 1040; **ȝif** 41
gyf(e) *v.* give 369, 1901, 2071 etc. *pr. 1 sg.* 371; **gyfue** 3304. **gyf(e)** *pr. 3 sg. subj.* 1373, 1744, 1764. **gyf** *imp. sg.* 1564, 1905, 2576. **gaf** *pa. 1 sg.* 2943. **gaf** *pa. 3 sg.* 1542, 1821, 2036 etc.; **gafe** 3237; misgave (of a person's heart) 3060
gyle *n.* trick 174, 2158, 2160; lie 252; treachery 1346, 2818; trick **gylle** 1380
gyle *v.* deceive 2635. **gyllyd** *pp.* 989; been false to **gylyd** 3075
gylt(e) *n. withouten ~* without guilt, innocent 671; undeservedly, unjustly 1028
gyn(e) *n.* device 2033, 2674
gyng *?pa. 3 sg.* ?became 1509n
gyrde *v.* strike 2402
glade *adj. mad ham ~* rejoiced, made merry 1790; *made hym ~* was pleased, rejoiced 3021; *~ forto, to* pleased or willing (to do sth.) 2995; **glad** 3163
glade *v. tr.* gladden, cheer up (sb.) 904, 1593, 1855, 2624; ~ *hom of hare lyfe* **gladen** 3341. **gladdyd** *pa. 3 sg. intr.* was gladdened, cheered up 1672, 2139, 2784
glidde *v.* glide 976; ~ *oppon* ?(of the eyes) fall upon (sb.), glance at (?*MED*) **glyede** 2097n
glotonye *n.* gluttony 3274
glowe *n.* glue 1232
gobettys *n. pl.* pieces, fragments 1706
gode *n.* see **good, gode**
god(e) *adj.* see **good, gode** *n.*; ~ *ynowe* see **inowe**; ~ *of lore* see **lore**
godman, goodman *n.* male head of a household 1345, 1371, 1422 etc.; burgess 2148, 2149, 2153 etc.; good man 2845
goldehord *n.* hoard of gold 2002n
gon(e) *v.* see **goon**
gon(n)e *pa. 3 pl. aux. with inf.* see **gan**
goo *adv.* formerly, in past times 1076

Good *n. by* ~ by God 686n, 989, 1440, 2133, 2231

good, gode *n.* good or useful knowledge 70, 1143, 2358; possessions or goods collectively, property, wealth 1268, 2868, 3039; good (as opposed to evil) 694; good fortune **goode** 791; money 1581; good words 1767; *leren* ~ gain knowledge **goode** 1049; *couthe so mykyl* ~ had so much knowledge or understanding 1115. **goodys** *pl.* ~ *lere* gain knowledge 1053

good, gode *adj.* (of animals, things) excellent, fine 738, 1697; beneficial **god** 1123; ~ *of* good with respect to (sth.) 740

good *adv.* ~ *inowe* see **inowe**

good wille *phr. with* ~ readily, heartily, enthusiastically 102

goon *v.* walk 144; go 549, 553, 650 etc.; **gon** 1157, 1599, 1695 etc.; **gone** 997, 1794, 1975, 2340, 2977; **goone** 1348, 2559, 2606; live *as I mot* ~ as I may live **go** 1729n; *so mot I* ~ so may I live **goo** 1779. **gooth** *pr. 3 sg. how hit* ~ how it is 1021; ~ *to grounde* (of the sun) sets **gos** 1609. **goon** *pr. 1 pl. wel we* ~ we fare well 2586. **ga** *imp. sg.* go 1429. **gawe** *imp. pl. with pron.* ~ *unto* let us go to (a person or place) 2335. **goon** *pa. 3 pl.* went 2017. **goon** *pp.* gone 161, 1229, 2024, 3061; **goo** 756; **go** 2128; *how his this game* ~ how has it happened **goone** 410

goon *pa. 3 pl. aux. with inf.* see **gan**

gospel *n.* words or statements that are as true as the gospel 1955

goune *v.* stare 1365. **gounde** *pp.* 1376

grace *n.* see **male grace**

gras *n.* plant, herb (of healing power) 1123, 1125, 1129, 1139

grauntit *pa. 3 sg.* granted 546

grestest *adj.* greatest 2378

gret *adj.* ?great 1509n

gretis *pr. 3 sg.* greets 320. **grette** *pa. 1 sg.* 433. **gret(e)** *pa. 3 sg.* 1011, 2103, 2328, 2521, 2856

grette *adj.* great (in degree), much 602, 871; big, large in size 610

grettir *pron.* larger, bigger (one) 585

greue *v.* injure (sb.) 2273; make (sb.) sorrowful, cause grief to 2470. **greuyd** *pa. 3 sg.* grieved 3224

gryse *v.* shudder, be frightened 2672

grote *n. euery* ~ every part 2069

grounde *n.* the bed of a pond **gronde** 885; *gos to* ~ (of the sun) sets 1609; *ȝeden to* ~ were defeated 2729

growe *pp.* grown 2882

gune *pa. 3 pl. aux. with inf.* see **gan**

Ȝ

ȝae *adv.* see **ȝe, ȝae**

ȝal *pa. 3 sg.* yelled, cried in pain 801

ȝare *adj.* ready, prepared 305

ȝare *adv.* quickly, without delay 289; (in rhyme) well 93

ȝate *n.* gate of a city 1296, 2417; gate 1343; *palyes* ~ palace gate 2095

ȝe *sub. pron. 2 sg.* you 88, 352, 913 etc.

ȝe *sub. pron. 2 pl.* you 238, 309, 359 etc.

ȝe, ȝae *adv.* yes 2375, 2525

ȝede *v.* be (in a certain place) 215. **ȝed(e)** *pa. 3 sg.* went 794, 943, 1784 etc. **ȝeden** *pa. 1 pl.* went 819. **ȝede** *pa. 3 pl.* went 391, 1417, 1962; ~ *to grounde* **ȝeden** see **grounde**

ȝelle *pr. 3 pl.* (of certain birds or animals) emit a loud cry, either as their actual utterance or when hurt or from rage 3242. *pr. p.* 805. **ȝal** *pa. 3 sg.* 801

ȝeme *v.* take care of, have charge of, have in keeping 99; give heed or attention to **geme** 100

ȝerd *n.* yard 795

ȝer(e) *n.* year; *as pl. with num.* 33, 161, 675, 2849

ȝif *conj.* see **gyf**

ȝyt *adv.* nevertheless, in spite of that 961, 1081, 1727, 2936; **ȝit** 2588; up to now, so far 1518; so soon as now 1599; again, in addition 1730; still 1734; also 3262

ȝong(e) *pron.* young one 618, 3305

ȝong(e) *adj.* young 83, 622, 732 etc.

ȝore *n.* see **hore** *n.*[2]

ȝore *adv.* for a long time 2151

ȝoure *poss. pron. 2 sg.* your 2338

ȝoure *poss. pron. 2 pl.* your 104, 240, 541 etc.

ȝow *obj. pron. 2 sg.* you 1020, 1447, 3356; **ȝou** 97; to you 1014

ȝow *obj. pron. 2 pl.* you 320, 321, 323 etc.; **ȝou** 369; **ȝoue** 2014; to you 106; **ȝou** 108

H

hadde *pa. 3 sg.* ~ *wondir* were greatly surprised, marvelled 3152. **hadde(n)** *pa. 3 pl.* ~ *wondire, wondyr* 526, 871
hagge *n.* age 732n
hayther *pron.* see **ayther, hayther**
haythyn, heythyn *adj.* heathen 2647, 2653, 2672, 2700
halden *v.* see **holde(n)**
half *n.* half **alf** 3231; *hon ilce* ~, *in ilce* ~ on each (every) side, in every direction, everywhere 153, 187; *on ilke* ~ 2564
halpe *pa. 3 sg.* helped 3051. **holpen, holpyn** *pa. 3 pl.* 2656, 3429
hals *n. by my* ~ by my neck 2221
ham *pr. 1 sg.* see **be**
ham *obj. pron. 3 pl.* them 168, 310, 545 etc.; **hom** 2302, 2486, 2938, 3341; **hem** 110, 1901, 2721; **hym** 1220
ham(e) *adv.* see **hom**
hange *pa. 3 pl.* were hanging 2545
happe *n.* luck, fortune 1744, 1764
hardylich *adv.* at once, immediately 3249, 3299
hare *poss. pron. 3 pl.* their 10, 111, 236 etc.; **hyr** 2314, 3357; **hir** 526; **or** 1354; **har** 3159; **hire** 3358
harlyche *adv. bothe* ~ *and latte* at all hours 600; ~ *or late* at any time **arly** 2373
harme, arme *n. the more* ~ *was* more was the pity 857, 1138; *hadde no* ~ sustained no harm or injuries 865
harmyd *adj.* armed 2726
has *adv. and conj.* as 490, 954, 1264 etc.; **ase** 38; as if, as though 2184; **as** 1235, 1885, 2692; in the same way as, just as **as** 2686; **as(s)tow** *with obj. pron.* as you 1549, 1761; **aste** *contr. of* as the 180n, 701n; *anon, anoon* ~ **(h)as, aste** see **anon**
hase *pr. 2 sg.* have 229, 266, 2965, 3258, 3375. **ase** *pr. 3 sg.* 1092; **haues** 3075
hastilich, hastylich *adv.* speedily, quickly 317, 1008, 1255, 1379, 1553; **hastilyche** 1263; **hastylych** 1695; **astiliche** 3335
hatte *pa. 3 sg.* see **hote**
he *n.* ~ *and lowe* people of all conditions, everyone 3202
he *pron.* see **ho**
he *adj.* see **hye**
hed(e) *n.*[1] *tak* ~ take heed, take notice 486; *to* ~ took heed 1432n; *take* ~ taken heed (of sth.) 2426; *nam* ~ took notice, saw 1710; paid attention to (sb. or sth.) **heed** 279
hede *n.*[2] see **heued**
hee *n.* eye 2094, 2830, 2877; **hye** 186, 663; **ee** 1404; **heye** 2440. **heyn** *pl.* 350
hee, heye, heygh(e), heyer *adv.* see **hygh(e)**
hegh, heye *adj.* see **hye**
heyre *n.* see **ayer(e)**
heythyn *adj.* see **haythyn**
helde *n.* old age 1158
heldest *n.* eldest member of a group 25
heldir, heldyr *pa. 3 sg. with obj. pron.* see **holde(n)**
hele *n.* cure, recovery 1092, 2319
hel(e), helle *v.*[1] heal 1091, 1547, 2316. **helyd** *pa. 3 sg.* 1108
hele *v.*[2] keep secret 1111. **helyd** *pa. 3 sg.* hid, concealed 1234. **helyd** *pp.* kept silent 1458
hem *obj. pron. 3 pl.* see **ham**
hende *n.* end 2886
hende, hynd *adj.* gracious, courteous 3002, 3045; helpful 3184
hendlych *adv.* graciously, courteously 2856
hent *pa. 3 sg.* grasped, took 866. *pp.* captured 1248, 1460; received 1658; ~ *harme* suffered harm 1401
heraudis *n. gen. pl.* heralds' 773
herber *n.* arbour 329, 595, 597, 1698; **erber** 1713
herborowe *imp. sg.* house, lodge 1431
herdeman *n.* herdsman *936
here *v.* hear 32, 120, 264 etc; **hyre** 3298; **heere** 132; *as ȝe mowe* ~ as you will hear 2645; **hyre** 457. **hyre** *imp. sg.* 2110. **herdyn** *pa. 3 pl.* 758
her(e) *adv.* see **ar(e)**
hereout *adv.* outside 1451
herkyn *imp. sg.* listen attentively, take heed 1675
hert *n.* the mind, understanding 44. *gen. sg.* ~ *blode* heart's blood 1766
hest *n.*[1] ~ *and weste* in all directions, everywhere 3276
hest(e) *n.*[2] command 518, 1639
het *pp.* see **hote**
hete *n.* (of emotions etc.) intensity, ardour 2496
hete *v.* ~ *brede* see **brede**

heued *n.* head 504, 2601; (in oaths and asseverations) as equivalent to life **hede** *by myn* ~ by my head 1164, 2591; *so I euer broke myn* ~, *so euer I broke my* ~ so may I keep (or have the use of) my head 1850, 2619; *for the* ~ *that I bere* by my head 3397

heuene *n.* see **euen**

heuene *n.* ~ *blys* see **blys**

heuen-riche *n.* kingdom of heaven 3450

hew *v.* tear with the teeth or tusks 965

hidyr to *adv.* to the present time, until now 95

hye *n.*[1] haste 1357

hye *n.*[2] see **hee**

hye *adj.* (of an ability, power) powerful **hyghe** 3135; *on* ~ up high, above 3125, 3181; **heye** 2988; **hygh** 3032; *of* ~ *lynage* noble 243; **he** 1556; *of* ~ *bloode* of noble rank, highborn **hegh** 1580; *of* ~ *blode* **hyghe** see **blode**

hye *v.* hasten, hurry 489, 841, 1553, 1966, 3165. *imp. sg.* 1914, 2602, 2900. **hyhyde, hyed** *pa. 3 sg.* 952n, 3108. **hiede** *pa. 3 pl.* 803; ~ *that* worked quickly (that sth. might be done) **hyeden** 393

hye *adv.* see **hygh(e)**

hyer *adv.* see **hire, hyre**

hygh(e) *adj.* see **hye**

hygh(e) *adv.* high **heye** 1725; **heyghe** 1881; high up **hye** 2878; *on* ~ high, far up, above, aloft 762, 809, 855 etc.; **heygh** 2873; *an* ~ **heygh** 2887; *on* ~ in heaven **hye** 3175; *low . . .* ~ high and low, everywhere **hee** 185. **heyer** *comp.* higher 1882

hight, hyght *pa. 3 sg., pp.* see **hote**

hilka *adj. in* ~ *syde* see **syde**

hym *refl. pron. 3 sg. masc.* himself 778n, 851, 975 etc.

hym *obj. pron. 3 sg. neut.* it 609n, 611, 633

hym *obj. pron. 3 pl.* see **ham**

hymp(e) *n.* tree 1697, 1704, 1724

hynd *adj.* see **hende, hynd**

hyng *pr. 3 pl.* hang 514. **angyd** *pp.*~ *and todrawe* hanged and dismembered (sb.) as a punishment, hanged and pulled apart 1611

hir(e), hyr *poss. pron. 3 pl.* see **hare**

hire *obj. pron. 3 sg. fem.* her 240, 257, 278 etc.; **hir** 248, 701, 828 etc.; **hyre** 278, 425, 573 etc.; **hyr** 1703, 1812, 1855 etc.; **hirre** 249

hire *poss. pron. 3 sg. fem.* her 278, 294, 479 etc.; **hir** 429, 431, 473 etc.; **hyre** 472, 484, 487 etc.; **hyr** 488, 684, 1368

hyre *v.* see **here**

hire, hyre *adv.* here 869, 1098, 1500, 3253, 3372; **hyer** 2495; *lo* ~ see here, behold, see 493

hyrefore *adv.* for this reason 3292

hyreseluene, hireselue *pron.* herself 1083, 2497

hys *poss. pron.* its 1915

his, hys *pr. 3 sg.* see **be**

hyt, hit *sub. and obj. pron. 3 sg. neut.* it 207, 218, 230 etc.; ~ *was* there was 928, 1676, 2141, 2289; ~ *his* there is 1254; as a subject of a *v.*: it, used with reference to a man ~ *hys* 1457

ho *sub. pron. 3 sg. fem.* she 472, 491, 568 etc.; **he** 827, 1703, 1704 etc.

hode, hoode *n.* hood 945n, 3169; *be myn* ~ by my hat, on my head (I swear) 2985n

hold(e) *pron.* old 619, 620

holde *adj.* old 623, 733, 1161 etc.; **hold** 2669

holde *n.* ~ *hor* grey, or old wood 929

holde(n) *v.* keep (a promise, pledge, an agreement, oath) 3258; ?govern (people) by law (?*MED*) 3447; hold, keep (sb.) in specified place **halden** 1233; ~ *lyf* preserve (sb.'s) life 1817; ~ *on lyue* keep (sb.) alive 2751. **hold(e)** *pr. 1 sg.* consider, think 269, 375. *pr. 3. sg. subj. refl.* ~ *hym stille* remain silent 1690. **heldyr, heldir** *pa. 3 sg. with obj. pron.* kept her 1600; *refl.* remained (in a state or condition) 1835. **holden** *pp. be* ~ be indebted (to sb.) 108

hole, ol *adj.* ~ *and sound(e)* completely healthy and well 869, 1108

hollys *n. pl.* eye sockets 2067

holpen, holpyn *pa. 3 pl.* see **halpe**

hom *n. at* ~ at home 1199

hom *obj. pron. 3 pl.* see **ham**

hom *adv.* (come or go) to one's home 286, 1112, 1140 etc; **ham(e)** 1264, 2145, 2197

hon *adj.* see **oon, o**

honde *n. brynge to* ~ see **bryng(e)**; *token on* ~ see **take**

hondis *n. pl.*[1] hounds 1752

hondis, hondys *n. pl.*[2] *hyr ~ forto wryng, hir, hyr ~ wronge* see **wryng**
honour *n. doost, dyde ~* honour, honoured (sb.) 531, 3435; *for gret ~* out of great honour, respect 433
hoppen *pa. 3 pl.* hoped 1963
hor *adj. holde ~* see **holde**
horchard *n.* orchard 882
hore *n.*[1] whore 1430
hore *n.*[2] *by God(d)ys ~* by God's mercy 1238, 2220, 2431; *thy ~* grant your help, favour **ȝore** 1493; *ask ~* beg for mercy **ȝore** 1826n
horlyng(e) *n.* fornicator, adulterer 2187, 2196, 2228
hoste *n.*[1] army 2638, 2733
hoste *n.*[2] host, innkeeper 2840
hote *adj. ~ of blode* see **blode**
hote *pr. 1 sg.* command 511. **hatte** *pa. 3 sg.* was named, called 223, 1878; **hight** 6. **hoten, hotyn** *pp.* named, called 92, 2323, 2444, 2752; promised, assured **hyght** 3258; **het** 3261
hoth *n.* oath 3102
hou *adv.* how 2192, 2269, 2412
hous(e) *n.* place of habitation, dwelling place, abode 2815; *to ~* into one's house 1370; *hadde hys ~ to kepe* managed the affairs of his household **hows** 1551
houede *pa. 3 sg.* lingered 2825; was situated **houyd** 2508
hurdom *n.* whoredom 1414

I

yfere, ifere *adv.* together 115, 451, 456 etc.
ile *n.* island 3140
ilyche *adj. euer ~* constant 3451
ilke *adj.* each, every 154, 581, 2564 etc.; **ilc(e)** 153, 179, 187, 384; **ilka** 1055; (as intens. with **this, that**) same, very 288, 1742, 1758 etc.; **ilk** 1917; *in ilke-a syde, in ilce-a syde, in hilka syde* see **syde**
ilkon *pron.* each one, every single one 219, 376, 383 etc.; **ilkone** 58, 106, 1586, 1795; **ilcon** 170, 3075; **ilcoon** 501; **elcon** 746; **ilchon** 2090
ylore *pp.* see **lese** *v*
in *n.* inn 1960, 2032, 2038; *took hys ~* found lodgings **ine** 2839; *hys ~ was nome* his lodgings were taken 3337
inne *adv.* inside 1409, 1427, 1452; on **in** 3141
ynome *pp.* see **nam(e)**
ynow(e), inowe *adj.* plenty of, abundant 229, 972, 1564, 2881, 3283; **inoughe** 969; enough, sufficient 615
inowe, ynowe *adv.* very much 850; enough, sufficiently **inowhe** 1565; *good ~* perfectly, very well 413; *god ~* all right 3036
inquere *v.* inquire 3324. **inqueryd** *pp.* inquired, investigated 901
inred *adj.* (of complexion) very ruddy 61
into *prep.* within 1388
iolyf *adj. ~ ob blode* see **blode**
iornay, iorne *n. out on ~ or twae, out a ~ or twae* away (on a journey of) one or two days 2150, 2410
is *poss. pron. 3 sg. masc.* his 4, 9, 44, 1875; **ys** 1766
ysped *pp.* see **spede**
isti *pr. 3 sg. with pron.* is thy 869
iuggement *n.* a penalty imposed by a court or someone in a position of authority, punishment 523, 1415, 1468 etc.; trial 3376; *passe thourgh ~* undergo trial 537; *passe by ~* 1461
iustay *adv.* yesterday 1973
iustis, iustys *n. pl.* jousts 802, 819
iuwel, iuel *n.* jewel 736, 2811, 2946
ivel *n.* disease, sickness 1521, 1522, 1535
iuel *adj.* hard, difficult 2809; *~ happe* ill fortune, bad luck 1744
iuel *adv. ~ dyght* see **dyght**
yuen-leues *n. pl.* ivy leaves 181
iwys *adv.* indeed, surely 75, 382, 444 etc.; **ywys** 220, 2708, 2845; **iwis** 283
ywroght *pp.* see **wyrke**

K

kam(e) *pa. 3 sg.* see **come**
kare *n.* anxiety, concern 1275; fear, dread 1420
karf *pa. 3 sg.* carved 3011
karole *n.* ?plait, braid (?*MED*) 2885n
kas *n.* see **cas**
kast *pp.* see **castyn**
kende *pa. 3 sg.* knew 2875
kenet *n.* small hunting dog 1740n, 1743, 1745, 1762
kepe *v.* abide by (sth. agreed to) 385; *hadde hys hows to ~* see **hous(e)**
kernelde *pp.* crenellated 2842
kest(e) *pa. 3 sg.* see **castyn**
kyd(e) *pp.* made known, revealed 1933; *~ was callid* his name was 28

kyng(e) *n. gen. sg.* king's 1058, 1070, 1532
kyrke *n.* church 1682
kyrkeȝarde *n.* churchyard 2480
kypyng *n. in* ~ in or into (sb.'s) personal charge or care 86
knaue *n.* male servant 2161n
knyght *n. pl.* knights 744n
knyt *pa. 3 sg.* fastened, tied 1262. *pp.* 181; (of a knot) tied 2993; fastened up, shut up **cnyt** 677
knote *n.* knot 2993
know(e) *v.* recognize (sth. or sb.), identify 1525, 2795, 2984
knowlech *n.* familiarity with things, places 3194
knowleched *pa. 3 sg.* acknowledged 3419

L

lad(e), ladde, laddyn *pa. 3 sg., pa. 3 pl., pp.* see **ledde**
lafte *pa. 3 sg.* see **leue** *v.*[3]
layed *pa. 3 sg.* ~ *on* gave (sth. to sb.) 3137; **layden** *contr. of* **layd on** struck (blows) 958
laysyr *n.* opportunity 1256
laytyd, layt *pa. 3 sg.* flashed lightning 2226, 2232
lake *n.* fault, misdeed, sin 2144
lange *adv.* long, a long time 1286, 1378, 2654, 2781. **langer** *comp.* longer, any longer 216, 2450, 2722; **lenger** 2742; **lengur** 2084; *no* ~ no longer, not any longer 215, 1408, 1462 etc.; **lenger** 3223
lappe *n.* fold in garment, loose, hanging sleeve used as pocket 1262; **lape** 1265; folded or extended skirt 1743, 1745, 1765
lare *n.* see **lore**
last(e) *n. at the* ~ in the end, finally, at last 280, 797, 874 etc.; *at(t)e the* ~ 2304, 2355
late *adj. hym thought to* ~ it seemed a long time to him 2418
lat(e) *v.* allow, permit 1752, 2011; ~ *be* desist from, cease (sth.) 2488. **lattist, lattys** *pr. 2 sg.* 1157, 2451. **late** *pr. 2 sg. subj.* 2771. **late** *pr. 3 pl.* ~ *be* desist from, cease (sth.) 1078. **lat(e)** *imp. sg.* 274, 534, 537 etc.; **latte** 615; *aux. with inf.* cause something to be done 289; **let(te)** 1585, 1913, 1972; ~ *be* desist from, cease (sth.) 698, 2573; **lete** 923; ~ *bee* leave (sb.) alone 2947. **lat(te), lete** *imp. pl. in exhortations* 590; ~ *be, been* desist from, cease (sth.) 2023, 2494. **lete** *pa. 1 sg. aux. with inf.* caused something to be done 1726. **let(e)** *pa. 3 sg.* caused something to be done 620, 1064, 1706 etc.; **lette** 618, 1228, 1586, 3097; ~ *blood* let blood 1814. **lete, late, letten** *pa. 3 pl. aux. with inf.* caused something to be done 138, 141, 2065. **latyn, lat** *pp.* ~ *blode, blood(e)* let blood 1811, 1825, 1834
late *adv. arly or* ~ see **arly**
lauedy, lauydy *n.* see **leuedy**
lawe *n.* the system of administering and enforcing the law, the practical operation of the law 1610; *proses of* ~ due process of law 533, 1647, 1871, 2075; *prossesse of* ~ 2118
leche *n.* physician 446; help, rescue **lyche** 354
led(d)e *v.* lead, bring, take, conduct (sb.) **leden** 1636; lead (a life) 232, 2218. **ledys** *imp. pl.* lead, bring, take, conduct (sb.) 514. **ladde** *pa. 3 sg.* led, brought, took, conducted (sb.) 1577, 1812; led (a life) 1204. **ladde** *pa. 3 pl.* led, brought, took, conducted (sb.) 114, 999, 1000; **lad** 1464; **laddyn** 523; **lede** 1294; led (a life) **lade** 3323. **lad(d)e** *pp.* led, brought, took, conducted (sb.) 658, 1068, 1530 etc.
lef *n.*[1] wife 1427; beloved person **leef** 2531
lef *n.*[2] *see* **lyue** *n.*[1]
lemman *n.* sweetheart, beloved 462, 2924, 2966 etc.; lover 1344, 1757, 2154, 2206
lenand *pr. p.* ~ *to* ?adjoining (sth.), being very near to (sth.) (?*MED*) 2895n
lene *adj.* thin, lean 27, 49
lenger, lengur *adv. comp.* see **lange**
lenkthe *n. in* ~ for the full length 2694
lent *pp.* come 3294
leppe *imp. sg.* ~ *to* jump onto (a horse) 2409. **lep(p)e** *pa. 3 sg.* leapt 885, 1245, 2543, 3066. **lopyn** *pa. 3 pl.* ~ *to* jumped onto (a horse) 2415. **lopon** *pp.* entered 627
lere *v.* teach 314, 324; receive instruction 116; learn 131; command, order 2682; ~ *goodys, goode* see **good, gode**
lerne *v.* ~ *of* learn from (sth.) 1143
lese *adj.* false 2468

lese *v.* lose 1276, 1471, 1626 etc.; ~ *lyf(f)e* lose (one's) life, die 1476; **lyse** 899; **lesyn** 1095. **lyse** *pr. 3 sg. subj.* ~ *lyfe* 1022. **les(e)** *pa. 3 sg.* 585, 921, 1619, 1874; ~ *lyf(e)* 2612; **lyse** 892; **lees** 3425. **lore** *pp.* 936, 2554, 2558 etc.; **lorne** 1989, 3065; destroyed 1148; *his* ~ is dead 343; **ylore** 346; *was* ~ was killed 742

lesyng *n.* lie, falsehood 458, 2082, 2230; lying 3356. **lesyngs** *pl.* lies, falsehoods 2116

lesse *pron. bothe more and the* ~ people of every estate and rank, everybody 1170. **lest** *comp. the* ~ *no the moste* (of persons) the lowest nor the highest, the humblest nor the greatest 519

lete *n.* delay 2437

let(e), lette(n) *v.* see **late**

lettyde *pa. 3 sg.* obstructed, impeded 611n. **let** *pp.* stopped 1323, 3347

leue *n.* see **lyue** *n.*[1]

leue *adj.* dear 54, 288, 1129, 1253, 2965. **leuer(e)** *comp. that were me* ~ I would prefer that, I would rather that 3083; *hym were* ~ he would rather 3212; *were he* ~, *were he loth* whether he liked it or not **lyf** 3103

leue *v.*[1] *pr. 3 sg. subj. God(e)* ~ may God grant 1657, 2761

leue *v.*[2] believe 581, 2274; **leuen** 1833. *pr. 1 sg.* 1313. **leuest** *pr. 2 sg.* 2349, 2756. **leue** *pr. 2 sg. subj.* 1506, 3073. **leuyd, leuede** *pa. 3 sg.* 2281, 2762, 3311

leue *v.*[3] remain 2400. **leued(e)** *pa. 3 sg.* remained, stayed 757; **lafte** 2422; left off, ceased, stopped (some activity) 160; left 1816

leue *v.*[4] live 534. *pr. 1 sg. subj.* 1830. **leuene** *pr. 2 sg. subj.* 3297. **leue** *pr. 3 sg. subj.* 2450. **lyueden, leuedyn** *pa. 3 pl.* 250, 3370

leuedy *n.* lady 2789, 2796, 2801 etc.; **lauedy** 432, 440, 477 etc.; **lauydy** 428, 823, 831. **leuedy** *gen. sg.* 2834. **leuedys** *pl.* 524

lybbe *v.* live 2771

lyche *n.* see **leche**

lyche, liche *adj.* like 2991, 2992, 3019, 3020

lycherye *n.* lechery 1079

lydyn *n.* language (of birds) 3238

lyees *pr. 3 sg.* lies 2220

lyf *adj.* see **leue**

lyf(e) *n.* living creature, esp. a human being 2816; *on* ~ alive **lyue** 56, 872, 1086 etc.; *lyse, lesyn, lese* ~ lose (one's) life, die 899, 1022, 1095; **lyffe** 1476; *lyse, lese, lees* ~ lost (one's) life, died 892, 2612, 3425; *dwelle, dwel on* ~ stay alive, live 1040, 2131, 2262; **lyue** 542, 2084; *of good* ~ virtuous 729; *in good* ~ 1393; *of olde* ~ of old age, old 1676; *on* ~ *go* go alive, stay alive 1752; *holde* ~ preserve (sb.'s) life 1817; *holden on* ~ keep (sb.) alive **lyue** 2751; *bere* ~ be alive, live 2813; *wan* ~ preserved (one's) life 3424

lygge *v.*[1] lie, recline 144, 216; be placed or located 1707; ~ *by* have sexual intercourse with (sb.) 1555; **ly** 1571; *by hyr flesche* ~ 684; ~ *aboue* (of a man) have sexual intercourse 1686. **lyes** *pr 3 sg.* is lodged, resides 1183. **lyge** *pr. 3 pl. subj.* lie down 1754. **lye** *pr. p.* lying down 805. **laye** *pa. 3 sg.* ~ *aboue* (of a man) have sexual intercourse 2541. **lyen, lyne** *pp.* ~ *by* raped (sb.) 496, 1310

lygge *v.*[2] ~ *my lyf* wager my life 692

lyȝt *n.* see **lyghtyn**

lyȝt *adj.* characterized by intense brightness, dazzling 2035

lyght *pa. 3 sg.*[1] ~ *adoun(e) (of)* dismounted (from a horse) 2519, 2839. **lyghte** *pa. 3 pl.* ~ *adoun* (of birds) flew down (to some place) 3147. **lyght** *pp.* dismounted (from a horse) 2418; (of God) descended (from heaven) 2713

lyȝt, lyght *pa. 3. sg.*[2] became light, dawned 555; shone, cast light 1899

lyghtyn, lyȝt *n.* lightning 2189, 2241n

lygnyd *pa. 3 sg.* flashed lightning 2211

lykkys *pr. 2 sg.* like 2412. **lykyde** *pa. 3 sg.* 978

lym *n.* lime, glue 1186

lynage *n. of hye, he* ~ of noble birth, lineage 243, 1556

lyste *n.* ?cunning or crafty person, evildoer (?*MED*) 1284n

lyther *adj.* wicked 2248

lytil, lytyl *in adv. phr. a* ~ a little way, a short distance 750, 2042, 2826

lyue *n.*[1] *took* ~ took leave 1568; *nam* ~ *at* took leave of (sb.) **leue** 1782; ~ *thay nome* they took leave **lef** 2031

lyue *n.*[2] see **lyf(e)**

lyueden *pa. 3 pl.* see **leue** *v.*[4]
lo *interj.* ah, see, behold, look 1618, 1749, 2423, 2609; indeed, surely, certainly 1837; (in combs.) ~ *hyre* see here, behold, see 493; ~ *were* see, behold, look where **loe** 1131
lodly, lothly *adj.* unpleasant 3207, 3244
loge *pa. 3 sg.* see **louke**
loke *v.* see, find out 1225, 1708, 2800. **lokkesttow** *pr. 2 sg. with pron.* look you 191. **lokyd** *pa. 3 pl.* ~ *that* took care (that sth. took place or did not take place) 1923; ~ *in* observed (the heavens, planets, etc.) **loked** 3383
loke *pp.* locked in a dwelling, prison, or the like 2898; locked **loken** 2951
lokyd *pa. 3 sg.* looked after, guarded 1222. **lokyd** *pp.* guarded 2658; preserved (virginity) **lokyn** 468
lome *adv. ofte and* ~ see **oft**
londe *n.* country, kingdom 5, 448, 454 etc.; landed property 2511, 3369; **lond** 2558; land, the earth 3056, 3361; population 3210. **londys, landys** *pl.* landed properties 2554, 2571, 2963; countries, kingdoms **londis** 229
longe *adj. thaym thought . . . ful* ~ it seemed a very long time to them 1997
longe on *prep.* dependent on, on account of (sb. or sth.) 475
loos *n. bare grete* ~ *of* was renowned for (sth.) 72; report, rumour **los** 1560
lopyn, lopon *pa. 3 pl., pp.* see **leppe**
lord(e) *n.* husband 568, 845, 1100 etc. **lordys, lordis** *gen. sg.* 565, 1685, 2952
lordyngs *n. pl.* lords, nobles 403; (as term of gracious or friendly address by a superior) gentlemen 238, 540
lore *n.* teaching, advice 1833, 2219; story 2763, 3311; knowledge, wisdom 176; *sette to* ~ set to learning, educated 16; *couthe of* ~ possessed learning, was learned **lare** 94; *gode of* ~ knowledgeable, well-informed 1080
lore, lorne *pp.* see **lese**
los *n.* see **loos**
lot *adj.* see **lothe**
lotby *n.* lover, paramour 2146
lothe *adj.* displeasing, unpleasant 1085; reluctant, unwilling **lot** 2470
lothly *adj.* see **lodly, lothly**
loude *adv.* ~ *or stille* under any circumstances, at any time, ever 372; ~ *and stille* at all times, always 2162
louke *pa. 1 sg.* laughed 3158. **loughe, loge** *pa. 3 sg.* 3154, 3156. **louhe** *pa. 3 pl.* ~ *to scorne* ridiculed 1993
loueden *pa. 3 pl.* see **louyste**
louerd *n.* lord 3002
louyste *pr. 2 sg.* love, care for 587. **louyd** *pa 3 sg.* 735, 737, 1193, 2492, 2867; **louyde** 739. **loueden** *pa. 3 pl.* *10
lowte, loute *v.* bow to 402, 428. **lowtid, loutyd** *pa. 3 sg.* 406, 2101

M

maane *n.* see **mane**
made *adj.* mad 2089, 2996, 3022
mageste *n. in* ~ (of God or Christ) by (His) might or power 558
maydenhod *n.* virginity 467
maynted *pa. 3 sg.* helped, assisted, supported 3426. *pp.* supported (an evildoer) 2369
mayntend *pa. 3 sg.* supported (an evildoer) *2302
maystyr *adj.* main, chief 2388
maystre *n. the* ~ *hadde* prevailed, was dominant 635; trick, piece of mischief **maystrie** 2178; *for the* ~ extremely **maystry** 2306
make *n.* (of birds) mate 3273, 3275, 3276 etc.; (of humans) spouse 239; lover 1338
makelees *adj.* without a mate 3307
makyst *pr. 2 sg.* make 575
male grace *n.* misfortune 2106
mane *n.* man 81, 1191, 1877 etc.; humankind **maane** 933; *no* ~ no one, nobody **man** 757, 763, 904 etc.; **mane** 2490. **manys** *gen. sg.* 1384, 1404. **mannys** *pl.* 1025; menservants **men** 1703; *with sg. v.* people 463, 646, 3400; men 2653, 2710
maner(e) *n. whilk(e)* ~ what kind 1513; in what manner 2960; *in alle* ~ in every way 1866; *wych* ~ what kind 2332; *on thys* ~ in this manner 3071
mannes *pr. 3 sg.* to behave like a man, act bravely *2851n
mare *pron.* see **mo**
markyd *pp.* rendered identifiable by physical or bodily features 2593
markys *n. pl.* markers indicating the location of something 1926

mas *n.* see **messe**
matyns *n. pl.* matins, the first canonical hour, recited at midnight or in the early morning 1631
maugre *n.* ~ *haue thow, thou* shame on you, bad luck to you 1013, 2106
maungerye *n.* feast, banquet 1789n
me *poss. pron.* my 354
mede *n.* meadow 1120
medycyne, medicyne *n.* cure, remedy 1149; ~ *ben don* cure be performed 2348
melodye *n. madyn myrth and* ~ see **myrthe**
membris *n. pl.* male genitalia 1525
merour *n.* mirror 2001
merryghe *n.* ?vital energy, virility, sexual potency (?*MED*) 1685n
merueyle, meruyle *n.* marvel, wonder 2360, 3031; *hadde* ~ *in thout* was greatly astonished or surprised 2931
merueyle *pr. 1 sg. refl.* am filled with wonder, surprise, or puzzlement 195
message *n. comen in a* ~ come with a message 2967
messe *n.* mass 1631, 1920; *here* ~ attend mass **mas** 1281
mete *n.* food 947, 3010, 3273, 3283; **met** 1821, 1823; meal 2933; **met** 2929; *cam to* ~ 3007; *gon to* ~ 3338
met(e) *pa. 3 sg.* dreamt 2788, 2797, 2801, 2822, 2828. **mete** *pp.* 1971
my *obj. pron.* me 496, 1760
myche *adj.* (of size) large, great 2566
myche *adv.* much, greatly 735, 847, 1405 etc.
myght *n.* an active power or faculty (of the heart, soul, brain etc.) *357n; physical energy, vitality, vigour 3272
mygtyst *pa. 2 sg.* see **moun(e)**
mykyl *adj.* (of amount) much 1115, 1219, 1567, 1581; **mykil** 58, 70, 580, 1774; great 937, 1420, 1466 etc.; **mykil** 26, 50, 258 etc.; **mikil** 2; **mykile** 557; **mykyle** 2846; (of size) large, great 614, 2424, 2895; **mykil** 634, 1384; ~ *deppe* very deep 1382
mykyl *adv.* much 36, 2876; far **mykil** 126; *for also* ~ *as* because, since 2479
myl *n.* a vague measure of time (the time spent in walking a mile; a period of twenty minutes) 1591
myn *poss. pron. 1 sg. of* ~ of mine (out of my money) 1937n
mynours *n. pl.* miners 2016, 2023, 2024
mynstralcie *n.* musical instruments 3049
mynt *pp.* intended 1660
myry *adj.* (of seasons, times, or days) delightful 261; merry, happy 1204; *refl. mad hym* ~ enjoyed themselves, revelled, made merry 1220
myry *adv. ferde* ~ was happy 3316
myrthe *n.* mirth, merriment 1962, 3051; happiness, state of happiness 3065; ~ *and solas* 3448; (sexual) pleasure **myrth** 1337; *maden* ~ *and solas* rejoiced **myrth** 1169; *madyn* ~ *and melodye* had sexual intercourse **myrth** 2155
mysbyleue *n. broghten in* ~ misled (sb.) into superstitious belief 2300
mysdyde *n.* misdeed, wrongdoing 1846
mysferde *pa. 3 sg.* fared badly 2765
mysgettyne *pp.* conceived out of wedlock 1075
myssayde *pp.* slandered 2247
myssyd *pa. 3 sg.* noticed to be absent or missing 1346. **mysde** *pp.* 1449
mytte *prep.* with *1399n
mo *n. no* ~ nothing more 2567
mo *pron.* more 1846; *no* ~ no more 282, 1753, 2948, 3442; **mare** 3366
mo, moo *adj.* more 673, 1829
mode *n.* disposition, temperament 695
modir *n.* mother 223, 1721, 1722 etc.; **moder** 1688, 1728, 1782, 3165; **modyr** 1683, 1684. **modyr** *gen. sg.* 1734
mon(e) *n.*[1] lamentation 575; complaint, lament 2550
mone *n.*[2] moon 332, 334, 338 etc.; *by sone and* ~ see **son(n)e**
more *n. by the* ~ by the root, completely 1726
more *pron. bothe* ~ *and the lesse* see **lesse**
more *adv.* again 2152
morne *n. on the* ~ on the morrow, next day 3007, 3038; *oppon the* ~ 1918; *o* ~ 2295
mornes *pr. 2 sg.* express grief or sorrow 1861. **morned** *pa. 3 sg.* 562
mornyng *n. in a* ~ on a certain morning *261
mornynge *n.* worry, anxiety 3015
morwen *n. o(n) (the)* ~ on the morrow, next day 555, 648, 1634 etc.; **morwe** 392; *oppon (the)* ~ 994, 3094; **morowen** 2478; *vppon* ~ 183, 911; *vppe o[n] the* ~ 1286n

moste *pron. comp. the lest no the* ~ see **lesse**

mot *pr. 1 sg.* must 370, 2524. **most** *pr. 2 sg. with implied inf.* are compelled or required (to do sth.) 1597n. **mot** *pr. 3 sg.* must 2970. **moten** *pr. 1 pl.* must 1969. **mot** *pr. 1 sg. subj.* may 1548, 1722, 1729 etc.; **mote** 1038; **moti** *with pron.* may I 1377. **mot** *pr. 2 sg. subj.* may 2526. **mot(e)** *pr. 3 sg. subj.* may 295, 582, 706 etc. **most** *pa. 3 sg.* might 683. *pa. 3 sg. subj.* 2501; *with v. of motion understood* must go 2816

moun(e) *pr. 2 sg.* may 2234; *here ȝe* ~, *as ȝe* ~ *here* as you will hear 788n, 1340; *as ȝe* ~ *see* as you will see **moue** 3267. **mow(e)** *pr. 1 pl.* 835, 2976. **mowe** *pr. 2 pl. as ȝe* ~ *hyre, here* as you will hear 457, 2645. **mou** *pr. 3 pl.* 2082. **mygtyst** *pa. 2 sg.* 234

mouthe *n. speke with* ~ spoken, said 121; speak, talk 3085; *sayed with* ~ said (sth.) 170; *telle with* ~ say (sth.) 2318; *comaunded with* ~ commanded with speech or words, orally 2679

N

na *adv.* ~ *hadde* had not, if it had not been that 3124

naddir *n.* adder 785, 798, 876; **nadder** 770, 774; **nedder** 769

nam(e) *pa. 3 sg.* took (sth.) 461, 852, 1265 etc.; *the way* ~ took the way, went, made the journey 401, 777, 940 etc.; **nome** 882; *the waye* ~ 2198, 2854; *hys way* ~ took his way, went 2804; ~ *heed, hed* paid attention to (sb. or sth.) 279; took notice, saw 1710; ~ *vp* (of a scream, sigh) raised 491, 2626; *in councel* ~ took (sb.) into a consultation 1683, 2840; ~ *leue at* took leave of (sb.) 1782. **nome(n)** *pa. 3 pl.* took (sb. somewhere) 125; *the way* ~ took the way, went, made the journey 317, 1918, 1922. **nome** *pp.* taken 1067, 1529; come, arrived *398n; *in concel* ~ taken into a consultation 2240; *oppe* ~ raised up (a sigh) **ynome** 2266; *hys concel was* ~ his advice was taken 2678; *pes was* ~ pardon was granted 2997; *parlement was* ~ assembly was convened 3221; *hys in was* ~ his lodgings were taken 3337

nas *pa. 3 sg. contr. of* **ne was** was not 139, 2055, 3014; **nastir** there was not 162

ne *adv. usually with another negative* not 204, 207, 248 etc.; ~ *hadde* had not, if it had not been that 1659, 1839, 2426

ne *conj. usually with another negative* nor 211, 216, 302, 2557; ~ . . . *no* 2232

ned *n. hit was* ~ it was necessary 1433. **nyddis, nedys** *pl. put forth thy, oure* ~ reveal your, our business 3248, 3250

nee *adv.* see **nyghe, nee, nye**

neghyd, neghid *pa. 3 sg.* approached, drew near (in time) **neght** 331; **neghyt** 1958; **neghit** 1990; *with adverbial constructions* approached, drew near (in space or position) ~ *nee, nye* 950, 3176, 3351

neye *adj.* close by 3124

nere *pa. 3 pl. contr. of* **ne were** were not 1700, 2056

ner(e) *adv.*[1] near 1751, 1895, 3337; ~ *wode* nearly mad 502; *fer no* ~, *fer and* ~ see **fer**

neuermore *adv.* at no time, never 466, 2820; never again 3310

nicote *n.* clever or skilful device 2890

nyddis *n. pl.* see **ned**

nyghe, nee, nye *adv.* close to 794, 1396, 3176, 3185; closely 3208; *neghyd, neghid* ~ **nee, nye** see **neghyd, neghid**

nigremancye, nigrimancye, nygrimancie *n.* sorcery, witchcraft, black magic, occult art 296, 344, 3381

nylle *pr. 1 sg. contr. of* **ne wylle** *(fut. aux.)* will not 104, 105, 1322 etc.; **nyl(l)** 1632, 2596. **nyl(le)** *pr. 3 sg.* 630; does not wish, desire 1583. **nult** *pr. 2 sg. subj.* would not 1626. **nolde** *pa. 3 sg.* would not 477, 938, 965, 1519. *pa. 1 pl.* would not wish, desire 122. **nolde(n)** *pa. 3 pl.* would not 215, 315, 1462

nys *pr. 3 sg. contr. of* **ne hys** is not 498. **nas** *pa. 3 sg.* 139, 2055, 3014; **nastir** *contr.* there was not 162. **nere** *pa. 3 pl.* 1700, 2056

no *adv. usually with another negative* not 163, 214, 233 etc.

no *conj. usually with another negative* nor 38, 60, 414 etc.; **na** 2742; *ne . . .* ~ 2232

nobil(e) *adj.* skilled, able 1527; good, choice 1701; valuable, precious 1953. **noblest** *comp.* valuable, precious 2003

non *n.* noon, or nones (3 p.m.) 2029

nones *n. pl. for the* ~ for the occasion 1913
noonekynne *adj. in* ~ *wyse* in no way, by no means 203
noris *n.* nurse 816. **noris(e)** *pl.* 803, 808n, 827, 829; **norises** 754
norische *v.* nourish 618
nortyre *n.* breeding, manners, courtesy 676
not(e) *pr. 1 sg. contr. of* **ne wot** do not know 126, 1450, 2773
nothyng *adv.* not at all 1593
nothir, noþer, nothyr *adj. no* ~ no other 478, 630, 1260, 2527
nou *adv.* now 2412
nought *n.* nothing 664, 694, 791 etc.; **nowt** 2134; **nouȝt** 1767; **noght** 1857; *bryng(e) to* ~ destroy, ruin 2739; **nowt** 304, 1117; **nouȝt** 459; *seruyd of* ~ was of no use, served no purpose **nouȝt** 767; *wente to* ~ became nothing, perished **nowt** 1213
nought *adj.* unavailing, useless 2489
nouȝt, nought *adv.* not 88, 119, 124 etc.; **nowt** 53, 405, 1085 etc.; **nout** 611, 2460, 2480 etc.; **noght** 165, 209; **nowght** 621, 1021; **nawt** 37, 38; **noughte** 430; **nowte** 2879; **nougt** 3168; not at all **nout** 2232
nowerware *adv.* nowhere 755
nowthir, nouthir, nowthyr *conj.* ~ . . . *no* neither . . . nor 60, 519, 1714, 2979

O

o *adj.* see **oon, o**
ob *prep.* see **of**
of *adv.* off 1187, 1255, 1261 etc.
of *prep.* during 2242, 2245; of **ob** (before **b**) 235n; with respect to, in 2367; from the surface of (a part of the body), off 2921; *lyght adoun* ~ dismounted from (a horse) 2519
oft *adv.* ~ *sythes* many times 1099, 2312, 2803; **of** 1492n; ~ *amange* all the while, continually **ofte** 571; ~ *tyme* many times **of** 601; ~ *and lome* frequently, often **ofte** 1890
oght *pron.* anything 2391
olde *n.* old age 641
on *n. at* ~ in agreement 388, 1240, 2056
on *adj.* see **oon, o**
on *indef. art.* a(n) 295, 1403, 3130, 3401
on *prep.* growing on (a tree etc.) 1706; ~ *wilk wyse* in what manner 1875; *crye* ~ cry at (sb.) 3227
ony adj. any 299, 419, 1610 etc.; **anny** 445, 1057, 2241, 2294
on(n)oon, onon *adv.* see **anon**
onour *n.* honour 3370
oon, on *pron.* one 160, 834, 1307 etc.; **oone** 143; *many* ~ many a one 234; *neuere* ~ nobody 396
oon, o *adj.* one 673, 1156, 1682 etc.; **on** 2150, 2698; **hon** 233; *that* ~ one (of two) 1902, 3270n; **on** 2008, 2911; *tha* ~ one (of several) 2706; *with partitive gen. hys* ~ *maystir* one of his masters 1297n; *pleonastically with superlatives* ~ *the fayerest* the fairest **on** 2812
oor *adj.* having white or grey hair or beard 27
or *poss. pron. 3 pl.* see **hare**
or *adv.* see **ar(e)**
ordeyn, ordayn *v.* arrange (sth.) 2009, 2033, 2903. **ordaynde** *pa. 3 sg.* appointed 744
ostage *n.* hostel 2039
otwo *adv.* (following verb of departing) from one another *wente* ~ 3053
oune, ouen *adj.* own 1783, 2142, 2675, 3052
ous *pron.* us 1944, 1946, 1973
oueral, oweralle *adv.* everywhere 774, 1224, 3282; all over **oueralle** 800, 1522

P

payed *pp. was* ~ *ful wel* was very well pleased, content, or satisfied 1954
payent *pp.* portrayed 148
paynyd *pa. 3 sg. refl.* strived, endeavoured (to do sth.) 3446
palas, palayes, paleys *n.* palace 400, 1168, 1640, 3096; ~ *ȝate* palace gate **palyes** 2095
paramour *adv.* for love, if it please you 1511
parfay *interj.* by my faith 628, 1584, 1828, 1969
parlement *n.* assembly 3115, 3220; ~ *was nome* assembly was convened 3221; *comuyn* ~ an open assembly **parlyment** 3214
parti *n.* claim 2986
party *v.* divide 104

passe ~ *thourgh iuggement,* ~ *by iuggement* see **iuggement**
pees *n.* peace 39, 1019, 1031; ~ *was nome* pardon was granted **pes** 2997
pepyl(e) *n.* people 771; subjects of a king etc. 3107, 3222; **pypyl** 3225
per *prep.* for 2108, 2359
pers *n. pl.* pears 1701n
persaued *pa. 3 sg.* perceived 2918
piger *n.* pitcher 2165
piler, pyler *n.* pillar or column 1881, 2001, 2017 etc.
pyne *n.*[1] bolt 1410, 1426, 1453
pyne *n.*[2] sickness 1532
pypyl *n.* see **pepyl(e)**
pyte *n. was* ~ was a pity 2610
pytte *n.* well 1400. **pyttys** *pl.* pits 1924
pytte *pp.* see **pute**
play(e) *n.* sexual play 2547; merriment, disport 3051; *a sory* ~ a bad course of action 1364
play(e) *v.* enjoy oneself, be merry 1100, 2149, 2308 etc.; **pleye** 1118; joust **play** 746; work tricks **play** 1921
plyght *n. good of* ~ faithful 1448
poynt *n. in* ~ *to* just about (to do or suffer sth.) 915, 1147
pole *n. fische* ~ fish pond 883
pomels *n. pl.* ornamental bosses on furniture 790
popyniay *n.* parrot 2143n
pouste *n.* power 3162, 3293
powerte *n.* poverty 3317
prentyse *n.* student, pupil 2100
pride, pryde *n.* glorious state, exalted position 585; splendour, opulence, magnificence 3112
pryked *pa. 3 sg.* rode rapidly 2549
prime, pryme *n.* prime, the canonical hour (6 a.m.) 1286, 2781, 3094
priuelyche, priuyliche, pryuyliche *adv.* cautiously, carefully, discreetly 763, 1910, 2891, 3324; privately, confidentially 1096
priuete *n.* private affairs, secrets 2162
profecye *n.* divine inspiration 1987
proses, prossesse *n.* ~ *of lawe* see **lawe**
proue *v.* test 175, 1696, 1730, 1781; **prouen** 182. *imp. sg.* 1693, 1777. *imp. pl.* 172
prowe *n.* profit, benefit, advantage 2281
purchasede *pa. 3 sg.* brought about 296
put *pa. 3 sg.* ~ *vp* put up (one's weapon), sheathed 2585
pute *pa. 3 sg.* ~ *at* struck at (sth.) 1357; thrust, pushed **putte** 2182. *pp.* thrust, pushed 3378; *oppon me* ~ imputed to me 3121n; *in wille* ~ determined, resolved **pytte** 670n
putrye *n.* lechery, adultery 1350

Q

queryd *pp.* inquired, investigated 691
queth *pr. 1 sg.* grant (sth. to sb.), give 97. **quod** *pa. 3 sg.* said 201, 291, 416 etc.
qweyntys(e) *n.* plan, trick, device 2693, 2880, 2897; ingeniousness, cleverness 378; **qweyntyes** 2637; **qweyntysse** 2904
qwentlyche, qwentilich, qweyntlich *adv.* ingeniously, cleverly 2908, 2912, 2917
qwyke *adj.* alive 2777

R

rade *adj.* ready, prepared 1290, 2088
rade *pa. 3 sg.* ~ *forth* continued or recommenced (one's) riding 664
raes *pa. 3 sg.* see **ryse**
raft *pp.* see **reuys**
rage *n.* trick 2175
ray *n.* preparation, arrangements 995
real *adj.* royal (one) 130
reche *v.* take 44n
red(e) *n.*[1] advice, counsel 1776, 2385, 2759; plan, course of action, way of proceeding 1252, 2592; a resolve, decision, purpose 226; plot 3416; *hit his no* ~, *thare was no nothir* ~ there is (was) no alternative 1254, 1260; *take* ~ follow counsel 1155; *at on* ~ in agreement 2062; *wyrke eftyr sory* ~ follow bad advice, counsel 579
rede *n.*[2] *at the* ~ ready 2579
red(e) *v.* to advise, counsel 1163, 1693, 1729. **rede, reed** *pr. 1 sg.* 1689, 1773, 2715. **reddyst** *pr. 2 sg.* 1253. **rede** *pr. 3 sg. subj.* (in asseverations) *so God the, my* ~ so God keep, save, direct you, me 1606, 1760
redy *adj.* convenient, easy, perspicuous 1926
redy, rydilich *adv.* readily 1916, 3254
refreynde *pa. 3 sg.* asked 22

reynned *pa. 3 sg.* rained 2226
remue *v.* remove 1228. **remou** *imp. sg.* 2350. **remoude** *pp.* 2351
rennyng *pr. p.* running 946
rent *pa. 3 sg.* tore 982. **rente** *pp.* 504
rere(n) *v.* erect 138, 141, 2894
resayued *pp.* welcomed (in a specified manner) 325, *3343
resoon *n.* speech, talk, discourse 2112; explanation **reson** 2707; **resoun** 3266
respyte *n. without* ~ without delay, at once 1660
reuthe *n. hadde* ~ *of* felt pity for 1389
reuys *pr. 3 sg.* deprives (sb.) of (a bodily ability) 2346. **raft** *pp.* 1015
rycher *adj. comp.* richer, more wealthy, more prosperous ~ *of tresour* 2367
ryclych, rychliche *adv.* richly, lavishly 1207, 3334
rydilich *adv.* see **redy, rydilich**
rygge-boon *n.* backbone, spine 859n
ryȝt, ryght *adv.* straight, directly 1941, 2518
ryghtys *n. pl.* the right side in a dispute 3099
ryghtwys *adj.* righteous 2754
ryse *v.* come into existence 1603, 1805; get (sb.) out of bed 1597n. **roos** *pa. 3 sg.* stood up 59; ~ *vppe* 1794; got out of bed **raes** 2436. **resyn, rysyn** *pp.* reached a higher position or level 199, 211
roche *n.* rock 3125, 3142n, 3176 etc.
Romauns *n.* romance language 1520
Romauns, Romans *adj.* in romance language 2688, 2922
rote *n.* source of a condition, origin, cause 624; *by the* ~ (dig up) by the root, uproot 631, 1126
rote-fast *adj.* securely rooted 960
rought *pa. 3 sg.* cared 1208

S

say *v.* command 651. **sayen** *pr. 3 pl.* express (a common opinion) *as men* ~ 594. **saye** *imp. sg.* tell 1860
saye *v.*[1] (shortened form of **assaye**) to sample, have a taste of, partake of (food) 3010
saye *v.*[2] see **see**
saylyd *pa. 3 sg.* ~ *ouer* sailed across (the sea etc.) 3055
sal *pr. 1 sg.* shall 373, 444. *pr. 2 sg.* 1663; **schaltou** *with pron.* shall you 596, 984, 1843; **saltow** 1622. *pr. 3 sg.* 268, 292, 443 etc. *pr. 1 pl.* 1499. *pr. 2 pl.* 309; **schulle** 567; *with v. of motion understood* 1017. *pr. 3 pl.* 1365. **schulde** *pa. 3 sg.* was about (to do sth.) 2093; **schul** 2692n
salt *adj.* ~ *flod(e)* see **flod**
Sarsyns, Sarzyns *n. pl.* saracens 2690, 2696, 2725, 2729
sate *pa. 3 sg.* see **sytys**
saue *adj.* see **vowch . . . saue**
saue *v.* protect (sth.) against attack etc. 2007, 2049, 2664; **sauen** 2513; hold (sth.) in safekeeping 1947; keep (sb.) in a state or condition 3429
schaft *n.* spear, lance 747
schaltou *pr. 2 sg. with pron.* see **sal**
schames *pr. 3 sg. impers. me* ~ it causes me to feel shame, embarrassment 3230. **schamyd** *pp.* ashamed, filled with shame 3211
sche *pron.* see **scho**
schende *v.* destroy, ruin, kill (sb.), bring about the death of (sb.) 501, 2735. **schent, schend** *pa. 3 sg.* 1796, 2638. **schent** *pp.* 367, 379, 536 etc.; **schend** 347; violated (sb.) 701
schentfol *adj.* ignominious, humiliating 3401
schete *n.* cloak, robe 2582n
schild(e) *pr. 3 sg. subj. so God(e)* ~ *me* as God may protect me (from sth.) 2085, 3364
schyreue, schyref *n.* sherrif 2469, 2476
scho *sub. pron. 3 sg. fem.* 225, 259, 265 etc.; **sche** 1681, 1818, *1832; **schoe** 818; **so** 1404
schodde *pp.* wearing shoes *that euer in erth ȝed* ~ who ever trod the earth (i.e. all mankind) 3453n
schof *pa. 3 sg.* shoved, pushed 1411
schort(e) *adj. at(te)* ~ *wordis* in few words 247, 2473, 2863; *at(e)* ~ *wordys* 2489, 2500; **schortys** 2329n
schreud *adj.* wicked 1785
schrewe *n.* wicked person 1705
schrewydschyp *n.* wicked deed 1737
schrewnes *n.* wicked deed 1739
schryue *v. refl.* confess or make confession 1087n
schulle, schul, schulde *pr. 2 pl., pa. 3 sg.* see **sal**

sciens *n. pl.* see **seuene sciens**
scole *n.* school 221
scout *n.* wretch, rascal, rogue (used of men and women) 2216
scryke *n.* scream, loud shout 491
se, see *n.* sea 3048, 3123, 3140 etc.; ~ *flood* 3040
seche *v.* seek, look for 242. **sowt** *pa. 3 sg.* 774, 1400, 3287. **sowt** *pp.* 2833
see *v.* see 603n. *pa. 1 sg.* 200, 212, 699. *pa. 2 sg.* 1724. *pa. 3 sg.* 351, 480, 763 etc.; **syghe** 854, 954, 3031, 3350; **segh** 827; **saye** 1601; **sygh** 3186. **seen** *pa. 3 pl.* 241, 756, 765; **seyen** 2019, 2703; **seghe** 808; **syghe** 3136
segyde *pa. 3 sg.* laid siege to (sth.) 2654
sely *adj.* see **syly, sely**
selue *adj. that ilke* ~ that very same 2249; *that* ~ that same **self** 2796
semyld *pp.* assembled 3107
semlant *n. made* ~ displaid (a certain) expression 905, 1791; feigned, pretended 3024
senescal *n.* seneschal 1550, 1614, 3044, 3062
serke *n.* ?nightshirt (?*MED*) 1391
sertis *adv.* see **certys, certis**
seruyd *pa. 3 sg.* ~ *of nouȝt* was of no use, served no purpose 767. *pp.* served (sb.) 93
seruys *n.* service, employment 1621
sesed *pp.* put in legal possession (of sth.) 3314
set(e), seten *pa. 3 sg., pa. 3 pl.* see **sytys**
seuen artis *n.* seven liberal arts 162
seuene sciens *n.* seven liberal arts 148
seuennyght *n.* week 1449, 2242, 2245
seuent, seuenet *adj.* seventh 91, 2750
sewed, sewyd *pa. 3 sg., pa. 3 pl.* see **suythe**
sexte *adj.* sixth 2443; as *n.* 83
syche *pron.* such 1406
syche *adj.* such 1076; *non, no* ~ no such 1700, 2570
sycurlyche *adv.* truly, certainly *685n, 846; **sykyrly** 123; **sycurliche** *734n; **sykirlich** 2277; without fail **sykyrlyche** 2491
syde *n. in ilke-a* ~ on every side, all around 638, 1463; *in ilce-a* ~ 141; *in hilka* ~ 939
sygge *v.* say 1708
sygh(e) *pa. 3 sg., pa. 3 pl.* see **see**
syght, syȝt *n. hadde (a)* ~ *of* got sight of (sth. or sb.) 948, 2837; *haues a* ~ gets sight 2983
syke *adj.* sick 1071
syked, sygkyd, sykkyd *pa. 3 sg.* sighed 571, 1492, 1592
sikere *v.* promise 47; ~ *hym trewly on honde* assure him truly, confirm truly **sykyr** 3232
sykyrd *pa. 3 sg.* assured, confirmed (a promise) 3264
sykyrly, sykirlich, sykyrlyche *adv.* see **sycurlyche**
syly, sely *adj.* ~ *man* good man, husband 1361, 1404
sylke *adj.* see **swylk(e)**
sympile *adj.* lowest in rank among a group 3098
synge *v.* lament, express sorrow 1367
sythen, sithen *conj.* since 94, 200, 212, 2233; **sythyn** 2201, 2988; at any time since, during the period after 3385
sythes *n. pl. oft* ~ see **oft**
sytys *pr. 3 sg.* (of God or Christ) to sit enthroned in Heaven 558; ~ *on hye* **syt** 3175. **set(e)** *pa. 3 sg.* was sitting **sate** 2471; *refl.* sat 2522; seated (sb.) 3009; ~ *(a)doun* sat down 2504, 3111, 3113. **seten** *pa. 3 pl.* ~ *adoun* sat down 3160. **syttyne** *pp.* been sitting 1074
skere *v.* defend oneself from a charge or accusation 3398
skil *n.* reason 163; *in* ~ by argument **skyle** 2336
skyrme *v.* fight with a weapon, fence 2691
slake *v.* diminish 1210, 1337. *pr. 2 sg. subj.* put an end to (sth.) 2770. **slakys** *pr. 3 sg.* neglects (to do sth.) 1686. **slakyd** *pa. 3 sg.* neglected (to do sth.) 1680
sle *v.* kill 671, 779, 1649, 2057, 2717; **sla** 2088, 3376; **slee** 997; **slae** 2394. **sle** *imp. sg.* 1753. **slow(e)** *pa. 3 sg.* 1028, 1138, 1745, 1765, 2250. **slawe** *pp.* 532, 1646, 1870 etc.; **yslawe** 876
sleppe *pa. 3 sg.* slept 793
smyt *v.* strike 2580; ~ *of* strike off 1187; **smytte** 2386. **smytte** *pr. 3 sg. subj.* 2695. **smyt(e)** *imp. sg.* ~ *of* 1255, 2379. **smot(e)** *pa. 3 sg.* 859; ~ *of* 1261. **smytyn** *pp.* afflicted, affected with feeling 1864
smyte *n. euery* ~ every part 1957n

snel(le) *adj.* swift 316, 738; prompt in performance of duties 1540
so *pron.* see **scho**
softe *adv.* in comfort, at ease 1858
sokur, sokyr *n.* aid, assistance, help 720, 3182, 3183
solace *pa. 3 sg.* ?cleaned (clothes) (?*MED*) 1801n
solas *n.* entertainment 753; joy, pleasure, happiness, state of happiness 50, 217, 1105, 1193; *myrthe and* ~ 3448; *make* ~ enjoy themselves 329; rejoice 856; *maden* ~ provided entertainment for someone 390; *maden myrth and* ~ rejoiced 1169
somthyng *adv.* rather 1605
somtyme *adv.* at one or some time in the past 1516, 2648
sonde *n.*[1] body of water 3055
sonde *n.*[2] a message containing a summons, command 340; *thourow Godys* ~ by God's favour or grace 3126
sone *adv.* soon 225, 253, 547 etc.; **son** 2038; at once 362, 616, 853 etc.; **soone** 1889; **soune** 2678, 3361; *ful* ~ right away, at once, immediately 458, 803; very soon 1977, 2159; *fol* ~ right away, at once, immediately 2207; *wille* ~ very soon 667
Sonenday *n.* Sunday 386
sonke(n), sonkon, sonkyn *pp.* sunk 198, 210, 1227, 3363
son(n)e *n.* sun 464, 1609; *vndir* ~ in the world 45, 2003; (as an element in oaths) *by* ~ *and mone* by sun and moon 2772
son(n)e *n. gen.* son's 1095, 2256
sooe *adv.* so 629
soone *adv.* see **sone**
sore *adv.* greatly, very much 15, 811, 964 etc.; keenly, bitterly 571, 690, 1492 etc.; painfully 900; terribly 1780; ~ *abought* see **abought**
sory *adj.* sad, sorrowful, grieved 743, 838, 850 etc.; **sori** 1853; evil, wicked, sinful 579; vexed, chagrined 2045; ~ *in thout, thought, thoght* sad 560, 654, 831, 906; *a* ~ *play* see **play(e)**
sorow(e) *n. do* ~ do harm, cause trouble 992; do harm, cause trouble (to sb.) 1282; *mad(d)e* ~ lamented, mourned 1592, 2264; *makes* ~ does harm, causes trouble 2433
soth(e) *n.* the truth 3241; ~ *forto, to telle* to tell the truth 3318, 3402
soth(e) *adj.* true 2193, 2775; ~ *hyt hys* it is true 2468, 3415; ~ *hit his* 817; ~ *tale* truth 76
soune *adv.* see **sone**
sowdyng, soudyng *n.* soldering 2021, 2041
sowdyt *pp.* soldered 2021
spak(e) *pa. 3 sg., pa. 3 pl.* see **speke**
spangel *n.* spaniel 1448
spare *v.* see **spere**
specialiche *adv.* only, exclusively 1097
spede *v.* achieve one's goal, succeed 1963. *pr. 3 sg. subj.* help (sb.), give success (to sb.) *God* ~ 2014. *pa. 3 sg.* fared 953. **speddyn** *pa. 3 pl.* fared 2304. **spede, ysped** *pp.* achieved one's goal, succeeded 1579, 2602
speke *v.* ~ *with mouthe* speak 121. **spake** *pa. 3 sg.* spoke 59, 409, 413 etc.; **spak** 418. **spake** *pa. 3 pl.* 421
spere *v.* excuse *1756n. **spare** *imp. sg.* hold back 843; delay 2899
spye *v.* look for (sb.) 3326. **spyde** *pp.* found out (sth.), ascertained 1771
spille, spyl(l)e *v.* kill 569, 682, 888, 911 etc.; be killed 658. **spylt** *pp.* killed 1029
sprede *v.* (of a tree, bough etc.) branch out, spread 622; (of a flower) bloom 1121. **spredis** *pr. 3 sg.* extends 639. **sprad(d)e** *pa. 3 sg.* (of a tree, bough etc.) branched out, spread 603, 607, 1725
sprong(e) *pa. 3 sg.* (of the day) dawned 1964, 1996; ~ (*out*) *of* (of a branch) sprouted, grew from (sth.) 605, 619, 633, 636; **sprange** 584. **sprong** *pp.* (of a word) issued from (sb.) 299
squyers *n. pl.* squires 525
stad *n.* see **stede**
stage *n.* a raised platform or base for a bed 177
stale *pa. 3 sg.* see **stele**
stede *n.* a position or place occupied by someone 2561, 2607; **stude** *1294n; town **stad** 3325; *in the* ~ straightaway, at once, immediately **stude** 1738
steke *pa. 3 sg., pp.* see **styked**
stele *v.* ~ *oppon* creep up stealthily on (a city etc.) with hostile intent 1893. **stelle** *pr. 3 sg. subj.* steal 2514. **stale** *pa. 3 sg.* 1236

stepmodir, stepmoder *n.* stepmother 344, 3433. **stepmodir** *gen. sg.* 1316
sternes *n. pl.* stars 335
styghe *pa. 3 sg.* ~ *oppon* climbed up on (a ladder) 2164; ~ *into* climbed up into (a tower) 2683
styked *pa. 3 sg.* was entangled so as to be unable to move or escape 1246; ~ *to* made (a door) secure **steke** 1352. **steke** *pp.* set in a specified place or position, put, placed 442; locked 1360; locked up, shut up (sb. in a place) 2910; (of a mouth) shut, kept silent **stoke** 434
stille *adj.* silent 1732, 3088; (of words) quietly spoken 101
stille *adv.* silently, quietly 277, 793, 1349 etc.; secretly 1910; **stylle** 2891; ~ *as (a) stoon(e), ston(e)* silently as a stone, perfectly silently 407, 427, 1069 etc.; secretly, covertly, privately ~ *a(s) ston, stoon* 1928n; **stylle** 2901; *dwel* ~ remain, be left 2495n; *loude or* ~, *loude and* ~ see **loude**
stilly *adv.* quietly 1493
styward *n.* steward 1508, 1566, 1594 etc.; **stywarde** 2870, 2981; **stiwarde** 1558. **stiward** *gen. sg.* 1602
stoke *pp.* see **styked**
stondis *pr. 3 sg.* (of a tree or plant) grows (in a place), is located 1131. **stoode** *pa. 3 sg.* 598
ston-stille *adv.* silently as a stone, perfectly silently 1735
stounde *n.* time, occasion **stonde** 818; *a lytil, lytyl* ~ a little while 1946, 1976, 2728; *anothir* ~ another time, once more **stound** 1730; *harde* ~ time of trial or suffering 2627; *in a* ~ in a short space of time 2885
stoute *adj.* sturdy, strong 1158
strange *adj.* sturdy 2509; (of an army or enemy) formidable in war or battle 2653
strange *adv.* sturdily, solidly 197; painfully, gravely **strong** 787
strangyl *pp.* strangled 495
strawyd *pp.* (of fighting men) deployed 2690
strem *n.* sea current 3191
strete *n. by the* ~ out about 1000
stryf(e) *n.* complaint 923, 2573; dissension, discord 1603, 2147; a disagreement, quarrel, dispute 1805
strong *adj.* (of weather) severe 2225
strong *adv.* see **strange**
stude *n.*[1] place of learning 129n, 134n; **studie** 133
stude *n.*[2] see **stede**
studye *v.* think, consider 590
suffyre, suffry *v.* permit, allow, let (sth. be done) 216, 532, 889, 3131, 3349. **suffry** *pr. 2 sg. subj.* 1844
suythe *pr. 3 sg.* goes 780. **sewed** *pa. 3 sg.* followed in pursuit, chased after 796; acceded to someone's will **sewyd** 1734. **sewyd** *pa. 3 pl.* followed 3208
susteyne *v.* support 234
swat *n.* sweat 1092n
sweuen(e) *n.* dream 1934, 2294, 2298 etc.
swylk(e) *adj.* such 1196, 1692, 2013 etc.; **swilk(e)** 1026, 1657, 1830, 1837; **sylke** 1983
swyte *adj.* (of Christ etc.) blessed, holy, gracious 2078
swyth *adj.* very 2, 133, 471 etc.; **swythe** 782, 1788, 2811, 2875
swone *v.* faint 3024
swoune *n.* loss of consciousness, faint 1820

T

taburne *n.* tabor 758
take *v.* give 99, 105; choose (sb. for a position, duty, etc.) 23; take (sb.) as one's spouse, marry 240; ~ *on honde* undertake (a task), engage in an undertaking 2512. **tak(e)** *imp. sg.* give 54, 63; send 1944; ~ *in kypyng* entrust (sb.) to someone's keeping 86. **took** *pa. 1 sg.* gave 1014; sent **toke** 1948. **took(e)** *pa. 3 sg.* engaged in an undertaking 160; (of sickness) took hold of, afflicted (sb.) 1521; took (sb.) as one's mate 3281; ~ *to hym sorowe* took sorrow to himself, felt sorrowful 2477. **tokyn** *pa. 3 pl.* took 520; ~ *on honde* undertook (a task), engaged in an undertaking **token** 1897
tale *n.* an event or experience which is related in the form of a set tale 713, 895. **talys** *n. pl.* stories 1023, 1279, 3430; rumours, gossip 2978
talent *n.* inclination, disposition 3375
tarye *pr. 3 sg. subj.* tarry, delay 516. **taryd** *pa. 3 sg.* 2383
te *obj. pron. 2 sg.* to thee 54

telle *v.* tell a story aloud 3092. **tellis** *pr. 2 sg.* ~ *of* tell about (sb.) 693. **tellys** *pr. 3 sg.* tells 3
tende *pa. 3 sg.* kindled 2181
tene *n.* trouble, harm 2846; *broght in* ~ got (sb.) into trouble 1797
tene *v.* trouble, harm 2432
tha, thad *rel. pron.* see **that**
tha *dem. adj.* that 2706, 3037
tha *conj.* see **that**
thay *dem. pron. 3 pl.* those 757
thaym *obj. pron. 3 pl.* them 7, 22, 23 etc.
than *adv.* then 117, 189, 213 etc.; **thanne** 238, 436, 672 etc.; **thane** 1080, 1269, 1539, 2394
than *conj.* when 145, 488, 564 etc.; **thane** 1268
thankit *pa. 3 pl.* thanked *544
thare *adv.* there 395, 764, 932 etc.; (expletive, or introdutory) 18, 598, 730 etc.; **thar** 1046, 3191; where 287, 514, 1230 etc.; **ther(e)** 116, 184, 368 etc.; though 1178
thareof *adv.* of that, of it 1702, 3210
thareto *adv.* to that end, for that purpose 909, 2592; to that 2391; **þerto** 291, 2426
tharevppon *adv.* about that 590
tharin *adv.* into that place 150
that *rel. pron.* who 1605, 1660; **tha** 3429; that which, what 2049, 2298, 2764, 3233; **tha** 1291; that **tha** 1698; **thad** 2293
that *conj.* with the result that 108, 1073, 1147 etc.; **tha** 2794; with the purpose that 393, 1324, 1886, 1970; **tha** 763n; when 535, 2043; that **tha** 16n
thau *conj.* see **thow**
the *n.* thigh 1384
the *obj. pron. 2 sg.* you 47, 80, 93 etc.; **þe** 1159; **thi** 1562
the *poss. pron. 2 sg.* your 2523; yours (?your war) **thyne** 2859n
the *sub. pron. 3 pl.* they 398n, 1918n
the *v.* thrive, prosper 611; *so mot I* ~ so may I thrive, as I may prosper 1548, 1722, 1806 etc.
the *conj.* see **thow**
thef(e), thyf(e) *n.* wretch, scoundrel, evildoer; a despicable person 681, 701, 1183, 3418; criminal 512; ~ *traytour* a false, duplicitous person; a liar 507, 1633. **thyfys** *pl.* criminals 514
þerbyne *adv.* therein 778
ther(e) *adv.* see **thare**
therfore, þerfore *adv.* because of that circumstance, in consequence of that 1275, 1727, 2556, 2557; *for . . .* ~ because of . . . for that reason 710
thermyde *adv.* along with that, at the same time 2169
therthourow *adv.* on account of that, because of that 1213
þerto *adv.* see **thareto**
thi see **the** *obj. pron. 2 sg*
thyderward(e), thydirward, thydyrward *adv.* thither, toward there 841, 1241, 2518, 3188
thydir, thydyr *adv.* thither, there 146, 952, 1443, 2932, 3335; **thyder** 3027, 3144; **thydyre** 1065; **thider** 1975
thydyraboute *adv.* thereabout 934
thyf(e) *n.* see **thef(e), thyf(e)**
thyne *poss. pron. 2 sg.* see **the**
thyn(e) *adv.* from that place 2484, 3320
thyng(e) *n.* that which is held in possession, chattel, property 3314; *of alle* ~ in every respect 1517
thynke *pr. 3 sg. impers. with dat.* seems 2709. **thought** *pa. 3 sg.* 944, 1301, 1451, 2418; **thout** 2531; resolved (that one will do sth.) **thout** 2893; intended (sth.) 694; **thouȝt** 440; intended (to do sth.) **thout** 1394; suspected **thout** 1346; ~ *on* fixed one's attentions on, concentrated on (sb. or sth.) **thouȝt** 476; ~ *tyme* thought it time **thout** 3095; *impers. with dat.* seemed 1997n. **thought** *pa. 3 pl.* made a plan, plotted, schemed 1965. **thought** *pp. was* ~ was decided 2159
thythyng *n.* tidings, news 1538
tho *sub. pron. 2 sg.* you 1430n, 1571
tho *dem. pron. pl.* those 870, 1077
tho *adv.* then 281, 576, 628 etc.
tho *conj.*[1] when 183, 241, 412 etc.
tho, thow *conj.*[2] even if 1690, 1732, 1754; **thau** 1780; notwithstanding the fact that 2935; **thau** 960, 2515; **the** 1741; if 1497; that (following a clause expressing wonder) *hit his no wondir* ~ 577; *as* ~ as if 2695
thole *v.* suffer, endure 1774; ~ *dethe* undergo the penalty of death, be executed 647. **tholyd** *pa. 3 sg.* ~ *deth* 2760
thonryd *pa. 3 sg.* thundered 2211

thorow *prep.* on account of, because of 1043, 1279, 1416 etc.; **thourow** 1874, 2251, 2634; **thorugh** 988; by means of 902, 2897, 3175; **thourow** 1880, 2063, 3126; **thourugt** 296; **thorug** 344; in response to, in obedience to (a command) 1043, 1200, 1329, 1670; **thourth** 522; **thourow** 722; through, throughout 2824; ~ *al thyng* in every point, thoroughly **thorou** 112; *passe* ~ *iuggement* undergo trial **thourgh** 537
thothyr, tothir, tohyr *pron.* other, second 1815, 2575, 3291
thow *conj.* see **tho, thow**
thowt *n.* thought 2889; *change, torne* ~ change (sb.'s) mind, purpose, opinion **thouht** 565; **thoght** 2490; *in hir* ~ to themselves, inwardly **thouth** 526
thrid *adj.* third 321
thrys, thryes, thrye *adv.* thrice 1776, 1810, 2177
thryue *v.* *so moti, mot I* ~ (in oaths and asseverations) so may I thrive, as I may thrive 1377, 2399
þrowe *n.* short period of time *2794
tie *n.* casket, small box or case for jewels and other valuables 2951
tylle *v.* persuade, entice 1563
tym *n.* *wan* ~ *was* when it was time 391
tyre *n.* outfit 2685, 2973
to *adv.* too 1003, 1731, 2219, 2418
to *prep.* for (sb.) 468; until 2265
toblaw *pp.* puffed up 1524
tobreke *v.* break in pieces 301, 1359
todon *pp.* undone, ruined 339n
todrawe *pp.* drawn apart 877; *angyd and* ~ see **hyng**
todryue *v.* break into pieces 2692
togydir *adv.* together 181, 250, 786, 1354; **togydyr** 149; **togidir** 442; **togyder** 1442
toȝode *pa. 3 sg.* approached 741
tohyr *pron.* see **thothyr, tothir, tohyr**
tohir *adj.* see **toþer**
tokast *pa. 3 pl.* cast 136
token, tokyn *pa. 3 pl.* see **take**
tolywryd *pa. 3 sg.* delivered 1974n
tollyd *pa. 3 sg.* led 3052n
tomorne *n.* tomorrow 993, 3006
ton *adj.* *the* ~ one 2548; one (of two), used in correlation with *the othir* 2886; one of two **tone** 2022
too *n.* toe 1131
toon *pron.* *the* ~ one 1444, 2566; one (of two), used in correlation with *the tothir* 2575; one of two **ton** 2000
torent(e) *pa. 3 sg.* tore apart 484. *pp.* 700
tormentour *n.* torturer 509. **tormentours** *pl.* 651, 1290, 2090, 2401; **tourmentours** 656
tormentrie *n.* torture 652
torne *n.* deed 1267
torne *v.* give new direction (to sth.), change; ~ *thoght* change (sb.'s) mind 2490. **tornys** *pr. 3 pl.* turn (to sth.) 1079. **tornyd** *pa. 3 sg.* changed the state of condition (of sth.) 1105. **tornyd** *pp.* transformed, changed 3388
toswal *pa. 3 sg.* swelled up 1523
toþer *adj.* *the* ~ the other 816; **tohir** 976n
tothes *n. pl.* tusks 956
tour(e) *n.* tower 762, 767, 1183 etc.
touryde *pp.* furnished with towers 2842
toward *prep.* at the point of (death) 660
tratour *n.* traitor 1307
tree *n.* a cross serving as means of execution, esp. the cross on which Christ was crucified 2760
trespas *n.* wrongful behaviour, wrongdoing 1437. *pl.* misdeeds 1830
trew *adj.* wise, discerning, learned 2358
trompe, trumpe *n.* trumpet *758, 772. **trumppys** *pl.* *3049
twa *adj.* two 1896, 1897, 1911 etc.; **tway(e)** 1737, 1924, 3048; **twae** 2150, 2410; **twayne** 441; **twey** 747; *in combs. as dual pers. pron. vs* ~ **twey** 1101; *thay* ~ **twey** 1119
twelmowth *n.* *a* ~ *holde* a year old 733
twynne *n.* *parten in* ~ part company, part 1499

U

veppe *pa. 3 pl.* see **wyppyng**
vnbore *adj.* never born (freq. in proverbs or prov. expressions) 3212
vndirgat *pa. 3 sg.* grasped the meaning of (what a bird said) 3151; saw, noticed **vndiryat** *2930n
vndirlayede *pp.* furnished with sth. laid below 213
vndirnam *pa. 3 sg.* understood 3236. **vndirnome** *pp.* undertook 2858
vndirtoke *pa. 3 sg.* undertook, began an enterprise 1106. **vndirtoke** *pa. 3 pl.*

2907. **vndirtake** *pp.* formally promised or pledged 66
vngyr *n.* hunger 3285
vnkynde *adj.* devoid of natural goodness; vile, bad, wicked, villainous *681
vnselde *pa. 3 sg.* opened (a book) 1054
uorthym *pr. 3 sg. subj. with pron.* see **worst**
vparaes *pa. 3 sg.* stood up 71
vpdrawe *pp.* drawn up 2406, 2603
vpe *adv.* up 2877
vpperyght *adv.* on one's back, face up 2540
vppesodoun *adv.* upside down 789
vryne *n.* urine 1533, 1534
vsage *n.* custom, practice 2292
vuele *adv.* unfortunately, unluckily 953, 1399; wickedly, evilly, treacherously **euyly** 457; painfully **euelle** 800

V

verrament *adv.* truly 2587
vertu *n.* unusual ability, distinction 3135, 3137; efficacious quality, medicinal potency 1135; strength **virtu** 626
vylany(e) *n.* shame, dishonour 3228, 3256; wickedness **vileny** 132; *do ~ by* violate (a woman) 1314
vysages *n.* face 487n
vowch . . . saue *pr. 1 sg. with separable adj. ~ on* confer, bestow on a person 452n

W

way *n. go thy ~* go away 1363
wayetys *n. pl.* watchmen 1886
wakken *v.* stir up 1803
wakmen *n. pl.* watchmen 1443, 1462
walaway *interj.* alas 1367, 3063
wald(e), walden *pa. 1 sg., pa. 3 sg., pa. 3 pl.* see **wil(e)**
wallis *n. pl.* walls 155
walme *n.* wave 2382, 2388. **walmes** *pl.* 2363, 2374, 2404
wan, wannyn *pa. 3 sg., pa. 3 pl.* see **wyn(n)e** *v.*
wan *adv.* when 391, 2977, 3449; **whan(e)** 154, 559; **whanne** 1609; **whent** *contr. of* **when the** 2153n
warden *n.* one who is in charge of a castle 3199, 3217
ware *adj.* aware 1702; watchful, cautious **were** 808
ware *pr. 1 sg.* warn 2277
ware *interrog. adv.* see **were**
warryson *n.* reward 1905
wars *adv.* worse 3365
wastir, wastyr, waster *pa. 3 sg. contr.* there was 164, 2244, 2465
wat *adj. ~ him, hym, hyre was* see **be**
waxe *v. so mot I ~* as I may prosper 2393. **waxist** *pr. 2 sg.* become 1824. **wax** *pr. 3 sg.* is becoming 171. **waxyn** *pr. p.* 813. **wax** *pa. 3 sg.* 634; developed, sprouted (up) 607; became 1063; (of a state or condition) grew 1101
wedyr *n.* weather 2225, 2244; spell of weather 3271. **wedirs** *pl.* 3284
welle *n.* happiness 3388
welles *n. pl.* springs of water 135
wellyde *pa. 3 pl.* welled up, gushed 135
welne *adv.* almost 1003, 1483, 1658 etc.; **welny** 1114, 2272
wende *v.* go, depart 2308, 2544, 3001, 3046; **wynde** 309; **whend** 2032. **wend(e)** *imp. sg* 451, 2409. **wentyst** *pa. 2 sg.* 2233. **went(e)** *pp.* 616, 1201, 2136, 2153, 2462; altered (one's mind or intention) 1484; *impers. with* **it** *hyt hys so ~* it has happened, it has come about 2633
wene *v.* believe 2980. **wenes** *pr. 3 sg.* 463n. **wende** *pa. 1 sg.* 1458. **wend(e)** *pa. 3 sg.* 1390, 1955, 1987, 3036; **whende** 2193
were *adj.* see **ware**
were *interrog. adv.* where 1129, 1711, 2941. *rel. adv. and conj.* where 915, 1131, 1416 etc.; **ware** 129, 832, 1229, 1984, 1985; **whare** 131; wherever 1769, 3209
wer(e)to *interr.* to what end, for what purpose 714, 1034
werfor *conj. do ~* provide compensation or payment in return for something *1937n
werys *pr. 3 sg.* makes war (upon sb.) 2848
werke *n.* sexual activity 1680; building, edifice 1879; deeds, actions 2731. **werkys** *pl.* deeds, actions 2366
wer(r)e *n.* war 2858, 2860
werrour *n.* warrior 2865
wet, wetyn *v., pr. 1 sg.* see **wyte(n)** *v.*[1]
whan, whan(n)e *adv.* see **wan**
whare *interrog. adv.* see **were**
wharefore *adv.* for what cause or reason, why (often coupled with **why** for emphasis) *why and ~* 2337

what *pron.* who 2791
whehir, where *conj.* whether 1225, 3014
whende *pa. 3 sg.* see **wene**
whent *adv.* see **wan**
where *pa. 3 sg. subj.* see **be**
where *conj.* see **whehir, where**
whethir *rel. pron.* which 3081, 3101
whyit *adj.* (of complexion) fair 60
whilk, wylk *rel. pron.* which 23, 387.
whilk(e) *adj.* ~ *maner(e)* what kind 1513; in what manner 2960; *on* ~ *wyse* in what manner **wilk** 1875
who *pron.* whoever 3226
wydir *adv.* whither 451
wydyrout *adv.* where, in the place in which 1927; ?of what material (?*MED*) 2893
wyduer *n.* widower 3438
wyel, wylle *n.* wile, stratagem 1212, 2157. **wylys** *pl.* 2731, 2735, 3069, 3074; *don* ~ engage in deceptions, play tricks **wylen** 121
wyes *adj.* wise 24, 171, 2865. **wyser** *comp.* 2915. **wysesde** *sup.* 375
wyet *v.* see **wyte(n)**
wyf(e) *n.* woman 2965; *good* ~ good woman 3340; *had(de) to* ~ had as (his) wife 728, 1677, 2812. **wyfys** *gen. sg.* wife's 503, 699; **wyues** 889; **wywys** 1844; **wyfvys** 2759; **wyfvis** 2763; **wyvys** 3069; **wyvis** 3389
wyght *n. no* ~ no one, nobody 298; *in adv. phr. a lytil* ~ a certain amount 609; a little way off 2507
wykkes *n. pl.* weeks 2802
wyl *n.* see **wyl(e), wile** *n.*[1], **wylle** *n.*[1]
wil, wyl *adv.* see **wylle, wille**
wil, wyl *conj.* while, during the time that 159, 221, 613, 2215, 3297; **wylle** 2546, 2547; **wyle** 1139; **wille** 2398
wildeliche *adv.* wildly 186
wyl(e), wile *n.*[1] *done thayre* ~ had sexual intercourse 1353; *do* ~ *by* have sexual intercourse with 1546; *at* ~ at will 1823; *at* ~ at (sb.'s) will 2161; (sexual) gratification, satisfaction **wylle** 2546
wyl(e), wile *n.*[2] see **wylle** *n.*[1]
wyle *adj.* see **wyly, wyle**
wil(e) *pr. 1 sg. (fut. aux.)* will 47, 65, 240, 540, 2236; **wyle** 369, 1693, 2362; **wole** 1937, 2392. **wolt** *pr. 2 sg.* 888, 2598; **wol** 2613; **woltow** *with pron.* will you 98; **woltu** 1274; **wyltou** 1470; **woltou** 2253. **wile** *pr. 3 sg.* 1846. **wylle(n)** *pr. 1 pl.* wish, desire 1903, 2977. **wyle** *pr. 3 pl.* will 513, 1159, 1162, 2734. **wol(e)** *pr. 2. sg. subj.* will 87, 3258. **walde** *pa. 1 sg.* would 69, 1729; would wish, desire **wolde** 2005, 3417. **woldestow** *pa. 2 sg. with pron.* would you 30. **walde** *pa. 3 sg.* would 494, 495, 496 etc.; **wald** 1567; wished, desired **wolde** 154, 2914; ~ *that* wished, desired that (sth. be in a specified manner) 1582, 3390; *with v. of motion understood* **wolde** 1409. **walden** *pa. 3 pl.* would 2649
wyle *adv.* see **wylle, wille**
wyle *conj.* see **wil, wyl**
wile a fyne, wylle a fyne *adv.* right well, well indeed 1064n, 2376
wylen *n. pl.* see **wyel, wylle**
wyly, wyle *adj.* wily, cunning 1395, 3432
wylys *n. pl.* see **wyel, wylle**
wylk *rel. pron.* see **whilk, wylk**
wilk *adj.* see **whilk(e)**
wylke *interrog. adj.* ~ *a* what a 2424
wylle *n.*[1] a while, a time 1221, 2524, 3130; **wyl(e)** 441, 1074, 1342, 2058; *within(ne), in a* ~ in a short time, soon 604, 1379; **wile** 173
wylle *n.*[2] see **wyel, wylle**
wylle *n.*[3] see **wyl(e), wile** *n.*[1]
wylle, wille *adv.* well 320, 452, 1541 etc.; **wyl** 1073, 1747; very 667; **wil** 332; *ful* ~ very well 431; **wyle** 954; ~ *a fyne* see **wile a fyne, wylle a fyne**
wille, wylle *conj.* see **wil, wyl**
williche *adv.* in a vile manner 1841
wyltou *pr. 2 sg. with pron.* see **wil(e)**
wymman, wymmen *n. pl.* women (in general) 695, 1517
wynde *v.* see **wende**
wyne *n. so God Almyghty gyf me* ~ as Almighty God may give me joy 1373
wyn(n)e *n.* profit, riches, wealth 2301; *wordlys* ~ worldly gain 2485
wyn(n)e *v.* get, obtain, acquire (sth. profitable or desired) 1572, 2319; get access (to sth.) 2809; obtain (a woman) as a wife or 'lady' by action or effort of some kind 2897. **wan** *pa. 3 sg.* ~ *lyf* preserved (one's) life 3424. **wannyn** *pa. 3 pl.* got, obtained, acquired (sth. profitable or desired) 2299
wyntirtyde *n.* winter time 2505
wypit *pp.* wiped 1800

wyppyng *pr. p.* weeping 2094. **wyp(p)e, wippe** *pa. 3 sg.* wept 570, 792, 2506. **veppe** *pa. 3 pl.* 833

wyrke *v.* ~ *eftyr* act according to 579. **wrout, wroght** *pa. 3 sg.* did 303, 3437; created, made, fashioned **wrought** 2133. **wrogten** *pa. 3 pl. subj.* brought about, caused 3443. **wrought** *pp.* created, made, fashioned 145, 149, 527, 2160, 2738; **wroght** 2231, 2676, 2900, 2917; **wrowt** 766; **ywroght** 2890; (of a person) done something, or done things generally **wrout** 303; **wroght** 1088; **wrogt** 3441; formulated, devised **wrouȝt** 458; done, performed **wroute** 2958

wys(e) *n. in noonekynne* ~ in no way, by no means 203; *on non* ~ in no way 207; *on al* ~ in all ways, in every way 1596; *on wilk* ~ in what manner 1875

wise *n.* wise man 1838

wyser, wysesde *adj. comp., adj. sup.* see **wyes**

wyssys *pr. 3 sg.* guides, directs 2366n

wyt *n.* intelligence, judgement 56, 2994, 3150, 3237; **wit** 182; knowledge, wisdom 676; **wit** 58, 131

wit *prep.* with 439, 2069, 3403

wyte(n) *v.*[1] know, know of 1061; learn 2052; **wet** 2372, 2780; **wyet** 3080; hear **wetyn** 2642; **wyt** 3215; *dyden hym to* ~ caused him to know, made known to him **wite** 1956. **wet, woot** *pr. 1 sg.* know 284, 587. **wost** *pr. 2 sg.* know 1021, 1103, 1691, 1733. **wyte** *pr. 1 pl.* know of 1930. **wyt** *pr. 1 sg. subj.* be informed of, learn 1032. **wyst** *pa. 3 sg.* knew, knew of 387, 665, 1104 etc.; **wyste** 2152, 3028; **wist** 293, 431; found out, discovered (sth.) 2144; was informed of, learned **wyste** 2621. **wyste** *pa. 3 pl.* knew 1984; were informed of, learned 1617; **wystyn** 3106

wyten *v.*[2] blame 349

withalle *adv.* therewith 782, 1267

withouten *adv.* outside 999, 1343, 2042 etc.; **without** 1640, 2417; on the outside, externally **witout** 2027

withsaye *v.* oppose 655. **wytsed** *pp.* denied, contradicted 214

withsytte *v.* oppose 518

wyues, wyvis, wyvys, wywys *n. gen. sg.* see **wyf(e)**

wo *n.* woe **woo** 358; *me hys* ~, ~ *hys me* woe is to me 1176, 2551, 2564; *me be* ~ woe be to me 577, 1497; *hym was* ~ woe was to him 703; *me schulde be ful* ~ woe should be to me completely 2578; the expression of grief or woe, lamentation *made* ~ 562; *euer uorthym* ~ see **worst**

wo *pron.* who 1093, 1421

wo *adj.* woeful 2556, 2623

wode *adj.* mad 499, 836, 958 etc.; **woode** 813, 848; **wodde** 806; (of the sea, a sea current) turbulent **wod(e)** 3173, 3191; (in phrases with adv. qualifiers) *nere* ~ nearly mad 502

wol(e), wolt, woltou, woltow, woltu, wolde, woldestow *pr. 1 sg., pr. 2 sg., pr. 2 sg. with pron., pa. 1 sg., pa. 3 sg., pa. 2 sg. with pron.* see **wil(e)**

womb *n.* belly 982

womman *gen. sg.* woman's 642, 825

wondid *pa. 3 sg.* wounded 787. **wondyd** *pp.* 800

wondir *adj.* wondrous, marvellous 1879, 2685; **woundir** 1059, 2703; **wundyr** 695; dreadful, dire 1214; **woundir** 1837; mentally challenging, difficult 67; ~ *kas, cas* wondrous, marvellous event, incident, occurrence 202, 330, 361 etc.; **wondyr** 1251, 1653, 2210; **woundir** 3206. **wonderest** *sup.* most wondrous, marvellous 2641

wondir(e), wondyr *n. hadde* ~ see **hadde**

wondyrful *adj.* wondrous, strange 2306

woned *pa. 3 sg.* lived 929

wont, wount *pp.* accustomed 942, 947

woo *n.* see **wo**

woode *adj.* see **wode**

wooke *pa. 3 sg.* was awake 159

word(e) *n.* things said, or something said 893, 898

wordlys *n. gen. sg.* ~ *wyne* see **wyn(n)e** *n.*

worme *n.* snake 794, 795

worst *pr. 2 sg.* come to be (sth.) 1505. **uorthym** *pr. 3 sg. subj. with pron., contr. of* **worth hym** *euer* ~ *wo* may woe betide him always 1130

worthy, worthe *adj.* deserving or meriting by fault or wrong-doing 2347, 2776

wost *pr. 2 sg.* see **wyte(n)**

wounde *v.* hesitate 1768. *pr. 2 sg.* 2633

woundyrlych *adv.* in a wonderful manner 2676

woundyt *pa. 3 sg.* wounded 2476. *pp.* 2456
wount *pp.* see **wont, wount**
wouwe, wowe *v.* to solicit or sue a woman in love; to court 230, 2533
wrat *n.* wrath 1142, 1483
wrathe *v.* anger 1827. **wrothe** *pr. 3 sg. subj. refl.* 1780
wreche *n.* vengeance 1775
wryng *v. hyr hondis forto* ~ to wring her hands 1368. **wronge** *pa. 3 sg. hir hondis, hyr hondys* ~ 570, 2506
wroght, wrogten, wrogt *pa. 3 sg., pa. 3 pl. subj., pp.* see **wyrke**
wronge *n. bodun* ~ harmed 632; *forto do the* ~ to act unjustly or unfairly to you 637; *hase the* ~ is in the wrong 3081; *wyth* ~ wrongfully, unjustly 3303
wroth(e) *adj.* angry 408, 696, 782 etc.
wrothe *pa. 3 sg.* twisted 1792
wrought, wrouȝt, wrout(e), wrowt *pa. 3 sg., pp.* see **wyrke**
wundyre *n.* marvel, object or cause of wonder 2052; *hadde* ~ **wondyr, wondir(e)** see **hadde**

INDEX OF PROPER NAMES